positions asia critique

T0311063

children and youth in asian migration:
states, families, and education

volume 30   number 2   may 2022

Contents

children and youth in asian migration: states, families, and education

Rhacel Salazar Parreñas, Nicola Piper, Sari K. Ishii, and Carolyn Areum Choi
Guest Editors' Introduction   219

Amanda R. Cheong
Deportable to Nowhere: Stateless Children as Challenges to State Logics of Immigration Control   245

Harriot Beazley and Jessica Ball
"I Can't Do Anything but Wait": The Lived Experiences of Children of Transnational Migrants in Lombok, Indonesia   277

Misaki Iwai
Barriers Faced by Returning Migrant Children in Vietnam: The Case of the Mekong Delta Region   301

Charlie Rumsby

Children's Experience and Practice of Belonging: The Realities of Integration among De Facto Stateless Vietnamese Children in Cambodia   323

Johanna L. Waters and Maggi W. H. Leung

Children's Bodies Are Not Capital: Arduous Cross-Border Mobilities between Shenzhen and Hong Kong   353

Carolyn Areum Choi

Transperipheral Educational Mobility: Less Privileged South Korean Young Adults Pursuing English Language Study in a Peripheral City in the Philippines   377

Contributors   409

Guest Editors' Introduction

Children and Youth in Asian Migration

Rhacel Salazar Parreñas, Nicola Piper, Sari K. Ishii, and Carolyn Choi

Beginning in the 1990s, migration scholars in the United States began to pay greater attention to the experiences of youth and the children of migrants. Heeding the call of Portes and Zhou (1993), many looked to the experiences of children to measure the extent of immigrant integration. In contrast, children including young persons have remained largely invisible in studies of migration in Asia (Alipio et al. 2015). Perhaps this is because most do not migrate but instead stay behind in the country of origin as members of transnational families (Beazley and Ball, this issue; Parreñas 2005). It is only in recent years that scholars have begun to focus on the question of youth and children in Asian migration. In 2015, *Children's Geography* dedicated a special issue to Asian children and transnational migration, which it identified as comprising four primary groups of left-behind children of migrant parents, educational migrants, child labor migrants, and adoptees.

positions 30:2   DOI 10.1215/10679847-9573315
Copyright 2022 by Duke University Press

This special issue advanced the literature by looking at migration from the point of view of children including "young people." Suggesting the continued need to rectify the absence of children and youth in the literature on Asian migration, *Children's Geography* in 2018 published another special issue that focused specifically on the emotional responses of South and Southeast Asian children to their experiences of migration.

Our special issue builds on these previous discussions and the knowledge they advance on the everyday experiences of Asian children and youth in two ways: in an expansionist sense and by adding more nuance. As for the former, we develop these discussions by foregrounding the macrostructures that shape migrant experiences. As we do so, we also include in our examination of migration the perspectives of children and youth, thus adding more nuance to existing debates and analyses. Articles in this special issue examine how states and economies shape migration through the experiences of children and youth. By foregrounding the macro in our analysis, we are able to provide a critical perspective on the structural inequalities that define migration in Asia. This special issue calls attention to the ethnic exclusion faced by Vietnamese settlers in Cambodia (Rumsby, this issue) and undocumented and stateless children in Sabah, Malaysia (Cheong, this issue), the gendered statelessness that confronts Korean-Vietnamese children when they return to Vietnam (Iwai, this issue), and the geopolitical and economic inequalities that shape migration flows within Asia including Indonesia-Malaysia (Beazley and Ball, this issue), Hong Kong–Mainland China (Waters and Leung, this issue), and South Korea–Philippines (Choi, this issue).

To call attention to the rise of South-to-South migration, this special issue solely examines migration flows within Asia. In doing so, we show the emergence of "unlikely" destinations, specifically drawing attention to the flow of Korean migrants to the Philippines, Vietnamese migrants to Cambodia, and Korean-Vietnamese children to Vietnam (see also Kondakci, Bedenlier, and Zawacki-Richter 2018; Yang 2018). As illustrated in this special issue, "youth and children in Asian migration" represent a diverse group. Educational migrants, for instance, are diverse in composition as they include daily border crossers between China and Hong Kong (Waters and Leung, this issue), primary and secondary students from mainland China in Singapore (Huang and Yeoh 2005), and Korean English-language learners in the Philippines (Choi, this issue). Likewise, the "second generation" includes not only children of immigrant parents but also children from international marriages, undocumented children of temporary labor migrants, children raised in transnational households, and stateless children born outside the territorial boundaries of their citizenship. Not all qualify for permanent residency. Some are authorized while others are unauthorized. And lastly, some have crossed borders while others have always been territorially bound (e.g., children of undocumented migrants in Cambodia or Malaysia; see Cheong and Rumsby, this issue). Their political status—whether as stateless children, children who are ineligible for sponsored migration, or undocumented children—is one we pay critical attention to in our analysis of their experiences.

Children of Migration and the State

Globally migrant and nonmigrant children and youth have become central to contests around national, ethnic or racial and class boundaries—and moral panics around them. In her pathbreaking book *Children and the Politics of Culture,* the anthropologist Sharon Stephens (1995) ventured the argument that children have emerged as important points of reference in the diverse identity claims that constitute various cultural contests around the world. Children have come to be included in the increasing preoccupation, if not obsession, with the guarding of boundaries and borders of national identity, ethnic purity, and the family—and, thus, the subject of various forms of exclusion. Such trends and developments warrant the need to bring the study of children and youth migration into the analysis of politics, economics, and culture globally as well as in regional contexts, as for example "Asia."

In many subregions of Asia, human mobility is typically perceived as a challenge to norms of state sovereignty and noninterference on which governments place high importance, partly as the result of unfinished nation-building projects in the context of decolonization (Asis, Piper, and Raghuram 2019). Intraregional migration in Asia has a long history but the increased involvement of nation-states in promoting, controlling, or limiting migratory movements has occurred on the basis of a specific regulatory framework: strictly temporary contract migration. Yet, while many Asian nations doggedly defend their national sovereignty, in reality management of cross-border migration has proven difficult. This can be attributed to physical geography and ethno-cultural composition of Asia's societies divided by artificially drawn and porous borders, faced with demographic challenges and the political economy of global supply and care chains—and migrants' ability to circumvent and navigate rigid and formal regulatory frameworks (Piper, Rosewarne, and Withers 2017). As far as regional governance of migration is concerned in a formal sense, however, the overall trend in Asia indicates the supremacy of economic interests and security concerns to which a rights-based approach to migration is typically subordinated, as evident from the difficulties encountered in adopting a declaration for migrant workers' rights and other rights-based frameworks that exist in most other regions in the world (Piper 2017).

In Asia, the prioritization of economics and security over rights manifests in the plight of stateless children, meaning "children without a state" (Bhabha 2011: 1). Statelessness emerges from either the absence of a legal identity (de jure and de facto statelessness) or from the inability to prove one's legal identity (effectively stateless). The issue of children's statelessness is one that migration scholars have ignored, since, according to Bhabha, "states have innocently overlooked the problems of migrant children and their correlative duties because of a dual perception lacuna: on issues of migration, they have focused on adults; on issues of child welfare, they have focused on citizens" (19).

As states prioritize economics and security over rights, temporary labor migration schemas may result in child statelessness as we see with the case of multigenerational transnational families in Indonesia (Ball, Butt, and Beazley 2017), children "born out of place" in Hong Kong (Constable 2014), or return migrants in Thailand (Ishii 2016). In their study of four known rural migrant-sending communities in East Lombok, Indonesia, Leslie Butt and her colleagues found a mere 12 percent rate of birth registrations among children in transnational families. Without legal documents, most children are rendered *effectively stateless*. Migrant workers from this area are often low-skilled laborers who, as part of multigenerational transnational families, are caught in a "cycle of high-risk mobility" (Ball, Butt, and Beazley 2017:

318–21) and a "multigenerational legacy of statelessness, poverty, and unauthorized migration" (321). They confront various structural barriers to child registration including the high registration fees required by the government, the stigma of single motherhood, or the fulfillment of traditional social norms such as meeting the requirement of the signature of both parents (Ball, Butt, and Beazley 2014: 9).

The trumping of security over rights also manifests in the legal status of children and youth "born out of place" to domestic workers in Hong Kong, who are rendered de facto stateless by their birth in a territory where jus sanguinis determines citizenship and where migrants are ineligible for permanent residency or are without rights to reproduction. According to Constable (2014), children born to domestic workers in Hong Kong live "bare lives" (Agamben 1998) in "zones of social abandonment" (Biehl 2005). Countries where we find a similar situation of statelessness among children of domestic workers would include most of their other known destinations including Malaysia, Singapore, and Taiwan in East Asia and Israel, Jordan, Lebanon, and among others Saudi Arabia in West Asia. In all of these countries, domestic workers not only are ineligible for permanent residency but also cannot sponsor the migration of their dependents. *De facto statelessness* applies to other groups of children of migration in Asia, including multigenerational ethnic Vietnamese in Cambodia whose ambiguous legal status results in discrimination against them in the labor market and schools (Rumsby, this issue). Korean-Vietnamese children including youth who return to the rural villages of their migrant mothers in Vietnam after growing up in South Korea also face de facto statelessness (Le 2016), as described by Iwai in this issue, because of gendered policies that require paternal consent for the registration of the child, which poses a challenge for mothers who flee situations of domestic abuse or nonconsensual divorce.

Finally, children and youth also experience *statelessness affectively* as it emerges in their feelings or experiences despite their legal claim to a territory. This is the case among Japanese-Thai children returning to Thailand with migrant mothers after the failure of a cross-border marriage. According to Ishii (2016), mismatched nationality results in feelings of exclusion from full citizenship for these children; they face exclusion for not being "proper" Thai (127), do not attain rights or privileges from having a Japanese nationality in a rural Thai village (131), and are at risk of becoming undocumented migrants in Thailand. Affective statelessness also applies to Japanese-Filipino children who confront feelings of "ambivalent citizenship" (Suzuki 2015). Beginning in 2008, children born out of wedlock to Filipino women and Japanese men could finally obtain Japanese nationality. However, legal membership in Japan has not protected them from ethnic discrimination, which they cannot flee by returning to the Philippines where they would no longer be considered citizens (Suzuki 2015: 130). This double displacement, according to Suzuki, renders these children effectively stateless.

Theorizing the affective statelessness of children, Allerton (2014: 8) asserts that "in considering statelessness, we must not neglect broader issues of justice and human rights, or the fact that children of migrants may not simply desire 'documents' but recognition of their right to be considered 'people from here.'" To write an ethnographic account of statelessness, it is not statelessness that must be overcome, but rather exclusion from the nationality to which migrants feel they belong (2). Stateless children do not suffer deprivation of a nationality, but an exclusion from the nationality/society in which they believe or want to belong to.

The specific way of state management of migration in Asia—as we see with the rise of statelessness among children of migration in the region—is, thus, related to specific constellations of state, market, and social relations linked to specific development pathways and ethno-cultural politics. The so-called national territories of modern South and Southeast Asia, for instance, were drawn after the departure of colonial powers several decades ago, when the new "developmental states and postcolonial imaginaries" also adopted the full package of Western governmentality, including the ideas of strict sovereignty and territorial delimitation. This provides a partial explanation for the tacit approval of refugee populations under conditions of nonratification of international instruments (Nah 2019; Moretti 2018).

International human rights treaties provide children and youth who reside outside of their country of origin, either accompanied by or separated from their parents or caregivers, with specific rights and obligate signatory states to provide for their protection. The 1989 United Nations Convention on the Rights of Children is an important codification of both children's age-distinctive entitlements and the responsibilities of duty bearers (i.e., states). The UNCRC happens to be the most widely (and rapidly!) ratified human rights treaty in history, with 194 countries as state parties, which means all countries in the world except for Somalia, South Sudan, and the United States. Yet the rights of children and youth in migration are only rarely asserted as such in Asia, either in courts or by civil society (although there is some variation across the subregions and individual countries in Asia). The main reason for this as suggested by Grugel (2015) is that migration is embedded culturally and in policy terms within the domain of labor markets and economic development, not as an established space where the rights of individuals are in play and asserted by law. Rights are typically equated with citizenship and citizenship in turn with nationality, while migration tends to be equated with economic processes that are seen as somehow beyond the control of states. Moreover, human rights debates are still primarily conducted by separating out civil and political liberties from social and economic rights. In Asia, the understanding is that the former cannot be granted before the latter are in place—that is, economic development has to precede the granting of civil and political liberties. In addition, the notion that migrants have everyday rights is a completely novel idea.

Despite the dominance of temporary migration and the insecurity involved in undocumented migration, migration is deeply embedded in economic, cultural, political, and educational life of a very large proportion of families in Asia. Its intraregional flows are deeply embedded in the lives of many poor families. The traditional pattern of migration, however, is seen as involving the departure of an adult—and given the feminization of migration in much of Asia, it is today more often the mother/wife—with children and youth being left behind. Yet children and youth are affected by migration in many other forms, through migration with their parents or having been born in the destination country but without recognition as citizens or as returnees to the country of origin or their mother's origin, but without holding their mother's or parents' citizenship. It is not known how many are affected by migration in these various forms in Asia and elsewhere. Children and youth are often obfuscated in statistics and thus from policy making. They are neglected as persons, participants, and the locus of important events in the process of culture and politics in academic studies also. Although there is a growing sociology of childhood and the new field of geographies of childhood has moved beyond the West, children had for long been absent from theoretical discussions about citizenship, democracy, and governance (Kehily 2004; Kulynych 2001). It has been only fairly recently that children and their claims to rights have become more prominent along with the issues of social exclusion and governance (James, Jenks, and Prout 1998). The specific circumstances and experiences of children and youth in migration, however, are still marginalized in such concerns. The fact that childhood functions as a particularly important site for expressions of national identity and nation-building projects requires the inclusion of migrant children and youth in such debates.

Educational Migration

There are currently 5 million international students enrolled in postsecondary educational institutions outside of their home country for degree courses or language acquisition (ICEF Monitor 2015; Institute of International Education 2017). More than 58 percent of international students are from the advancing capitalist Asian economies of China, India, Saudi Arabia, and South Korea, where global and technological transformations of the political economy have paralleled major changes in the class structure of various Asian societies (Chu 1996). The continent of Asia has played an important role in the aspirations and imaginations of students and continues to operates as the largest regional sender of international students for institutions of higher education (Brooks and Waters 2011; Collins 2013). Western imaginaries and languages continue to inform the national development projects of postcolonial and postimperial states (N. Kim 2008; Park 2011), with the most popular destinations concentrated in North America and western Europe (Waters 2005, 2006). The increasingly disparate pathways of migration to places beyond traditional destinations in the West/Global North offer a window into understanding the larger hierarchical landscape of educational destinations in the global economy.

Earlier literature examined educational migration as a lens for understanding the cultural reproduction practices of what Robinson and Goodman (1996) have called Asia's new rich. Contemporary Asian elites, faced with low college admission rates, began to send their children abroad to Western countries to reproduce their privileged status (Brooks and Waters 2011; Waters 2006; Ong 1999) distinguishing their families from the expanding local middle classes through the acquisition of Western credentials. These "flexible citizens," as Aihwa Ong (1999) has called them, enjoyed documented status and were best positioned to maximize opportunities for social reproduction through specific credentials either by returning to their home country to be part of the elite or by leading flexible lives across borders. Because initial studies were concerned with a small "flexible minority" who had the freedom of "choice" to appreciate the trappings offered by an increasingly globalized world, critical research on educational migration was delayed, which Findlay (2011: 165) argued "treat the topic in an unproblematic fashion seeing the process as temporary, invisible and not worthy of theorization."

Contemporary works have unpacked some of the earlier assumptions of educational migration as a phenomenon of the elite. Following the 1997 Asian financial crisis, educational migration grew dramatically among first-generation middle-class and working-class families who, despite being some of the hardest hit, viewed it as their only recourse in securing economic futures for their children in uncertain times (Huang and Yeoh 2005; Kang and Abelman 2011; Park and Abelmann 2004; Park and Bae 2009). With their heavy focus on the reorganization of families across space (E. Ho 2002; Jeong, You, and Kwon 2014; Le 2016), these works were some of the first to interrogate the broader scope of the global educational landscape, documenting the rise of budget-friendly localized higher educational zones (Waters and Leung 2013) or "regional educational hubs" (Collins et al. 2014; Mok 2011; Sidhu, Ho, and Yeoh 2011) as alternatives to the West and underscoring critical ways that student migration regimes produce stratified pathways for social mobility and for residency in receiving destinations (Luthra and Platt 2016; Pan 2011; Wilken and Ginnerskov-Dahlberg 2017). Incorporating the larger landscape of student demographic and geographic diversity, these studies served as a starting place for exposing the inherent contradictions of capitalistic international education as a neutral or even liberatory process as well as the ways that differential pathways can also mirror the class and gender stratification in home societies (Park and Abelmann 2004).

In this issue, Johanna Waters and Maggi Leung's article on mainland Chinese children's commutes to schools in Hong Kong is an important update to the literature on children's educational migration/mobilities. Challenging dominant paradigms of educational migration as a unidirectional country-to-country phenomenon, this article exposes structural challenges of inter-regional, cross-border educational mobilities within Asia and the underlying ways it can produce class, educational, and regional inequalities. Their article demonstrates this through the case of "double not" children—that is, children born in Hong Kong to mainland Chinese parents—and how it has given rise to the phenomenon of cross-boundary student migration as those residing in the mainland are ineligible to attend mainland schools because of their Hong Kong citizenship. While attending schools in Hong Kong signals their participation in a localized form of elite education, their experiences as working-class and rural children confronted them with the everyday realities of state governance of children's bodies and futures.

Parallel to the scholarship on educational migration, researchers of youth mobilities and children's geographies have introduced key conversations to existing debates that have challenged the dominant assumptions about the temporality, directionality, and linearity of young people's moves. By centering on the lived experiences of children and young people themselves, these works have highlighted the growing fragmentation and discontinuities of young people's transitions in rapidly changing late capitalist societies and how the structural shift toward flexible labor models has transformed the meaning of adolescence, adulthood, and the life course. Concepts such as "emerging adulthood" (Arnett 2000) and "mobile transitions" (Robertson, Harris, and Baldassar 2018) highlight the ways in which traditional linear pathways from youth to adulthood have become prolonged, destandardized, inverted (Frändberg 2014), and increasingly mobile. Anthropologist Cho Hae-joang (2015), for instance, explains how in South Korea people in their thirties and forties perceive themselves as youth because of their difficulties in securing long-term employment during the current economic crisis and their political opposition to an authoritarian developmentalist regime.

In the last couple of decades, we have also borne witness to the ways in which young people have become a key cornerstone in the disciplining and development of new-age forms of citizenship and membership within governmentality regimes of postcolonial and postauthoritarian states. Johanna Waters and Maggi Leung point out in their article in this issue how children's mobilities are linked to the idea of what Mitchell and Kallio (2017) refer to as "embodied statecraft," whereby states are produced through the everyday movements of ordinary people. For instance, young people are becoming increasingly linked to national and regional policies for migration such as working holiday programs and the EU Erasmus Program (Robertson, Harris, and Baldassar 2018) to advance national interests for economic development, cultural diplomacy, and global competitiveness. While such institutional moves have indeed smoothed existing channels for travel and lowered costs and barriers to entry, they have also produced multiple, overlapping structural challenges to navigating the legal, racial, gender, and status-based barriers of receiving societies and regions, challenges faced as well by those who have "voluntarily returned" (Lachica Buenavista 2018) to originating societies.

Young people are no longer going abroad just to gain competitive advantage through education but also to earn an income, develop global skill sets (i.e., language), gain cosmopolitan exposure, and seek new freedoms within a variety of different migratory configurations such as working holiday makers, volunteers, tourists, and English-language learners (Chun and Han 2015; Inkson and Myers 2003; Jones 2011; Kawashima 2010; Loker-Murphy and Pearce1995; Yoon 2014). With the length of migration becoming increasingly shorter, multistep, and multidirectional, much of the research on youth mobilities has focused on documenting the diversity of young people's movements and the ways in which they respond to global flows of information, goods, and capital with the liberalization of borders across the Global North and Global South. In particular, the expansion of the global educational marketplace to destinations in the Global South has allowed for a clearer observation of the stratified educational mobilities that can arise under a deregulated and global capitalist model of education. For instance, Carolyn Choi's article in this special issue examines the regionally segmented mobilities of South Korean working-class youth who learn English in cost-effective rural destinations in the Philippines as they aspire to meet growing demands for English-language competency in a globalizing South Korea. Her article establishes the stratification of mobility among English-language learners from South Korea with the haves likely to migrate to the Global North and the have-nots limited to the Global South.

With education as a central theme, this special issue will focus on the intersections of children's geographies, student and educational mobilities, and youth mobilities and how the repositioning of Asia (and Asian educational destinations) in the shifting topographies of the global educational landscape has shed light on the new stratifications and inequalities that arise in an increasingly deregulated neoliberal global educational marketplace. In these new circumstances of increased regional and national competition and global literacy, there is a need to challenge our previous assumptions of educational mobilities/migration as East to West/South to North, youth to adulthood, and mobile/immobile and ground our theorizations within the everyday experiences of the young people who take more diverse pathways.

Children, Youth, and Transnational Families

The limited rights of migrant workers clearly manifest in the emergence of transnational families, which results from the ineligibility of migrant workers to sponsor their dependents, the lesser cost of reproduction in sending societies, the attachment of migrants to their country of origin, or the conflicts posed by workplace demands (Parreñas 2005; Parreñas 2015). Family separation across international borders is the norm for migrant workers all over the globe. In the Philippines, approximately 25 percent of children have at least one migrant parent abroad (Parreñas 2005). In Moldova, it is believed that 31 percent of children younger than the age of fifteen are left behind by a migrant parent (Salah 2008). The parents of these children are likely to be unskilled temporary migrant workers who are disqualified from sponsoring the migration of their dependents. Indeed, this is true for construction workers in the Middle East; farm workers in Canada, United States, and European countries; factory workers in South Korea and Taiwan; and domestic workers across the globe.

In the last decade, we have seen an explosion of studies on the separation of migrant families. Categorically labeling them "transnational families," studies have been primarily attuned to the question of gender. Empirically, studies have asked two primary questions to get to the heart of gender relations in transnational migrant families. First, they have raised the question of "who cares for the children" (Abrego 2014; Dreby 2010; Lam and Yeoh 2018; Mazzucato and Schans 2011; McKay 2007). Second, they have asked, "How is mothering practiced"? (Hondagneu-Sotelo and Avila 1997; Madianou and Miller 2012. With limited exceptions (see Abrego 2014; Dreby 2010; Mazzucato and Schans 2011), most studies focus almost exclusively on the transnational households of migrant women. Additionally, few address the situation of children (for exceptions, see Abrego 2014; Beazley, Butt, and Ball 2018; Dreby 2010; Graham et al. 2012; Parreñas 2005), as more focus has been given on the experiences of the migrant parents or the left-behind caregivers (Bastia 2015). While this is the case, studies that do focus on children do not necessarily provide their perspective as some continue to rely on the opinions of caregivers to account for their welfare (Dobson 2007).

Studies initially attended to the question of children's well-being by asking the question of who provides care, particularly examining whether or not men provide care if children have been left behind by a migrant mother. One group led by the likes of McKay (2012) and Manalansan (2006) maintains that men do. Drawing from her ethnography of a migrant sending community in the Philippines, the geographer Deirdre McKay (2012) asserts that men respond positively to women's out-migration and accordingly care for children. Interestingly, she argues that those who would otherwise insist on women's continued maternal responsibilities upon migration assume "a universal understanding of intimacy" and reflect "contemporary, commonsense understandings of gendered family roles that predominate in the middle-class northern European West" (116). By advancing this argument, McKay assumes a universal difference between the West and the Rest. In so doing, she romanticizes the Philippines as a non-Western space inhabited by the Other and thus believes women in the Philippines must have uniquely different problems from women in the West. This is actually an exemplary example of Orientalism.

Not surprisingly, most studies disagree with McKay and found that women and not men are more likely to care for children in transnational migrant families. In her comparative study of children of migrant fathers and mothers in the Philippines, Parreñas (2005) found that men left behind in the Philippines fail to reciprocate for the income contributions of migrant women as most relegate the primary care duties of their children to extended female kin. Lam and Yeoh (2018) add nuance to the discussion as they found that men will perform some traditional women's work if women are not available to do it. Yet, in most instances, "other" women are available to do the work of mothers. Dreby (2010), who in her study of Mexican transnational families, also found that it is "middlewomen" who likely care for children in transnational families. More specifically, Dreby found that the vast majority of children of migrant mothers who are left behind in Mexico are cared for not just by a grandmother but in particular a maternal grandmother. Maternal grandmothers are those likely to care for children because migrant women, similar to the working women that Cameron Macdonald (2011) observed in Boston, are likely to seek those who can act as their extension or temporary replacement, which in effect magnifies not just women's but the mother's continued responsibility as the primary nurturer of children.

Also examining gender's constitution in transnational families are those who examine the practice of transnational mothering. Coined by Hondagneu-Sotelo and Avila (1997), "transnational mothering" refers to the organizational reconstitution and rearrangement of motherhood to accommodate the temporal and spatial separations forced by migration. Transnational mothering is not an exception but instead a normative feature of the experiences of migrant women, including among others, Ukranian migrant mothers employed as domestic workers in Italy (Solari 2006), Polish migrants in Germany (Lutz 2011), migrant women in the United States from Mexico (Dreby 2010), El Salvador (Abrego 2014), and Honduras (Schmalzbauer 2005), and migrant women in the Philippine diaspora (Parreñas 2005). According to Hondagneu-Sotelo and Avila (1997), transnational mothering signals a new form of motherhood that specifically expands the definition of mothering to encompass breadwinning, which in turn signals an advancement for women. Similarly, Madianou and Miller (2012), who advanced our understanding of transnational communication with their notion of polymedia (i.e., the view that the contours of intimate relations in transnational families change from one medium to the next), found that transnational migrant mothers neither reject nor fully retain their nurturance of children but instead maintain feelings of ambivalence. In doing so, they are said to question traditional notions of child-rearing.

Missing from discussions on transnational mothering is its reception by both society and the family, including the caregivers and children left behind. How does society receive the efforts of migrant mothers to reconfigure mothering? Although transnational mothers might redefine mothering as breadwinning for themselves, we should recognize that society back home might not necessarily accept their efforts. Indeed, they may reject such a redefinition. The backlash confronting migrant mothers in various home societies indicates this to be the case. In the Philippines, the public sees children of transnational mothers as victims who have been abandoned by their mothers (Parreñas 2005). This view is shared in many other sending countries of domestic workers, including Poland and Romania. A newsprint article on "Euro-orphans," meaning children who have been orphaned by the outflow of migrant mothers to western Europe, for instance, quotes the minister of education in Poland as blaming failing test scores and growing truancy on parental migration. As she notes, "Kids get into trouble with the law, have social problems, behavior and attitude problems in school, and absences" (*Chicago Tribune* 2008). Likewise, an article in the *New York Times* describes the out-migration of women as a "national tragedy" that has triggered social upheaval in Romania. The article blames not only the collapse of the Romanian family but also the abandonment and delinquency of children on the migration of women (Bifelski 2009). In this article, the migration of mothers is said to result in severe psychological difficulties among children, which can cause a number of them to commit suicide. However, academic studies do not necessarily support the negative assertions frequently associated with women's migration in news reports. Instead, they show that the maintenance of transnational families does not result in either the poorer performance of children in school or their increased criminal activities (Parreñas 2005; Urbańska 2009).

A third body of research advances discussions on transnational families with their singular focus on the well-being of children. One set of studies addresses the question of how children are responding to the reconstitution of their families, specifically the absence of migrant mothers from their everyday lives. Contrary to mainstream media reports on the adverse effects of transnational families on children, social science studies generally find that children are resilient and accordingly adjust to their circumstances

(Dreby 2010; Hoang, Yeoh, and Graham 2014). In Vietnam, children are said to recognize their parent's migration and their household formation as a necessary livelihood strategy (Hoang and Yeoh 2014). In the Philippines, children of migrant fathers are those more likely to recognize the necessity of parental migration (Parreñas 2005). Finally, research studies also examine the health of children in transnational families, finding that their health is not necessarily better than that of children in nonmigrant families (Graham and Jordan 2013). For instance, exposure to tobacco does not differ for children in migrant and nonmigrant households (Sukamdi and Wattie 2013).

The robust literature on transnational families, which has dominated discussions of "children and youth in Asian migration," suffers, however, from its singular concern with gender, a focus that has arisen with the increase in women's migration. Interestingly, the rise of transnational families from male migration has not elicited the same concern or interest from scholars, as this did not disrupt traditional notions of the family. Yet, the focus on gender has come at the expense of ignoring other factors that likewise shape household dynamics, including class and legal status. While cross-class comparative studies on transnational families remain thin, studies that examine how household dynamics would differ for authorized and unauthorized migrant parents and their children is missing in the Asian context (see Abrego 2014 for the case of El Salvador). Addressing this absence is the article by Beazley and Ball in this special issue; they describe the temporal limbo of "waiting" that confronts Indonesian children with unauthorized migrant parents.

The articles in this special issue expand our knowledge of children and youth in Asian migration as they move beyond discussions of educational migration from East to West and those concerning gender and the transnational family. They expand our knowledge on educational migration by focusing on "unusual" destinations such as the Philippines (Choi) and highlight the short-term migrations of children and youth (Choi, Waters and Leung). They also foreground the politics of citizenship and illustrate boundaries that delimit the membership of children and youth including (1) children from Vietnamese-Taiwanese and Vietnamese-Korean marriages who confront "legal ambiguity" in Vietnam following the dissolution of their parents' marriage (Iwai); (2) Hong Kong–born Chinese from the mainland whose citizenship in Hong Kong mandates that they attend school in the territory as daily border crossers (Waters and Leung); (3) undocumented youth rendered stateless in Malaysia (Cheong) and Cambodia (Rumsby); and (4) children of undocumented parents who face the temporal displacement of perpetually waiting for family reunification (Beazley and Ball).

The articles also expand the parameters of migration studies to include children who have never moved as they highlight the existence of multigenerational undocumented settlement, in this case of "stateless" children (Cheong, Rumsby), and the temporal displacement of children waiting in limbo for the return of undocumented transnational migrant parents (Beazley and Ball). Overall, this special issue calls for more studies that document inter-Asian cross-border connections as the articles highlight distinct pathways of inter-Asian migration, underscore the ethnic (Rumsby, Cheong) and gender (Iwai) boundaries that lead to the marginalization of children and youth in Asian migration, and the stratifications that shape cross-border movements within Asia (Choi, Waters, and Leung).

Note

This work was supported by the Japan Society for the Promotion of Science (JSPS) under Grant # 16H02737.

References

Abrego, Leisy J. 2009. "Economic Well-Being in Salvadoran Transnational Families: How Gender Affects Remittance Practices." *Journal of Marriage and Family* 71, no. 4: 1070–85.

Abrego, Leisy J. 2014. *Sacrificing Families: Navigating Laws, Labor, and Love across Borders.* Stanford, CA: Stanford University Press.

Agamben, Giorgio. 1998. *Homo Sacer: Sovereign Power and Bare Life.* Stanford, CA: Stanford University Press.

Alipio, Cheryll, Melody C. W. Lu, and Brenda S. A. Yeoh. 2015. "Asian Children and Transnational Migration." *Children's Geographies* 13, no. 3: 255–62.

Allerton, Catherine. 2014. "Statelessness and the Lives of the Children of Migrants in Sabah, East Malaysia." *Tilburg Law Review: Journal of International and European Law* 19, nos. 1–2: 26–34.

Arnett, Jeffrey Jensen. 2010. "Emerging Adulthood(s)." In *Bridging Cultural and Developmental Approaches to Psychology: New Syntheses in Theory, Research, and Policy*, edited by Lene Arnett Jensen, 255–75. New York: Oxford University Press.

Asis, Maruja. 2006. "How International Migration Can Support Development: A Challenge for the Philippines." *Migración y desarrollo*, no. 7: 96–122.

Asis, Maruja, Nicola Piper, and Parvati Raghuram. 2019. "Asian Contributions to Global Migration Research: Current Contributions and Future Avenues." *Revue Européenne des migrations internationales* 35, nos. 1–2: 13–37.

Bae, So Hee. 2015. "Complexity of Language Ideologies in Transnational Movement: Korean Jogi Yuhak Families' Ambivalent Attitudes towards Local Varieties of English in Singapore." *International Journal of Bilingual Education and Bilingualism* 18, no. 6: 643–59.

Ball, Jessica, Leslie Butt, and Harriot Beazley. 2014. "Children and Families on the Move: Stateless Children in Indonesia." Preliminary Field Research Report, Lombok and Jakarta, May. www.ecdip.org/docs/pdf/Research%20Report%201%20Stateless%20Children%20Indonesia%20UVic%20USC%20Sept%202014.pdf.

Ball, Jessica, Leslie Butt, and Harriot Beazley. 2017. "Birth Registration and Protection for Children of Transnational Labor Migrants in Indonesia." *Journal of Immigrant and Refugee Studies* 15, no. 3: 305–25.

Ball, Jessica, Leslie Butt, Harriot Beazley, and Natasha Fox. 2014. "Advancing Research on 'Stateless Children': Family Decision Making and Birth Registration among Transnational Migrants in the Asia-Pacific Region." CAPI Working Paper No. 2014-2, January 12. dspace.library.uvic.ca/bitstream/handle/1828/6522/Ball_Jessica_CAPI_2014a.pdf?sequence=1&isAllowed=y.

Bastia, Tanja. 2015. "'Looking after Granny': A Transnational Ethic of Care and Responsibility." *Geoforum* 64: 121–29.

Beazley, Harriot, Leslie Butt, and Jessica Ball. 2018. "'Like It, Don't Like It, You Have to Like It': Children's Emotional Responses to the Absence of Transnational Migrant Parents in Lombok, Indonesia." *Children's Geographies* 16, no. 6: 591–603.

Bhabha, Jacqueline, 2011. "From Citizen to Migrant: The Scope of Child Statelessness in the Twenty-First Century." In *Children without a State: A Global Human Rights Challenge*, edited by Jacqueline Bhabha, 1–39. Cambridge, MA: MIT Press.

Biehl, João. 2005. *Vita: Life in a Zone of Social Abandonment*. Berkeley: University of California Press.

Bifelski, Dan. 2009. "In Romania, Children Left Behind Suffer the Strains of Migration." *New York Times*, February 14. www.nytimes.com/2009/02/15/world/europe/15romania.html.

Brooks, Rachel, and Johanna Waters. 2011. *Student Mobilities, Migrations, and the Internationalization of Higher Education*. Basingstoke, UK: Palgrave Macmillan.

Castles, Stephen, and Mark J. Miller. 1993. *The Age of Migration: International Population Movements in the Modern World*. Basingstoke, UK: Palgrave Macmillan.

Chakraborty, Kabita, and Shanthi Thambiah. 2018. "Children and Young People's Emotions of Migration across Asia." *Children's Geographies* 16, no. 6: 583–90.

Chiang, Lan-Hung Nora. 2008. "'Astronaut Families': Transnational Lives of Middle-Class Taiwanese Married Women in Canada." *Social and Cultural Geography* 9, no. 5: 505–18.

Chicago Tribune. 2008. "Poland Sees Host of Problems among Euro-Orphans." September 21.

Cho, Hae-joang. 2015. "The Spec Generation Who Can't Say 'No': Overeducated and Underemployed Youth in Contemporary South Korea." *positions* 23, no. 3: 437–62.

Chu, J. J. 1996. "Taiwan: A Fragmented 'Middle' Class in the Making." In *The New Rich in Asia: Mobile Phones, McDonalds, and Middle-Class Revolution*, edited by Richard Robison and David S. G. Goodman, 207–22. London: Routledge.

Chun, Jennifer Jihye, and Ju Hui Judy Han. 2015. "Language Travels and Global Aspirations of Korean Youth." *positions* 23, no. 3: 565–93.

Collins, Francis Leo. 2013. "Regional Pathways: Transnational Imaginaries, Infrastructures, and Implications of Student Mobility within Asia." *Asian and Pacific Migration Journal* 22, no. 4: 475–500.

Collins, Francis Leo, Ravinder Sidhu, Nick Lewis, and Brenda S. A. Yeoh. 2014. "Mobility and Desire: International Students and Asian Regionalism in Aspirational Singapore." *Discourse: Studies in the Cultural Politics of Education* 35, no. 5: 661–76.

Constable, Nicole. 2014. *Born out of Place: Migrant Mothers and the Politics of International Labor*. Berkeley: University of California Press.

Derné, Steve. 2005. "The (Limited) Effect of Cultural Globalization in India: Implications for Culture Theory." *Poetics* 33, no. 1: 33–47.

Dobson, Madeleine E. 2009. "Unpacking Children in Migration Research." *Children's Geographies* 7, no. 3: 355–60.

Dreby, Joanna. 2010. *Divided by Borders: Mexican Migrants and Their Children*. Berkeley: University of California Press.

Findlay, Allan M. 2011. "An Assessment of Supply and Demand-Side Theorizations of International Student Mobility." *International Migration* 49, no. 2: 162–90.

Frändberg, Lotta. 2014. "Temporary Transnational Youth Migration and Its Mobility Links." *Mobilities* 9, no. 1: 146–64.

Graham, Elspeth, and Lucy P. Jordan. 2013. "Does Having a Migrant Parent Reduce the Risk of Undernutrition for Children Who Stay Behind in South-East Asia?" *Asian and Pacific Migration Journal* 22, no. 3: 315–48.

Graham, Elspeth, Lucy P. Jordan, Brenda S. A. Yeoh, Theodora Lam, Maruja Asis, and Su-Kamdi. 2012. "Transnational Families and the Family Nexus: Perspectives of Indonesian and Filipino Children Left Behind by Migrant Parents." *Environment and Planning A: Economy and Space* 44, no, 4: 793–815.

Grugel, Jean B. 2015. "Unaccompanied Child and Adolescent Migrants in Latin America: From Mapping Migration to the Assertion of Migrants' Rights." Paper presented at the International Workshop on Addressing Multiple Forms of Migrant Precarity—Beyond Management to an Integrated Rights-Based Approach, United Nations Research Institute for Social Development, Palais des Nations, Geneva, September 24.

Ho, Chaang-luan, Pi-Yueh Lin, and Shu-Chin Huang. 2014. "Exploring Taiwanses [*sic*] Working Holiday-Makers' Motivations: An Analysis of Means-End Hierarchies." *Journal of Hospitality and Tourism Research* 38, no. 4: 463–86. doi.org/10.1177/1096348012461549.

Ho, Elsie. 2002. "Multi-Local Residence, Transnational Networks: Chinese 'Astronaut' Families in New Zealand." *Asian and Pacific Migration Journal* 11, no. 1: 145–64.

Hoang, Lan Anh, and Brenda S. A. Yeoh. 2014. "Children's Agency and Its Contradictions in the Context of Transnational Labour Migration from Vietnam." *Global Networks* 15, no. 2: 180–97.

Hoang, Lan Anh, Brenda S. A. Yeoh, and Elspeth Graham. 2014. "Transnational Migration, Changing Care Arrangements, and Left-Behind Children's Responses in South-East Asia." *Children's Geographies* 13, no. 3: 263–77.

Hondagneu-Sotelo, Pierrette, and Emestine Avila. 1997. "'I'm Here but I'm There': The Meanings of Latina Transnational Motherhood." *Gender and Society* 11, no. 5: 548–71.

Huang, Shirlena, and Brenda S. A. Yeoh. 2005. "Transnational Families and Their Children's Education: China's 'Study Mothers' in Singapore." *Global Networks* 5, no. 4: 379–400.

ICEF Monitor. 2015. "The Number of Korean Students Abroad Declines for the Third Straight Year." ICEF Monitor, February 10. monitor.icef.com/2015/02/number-korean-students-abroad-declines-third-straight-year/.

Institute of International Education. 2017. *Open Doors: Report on International Educational Exchange.* New York: Institute of International Education.

Ishii, Sari K. 2016. "Child Return Migration from Japan to Thailand." In *Marriage Migration in Asia: Emerging Minorities at the Frontiers of Nation-States*, edited by Sari K. Ishii, 118–34. Singapore: National University of Singapore Press.

James, Allison, Chris Jenks, and Alan Prout. 1998. *Theorizing Childhood.* Cambridge, UK: Polity Press.

Jeong, Yu-Jin, Hyun-Kyung You, and Young In Kwon. 2014. "One Family in Two Countries: Mothers in Korean Transnational Families." *Ethnic and Racial Studies* 37, no. 9: 1546–64.

Jones, Andrew. 2011. "Theorising International Youth Volunteering: Training for Global (Corporate) Work?" *Transactions of the Institute of British Geographers* 36, no. 4: 530–44.

Kang, Jiyeon, and Nancy Abelmann. 2011. "The Domestication of South Korean Pre-College Study Abroad in the First Decade of the Millennium." *Journal of Korean Studies* 16, no. 1: 89–118.

Kang, Yoonhee. 2012. "Singlish or Globish: Multiple Language Ideologies and Global Identities among Korean Educational Migrants in Singapore." *Journal of Sociolinguistics* 16, no. 2: 165–83.

Kawashima, Kumiko. 2010. "Japanese Working Holiday Makers in Australia and Their Relationship to the Japanese Labour Market: Before and After." *Asian Studies Review* 34, no. 3: 267–86.

Kehily, Mary Jane, ed. 2004. *An Introduction to Childhood Studies*. Maidenhead, UK: Open University Press.

Kim, Dong-One, and Seongsu Kim. 2003. "Globalization, Financial Crisis, and Industrial Relations: The Case of South Korea." *Industrial Relations: A Journal of Economy and Society* 42, no. 3: 341–67.

Kim, Nadia Y. 2008. *Imperial Citizens: Koreans and Race from Seoul to LA*. Stanford, CA: Stanford University Press.

King, Russell, and Eric Ruiz-Gelices. 2003. "International Student Migration and the European 'Year Abroad': Effects on European Identity and Subsequent Migration Behaviour." *International Journal of Population Geography* 9, no. 3: 229–52.

Kondakci, Yasar, Svenja Bedenlier, and Olaf Zawacki-Richter. 2018. "Social Network Analysis of International Student Mobility: Uncovering the Rise of Regional Hubs." *Higher Education* 75, no. 3: 517–35.

Koo, Hagen. 2007. "The Changing Faces of Inequality in South Korea in the Age of Globalization." *Korean Studies* 31, no. 1: 1–18.

Kulynych, Jessica. 2001. "No Playing in the Public Sphere: Democratic Theory and the Exclusion of Children." *Social Theory and Practice* 27, no. 2: 231–64.

Kuper, Andrew, ed. 2005. *Global Responsibilities—Who Must Deliver on Human Rights?* London: Routledge.

Lachica Buenavista, Tracy. 2018. "Model (Undocumented) Minorities and 'Illegal' Immigrants: Centering Asian Americans and US Carcerality in Undocumented Student Discourse." *Race, Ethnicity, and Education* 21, no. 1: 78–91.

Lam, Theodora, and Brenda Yeoh. 2018. "Migrant Mothers, Left-Behind Fathers: The Negotiation of Gender Subjectivities in Indonesia and the Philippines." *Gender, Place, and Culture* 25, no. 1: 104–17.

Le, Hien Anh. 2016. "Lives of Mixed Vietnamese-Korean Children in Vietnam." In *Marriage Migration in Asia: Emerging Minorities at the Frontiers of Nation-States*, edited by Sari K. Ishii, 175–86. Singapore: National University of Singapore Press.

Lee, Hakyoon. 2010. "'I Am a Kirogi Mother': Education Exodus and Life Transformation among Korean Transnational Women." *Journal of Language, Identity, and Education* 9, no. 4: 250–64.

Liu-Farrer, Gracia, and Brenda S. A. Yeoh. 2018. "Introduction: Asian Migrations and Mobilities: Continuities, Conceptualisations, and Controversies." In *Routledge Handbook of Asian Migrations,* edited by Gracia Liu-Farrer and Brenda S. A. Yeoh, 1–18. New York: Routledge.

Loker-Murphy, Launie, and Philip L. Pearce. 1995. "Young Budget Travelers: Backpackers in Australia." *Annals of Tourism Research* 22, no. 4: 819–43.

Luthra, Renee, and Lucinda Platt. 2016. "Elite or Middling? International Students and Migrant Diversification." *Ethnicities* 16, no. 2: 316–44.

Lutz, Helma. 2011. *The New Maids: Transnational Women and the Care Economy*, translated by Deborah Shannon. London: Zed Books.

Macdonald, Cameron Lynne. 2011. *Shadow Mothers: Nannies, Au Pairs, and the Micropolitics of Mothering*. Berkeley: University of California Press.

Madianou, Mirca. 2012. "Migration and the Accentuated Ambivalence of Motherhood: The Role of ICTs in Filipino Transnational Families." *Global Networks* 12, no. 3: 277–95.

Madianou, Mica, and Daniel Miller. 2012. *Migration and New Media: Transnational Families and Polymedia*. London: Routledge.

Manalansan, Martin F., IV. 2006. "Queer Intersections: Sexuality and Gender in Migration Studies." *International Migration Review* 40, no. 1: 224–49.

Mazzucato, Valentina, and Djamila Schans. 2011. "Transnational Families and the Well-Being of Children: Conceptual and Methodological Challenges." *Journal of Marriage and Family* 73, no. 4: 704–12.

McKay, Deirdre. 2012. *Global Filipinos: Migrants' Lives in the Virtual Village*. Bloomington: Indiana University Press.

Mitchell, Katharyne, and Kirsi Pauliina Kallio. 2017. "Spaces of the Geosocial: Exploring Transnational Topographies." *Geopolitics* 22, no. 1: 1–14.

Mok, Ka Ho. 2011. "The Quest for Regional Hub of Education: Growing Heterarchies, Organizational Hybridization, and New Governance in Singapore and Malaysia." *Journal of Education Policy* 26, no. 1: 61–81.

Moretti, Sebastien. 2018. "Keeping up Appearances: State Sovereignty and the Protection of Refugees in Southeast Asia." *European Journal of East Asian Studies* 17, no. 1: 3–30.

Nah, Alice M. 2019. "Constructing Refugees: Negotiating Asylum in the Complexities of Migration in Southeast Asia." *Revue Européenne des migrations internationales* 35, no. 2: 63–87.

Newman, Philip R., and Barbara M. Newman. 2009. "Self-Socialization: A Case Study of a Parachute Child." *Adolescence* 44, no. 175: 523–37.

Ng, Pak Tee, and Charlene Tan. 2010. "The Singapore Global Schoolhouse: An Analysis of the Development of the Tertiary Education Landscape in Singapore." *International Journal of Educational Management* 24, no. 3: 178–88.

Ong, Aihwa. 1999. *Flexible Citizenship: The Cultural Logics of Transnationality*. Durham, NC: Duke University Press.

Orellana, Marjorie Faulstich, Barrie Thorne, Anna Chee, and Wan Shun Eva Lam. 2001. "Transnational Childhoods: The Participation of Children in Processes of Family Migration." *Social Problems* 48, no. 4: 572–91.

Pan, Darcy. 2011. "Student Visas, Undocumented Labour, and the Boundaries of Legality: Chinese Migration and English as a Foreign Language Education in the Republic of Ireland." *Social Anthropology* 19, no. 3: 268–87.

Park, Joseph Sung-Yul. 2011. "The Promise of English: Linguistic Capital and the Neoliberal Worker in the South Korean Job Market." *International Journal of Bilingual Education and Bilingualism* 14, no. 4: 443–55.

Park, Joseph Sung-Yul, and Sohee Bae. 2009. "Language Ideologies in Educational Migration: Korean Jogi Yuhak Families in Singapore." *Linguistics and Education* 20, no. 4: 366–77.

Park, So Jin, and Nancy Abelmann. 2004. "Class and Cosmopolitan Striving: Mothers' Management of English Education in South Korea." *Anthropological Quarterly* 77, no. 4: 645–72.

Parreñas, Rhacel. 2005. *Children of Global Migration: Transnational Families and Gendered Woes*. Stanford, CA: Stanford University Press.

Parreñas, Rhacel. 2015. *Servants of Globalization: Migration and Domestic Work*. Stanford, CA: Stanford University Press.

Piper, Nicola, 2017. "Global Governance of Labour Migration: From 'Management' of Migration to an Integrated Rights-Based Approach." In *Regulatory Theory: Foundations and Applications*, edited by Peter Drahos, 377–94. Acton: Australian National University Press.

Piper, Nicola, Stuart Rosewarne, and Matt Withers. 2017. "Migrant Precarity: 'Networks of Labour' for a Rights-Based Governance of Migration." *Development and Change* 48, no. 5: 1089–1110.

Popadiuk, Natalee E. 2009. "Unaccompanied Asian Secondary Students Studying in Canada." *International Journal for the Advancement of Counselling* 31, no. 4: 229–43.

Portes, Alejandro, and Min Zhou. 1993. "The New Second Generation: Segmented Assimilation and Its Variants." *Annals of the American Academy of Political and Social Science* 530, no. 1: 74–96.

Robertson, Shanthi. 2014. "Time and Temporary Migration: The Case of Temporary Graduate Workers and Working Holiday Makers in Australia." *Journal of Ethnic and Migration Studies* 40, no. 12: 1915–33.

Robertson, Shanthi. 2016. "Student-Workers and Tourist-Workers as Urban Labour: Temporalities and Identities in the Australian Cosmopolitan City." *Journal of Ethnic and Migration Studies* 42, no. 14: 2272–88.

Robertson, Shanthi, Anita Harris, and Loretta Baldassar. 2018. "Mobile Transitions: A Conceptual Framework for Researching a Generation on the Move." *Journal of Youth Studies* 21, no. 2: 203–17.

Robison, Richard, and David S. G. Goodman. 1996. "The New Rich in Asia: Economic Development, Social Status, and Political Consciousness." In *The New Rich in Asia: Mobile Phones, McDonalds, and Middle-Class Revolution*, edited by Richard Robison and David S. G. Goodman, 1–16. New York: Routledge Press.

Salah, Mohamed Azzedine. 2008. "The Impacts of Migration on Children in Moldova." UNICEF Working Paper, October. cdn.oneworld.nl/app/uploads/2015/05/07102525/www.unicef.org_The_Impacts_of_Migration_on_Children_in_Moldova(1).pdf.

Schmalzbauer, Leah. 2005. "Searching for Wages and Mothering from Afar: The Case of Honduran Transnational Families." *Journal of Marriage and Family* 66, no. 5: 1317–31.

Sidhu, Ravinder, K.-C. Ho, and Brenda Yeoh. 2011. "Emerging Education Hubs: The Case of Singapore." *Higher Education* 61, no. 1: 23–40.

Solari, Cinzia. 2006. "Professionals and Saints: How Immigrant Careworkers Negotiate Gendered Identities at Work." *Gender and Society* 20, no. 3: 301–31.

Stephens, Sharon, ed. 1995. *Children and the Politics of Culture.* Princeton, NJ: Princeton University Press.

Sukamdi, and Anna Marie Wattie. 2013. "Tobacco Use and Exposure among Children in Migrant and Non-Migrant Households in Java, Indonesia." *Asian and Pacific Migration Journal* 22, no. 3: 447–64.

Suzuki, Nobue. 2015. "Troubling *Jus Sanguinis*: The State, Law, and Citizenships of Japanese-Filipino Youth in Japan." In *Migrant Encounters: Intimate Labor, the State, and Mobility across Asia*, edited by Sara L. Friedman and Pardis Mahdavi, 113–32. Philadelphia: University of Pennsylvania Press.

Tsong, Yuying, and Yuli Liu. 2008. "Parachute Kids and Astronaut Families." In *Asian American Psychology: Current Perspectives*, edited by Nita Tewari and Alvin N. Alvarez, 365–80. New York: Psychology Press.

Urbańska, Sylwai. 2009. "'Mothers of the Nation as a Target of Public Therapy': Transnational Parenting and Moral Panic in Poland." Paper presented at Mosaics of Transnational Spaces Workshop, Krakow, Poland, May 9.

Waters, Johanna L. 2002. "Flexible Families? 'Astronaut' Households and the Experiences of Lone Mothers in Vancouver, British Columbia." *Social and Cultural Geography* 3, no. 2: 117–34.

Waters, Johanna L. 2005. "Transnational Family Strategies and Education in the Contemporary Chinese Diaspora." *Global Networks* 5, no. 4: 359–77.

Waters, Johanna L. 2006. "Geographies of Cultural Capital: Education, International Migration, and Family Strategies between Hong Kong and Canada." *Transactions of the Institute of British Geographers* 31, no. 2: 179–92.

Waters, Johanna, and Maggi Leung. 2013. "Immobile Transnationalisms? Young People and Their *In Situ* Experiences of 'International Education' in Hong Kong." *Urban Studies* 50, no. 3: 606–20.

Wilken, Lisanne, and Mette Ginnerskov-Dahlberg. 2017. "Between International Student Mobility and Work Migration: Experiences of Students from EU's Newer Member States in Denmark." *Journal of Ethnic and Migration Studies* 43, no. 8: 1347–61.

Yang, Peidong. 2018. "Compromise and Complicity in International Student Mobility: The Ethnographic Case of Indian Medical Students at a Chinese University." *Discourse: Studies in the Cultural Politics of Education* 39, no. 5: 694–708.

Yoon, Kyong. 2014. "Transnational Youth Mobility in the Neoliberal Economy of Experience." *Journal of Youth Studies* 17, no. 8: 1014–28.

Yoon, Kyong. 2015. "A National Construction of Transnational Mobility in the 'Overseas Working Holiday Phenomenon' in Korea." *Journal of Intercultural Studies* 36, no. 1: 71–87.

Deportable to Nowhere:

Stateless Children as Challenges to State Logics of Immigration Control

Amanda R. Cheong

An estimated 281 million people (3.6 percent of the global population) were living outside of their country of birth in 2020, of whom 36 million were younger than the age of 18 (UNICEF 2021a). The global migrant population at the end of 2020 included a record-high 33 million refugees, approximately 36 percent of whom were children (UNICEF 2021b). An estimated 153,300 of these children crossed an international border unaccompanied by or separated from family members (UNHCR 2021a). Nearly 14 million (39 percent of the world's child migrants) reside in Asia, making it the region that hosts the highest number of child migrants (UNICEF 2021a). Of the United Nations Refugee Agency's (UNHCR) identified populations of concern in the Asia-Pacific region in 2017 (including refugees, asylum seekers, stateless persons, and internally displaced persons, among other vulnerable groups), 38 percent were children (UNHCR 2021b).

positions 30:2 DOI 10.1215/10679847-9573331
Copyright 2022 by Duke University Press

The protection of children on the move has become an issue of concern for international bodies in recent years. For example, as part of the 2018 Global Compact for Safe, Orderly, and Regular Migration (henceforth the Global Compact for Migration), UN member states resolved to establish child-sensitive migration "management" procedures, including the eradication of the practice of child detention.[1] These commitments, however, are nonbinding and therefore unenforceable, and we have witnessed in recent years a scaling up of receiving states' border control and surveillance infrastructures in response to irregular migration (Bennett and Lyon 2008; Broeders 2007; Massey, Durand, and Malone 2002). The securitization of migration is a process that has largely overlooked the particular vulnerabilities of children and the potential long-term consequences of detention and deportation on their well-being and life course trajectories.

Outside of the field of public health (see, for example, Dudley et al. 2012; Ehntholt et al. 2018; Fazel, Karunakara, and Newnham 2014; Kronick, Rousseau, and Cleveland 2011; Linton, Griffin, and Shapiro 2017; Lorek et al. 2009; Mares and Jureidini 2004; Shields et al. 2004), less empirical research has been conducted on the experiences and impacts of child detention and deportation (see note for exceptions).[2] This is despite estimates that millions of children worldwide have been affected by immigration detention—a figure referring not only to children who have a parent or relative who has been detained but also to children who have been detained themselves (Inter-Agency Working Group to End Child Immigration Detention 2016). It is also worthwhile to focus on children because immigration and asylum policies and practices have historically been modeled after the archetypical image of the migrant as being alone, unmarried, and male (Bhabha 1996; Garip 2017; Kelly 1993). An analytical focus on children serves to denaturalize this image as well as the legitimacy of the institutions that have been developed to "manage" it.

In this article I draw on ethnographic fieldwork with legally marginalized families in Malaysia—including undocumented migrants, stateless persons, asylum seekers, and their descendants—to examine how the specters of detention and deportation shape children's lives and their relationships with the Malaysian state. I conducted my fieldwork in Kuala Lumpur and Sabah over eighteen months between 2016 and 2017 as part of a larger qualitative study on access to identity documentation and legal personhood among legally marginalized families. In conducting this study, I built on a much longer academic and civil society–based engagement with questions of citizenship and statelessness in the Malaysian context dating back to 2012. A major theme that emerged from 105 household interviews as well as observations of families going through the process of applying for basic documents was the legal paradox that stateless children found themselves in: Denied acceptance as citizens of Malaysia despite their substantive connection to the country, and often without a viable pathway to obtaining citizenship from their ancestral countries, stateless children constitute a "problem of organization" to the contemporary nation-state system (Malkki 2002). I argue that the figure of the stateless child challenges state logics of immigration control in two ways: First, born in Malaysia but without proper identity documentation or legal status from any nation, stateless youths in the study were "deportable to nowhere." Second, Malaysian detention and deportation systems—designed to deter "illegal" immigration—inadvertently transform stateless children into illegal migrants: for some, expulsion to their ancestral country and eventual illicit return to Malaysia marked the first time they crossed an international border.[3]

This study is organized as follows: First, I theorize how stateless children pose challenges to the immigration policies and systems that have been modeled on the archetype of the lone male migrant. Second, I contextualize Malaysia's detention and deportation apparatus within its ongoing racialized nation-building project and its development as a major migrant destination in the ASEAN region. Third, I provide an overview of the multiple pathways into statelessness that exist within the legal framework governing Malaysian nationality. Fourth, I flesh out the concept of being "deportable to nowhere," drawing on ethnographic data to demonstrate the legal quandaries faced by stateless children who are simultaneously denied political membership in Malaysia while being unable to claim, on a practical basis, the nationality of their ancestral countries. Fifth, I illustrate how states' efforts to crack down on illegal immigration may produce illegality domestically, given that Malaysian-born stateless children who are expelled may illicitly repatriate themselves to reunite with family and friends, and continue their lives in the country with which they most identify. I conclude by discussing the broader implications of this study with regard to the defensibility of violent and carceral tactics for upholding states' territorial sovereignty.

Stateless Children as Challenges to State Logics of Immigration Control

Despite mounting research since the 1970s that has drawn attention to the feminization of migration flows (Donato and Gabaccia 2015; Morokvasic 1984; Ong 1991; Pedraza 1991), and that has decentered the analytical focus on men as the protagonists of migration processes (Brettell and deBerjeois 1992; Pessar 1986), the archetype of the lone male migrant has endured (Pessar and Mahler 2003). This bias informs and is reflected in immigration policies, which often overlook the specific migratory modalities, interests, and needs of women and children. For example, Crawley (2000) argues that the subordination of women's experiences of gender-related persecution to the private and cultural, as opposed to the political, sphere has resulted in the discounting of their asylum claims across various national contexts. In the United States (US), only 68 percent of unaccompanied children (UACs) had legal representation in immigration proceedings during the 2019 fiscal year.[4] The particular vulnerabilities of UACs—given that they are separated from their families and/or guardians, have likely endured trauma in their origin countries and throughout the migration process, are less likely to be able to afford legal fees, and are still in the process of growth and maturation—render the practice of expecting UACs as young as toddlers to plead their own asylum cases before immigration court particularly absurd.[5] Indeed, UACs appearing in US immigration court without an attorney are much more likely to be ordered to be deported.[6] Furthermore, Galli (2020) shows how the asylum-seeking process in the US—even while recognizing and making accommodations for the vulnerabilities of migrant children— incentivizes the infantilization and victimization of UACs in ways that deny their agency.

Logistical dilemmas also arise when irregular migrant parents and their accompanying children are arrested together. Some states detain children along with their parents under the rationale that this practice adheres to Article 9 of the Convention on the Rights of the Child, which advises against the separation of children from parents (Gros and Song 2016). At the same time, however, international agencies such as the UN Refugee Agency have argued that detention for immigration-related purposes is a violation of the best interests of the child.[7]

A lack of regard for the heterogeneity of migrants also inheres in the design of the systems and physical structures used in immigration control, with adverse consequences for those who do not fit the archetype of the lone male migrant. For example, inadequate health care services for women in immigration detention, including pregnant women, have been documented in the United States (Brané and Wang 2013; Human Rights Watch 2009; Rabin 2009). The influx in recent years of UACs into the United States and the European Union has been met with screening and detention processes that have been criticized for the negative physical and psychological impacts wrought on the youth subjected to them (Menjívar and Perreira 2019). A 2019 report by the US Department of Homeland Security, based on inspections of five Border Patrol facilities in the Rio Grande Valley, warned of the "dangerous" overcrowding, prolonged detention, and substandard provision of hygiene and nutrition for UACs and families.[8]

Many parallels can be drawn between the struggles faced by stateless people children and irregular migrant children, the latter having become the subject of a large and growing body of literature. This is partly because of the blurriness of the definitional boundary between the two groups: certain types of irregular migrant children, such as asylum seekers, might be considered to be de facto or functionally stateless because of an inability to actualize their formal nationality rights (Bhabha 2009). Similarities can also be drawn with undocumented 1.5-generation immigrants in the United States, who have been identified by researchers as inhabiting a liminal existence characterized by a substantive principal connection to, but simultaneous denial of legal membership of, the United States (Gonzales 2011; Gonzales and Chavez 2012). In Hong Kong, children born to Indonesian and Filipino women labor migrant workers have been described by Constable (2014) as being "born out of place," owing to the Hong Kong state's view of temporary labor migrants as strictly workers without regard to their multifaceted identities as women, mothers, and partners.

At the same time, stateless people, including children, represent "problems of organization" for states that are distinct from those associated with irregular migrants (Malkki 2002). From a legal standpoint, stateless children are not considered to be nationals of any state, and consequently lack the formal rights associated with citizenship. Additionally, some people can be stateless while they are migrants but can gain or regain a national affiliation, as in the case of children born "out of place" to temporary women labor migrants whose irregular statuses can presumably be resolved when their mothers bring them back to their home countries (Constable 2014). Others, though, are stateless in situ, as in the case of Rohingya minorities living within Myanmar (Kyaw 2017). That is, they may have durable and meaningful ties to the country in which they were born and from which they may have never traveled out of, and yet are not considered to be citizens of that or any other country (UNHCR 2014; Vlieks 2017).

International organizational problems arise when stateless children become caught up in countries' immigration control systems. Beyond the aforementioned risks and dangers faced by children subject to immigration processing, the status of statelessness is associated with additional vulnerabilities. Stateless children can be conceived of as being what I term "deportable to nowhere": they are denied legal membership of the country to which they are most substantively connected to, and yet may have no actionable political membership claims or substantive ties to any other country. In her ethnographic study of children or migrants in Sabah, East Malaysia, Allerton (2017) describes them as "impossible children," which is an adaptation of Ngai's (2014) history of the legal construction of "illegal aliens" in the US in her book *Impossible Subjects*. With the term *impossible children*, Allerton (2017) refers to the legal denial of children of irregular migrants' existence by the Malaysian government, and their discursive portrayal as immutably foreign and unassimilable within Malaysian society. These characteristics speak to the first condition of being "deportable to nowhere"—that is, the rejection of stateless children from the formal polity and national imaginary of the country in which they were born, and to which they most strongly identify. The novel utility of the concept of "deportability to nowhere" broadens the analytical scope of research on stateless children by considering their liminal positionality within the international nation-state system. Not only do they face exclusion from the country they have the greatest attachment to, but also they stand, as I will demonstrate, to be legally and symbolically rejected from their putative homeland. In the next section, I turn to the institutional apparatuses that the Malaysian state has erected to "manage" its migration flows in order to contextualize the empirical findings of this article.

Migrant Expendability and Deportability in the Malaysian State

Texts such as the 2018 Global Compact for Migration signify a popularization over the past decade and a half of the language of "migration management," which the International Organization for Migration defines as "planned approaches to the implementation and operationalization of policy, legislative, and administrative frameworks developed by the institutions in charge of migration."[9] I put the term *management* in quotation marks to underscore how its seeming neutrality euphemizes the often violent nature with which states police the movement of people in and out of their borders. The ideal of international migration becoming a rationalized matter of administration is a stark contrast to the punitive and carceral nature of the administrative practices currently employed by many states to "manage" migration flows. Scholars have pointed out the increased routine use of detention as a mechanism of population control, whereby immigration enforcement and criminal punishment have become increasingly homologous in form despite their discrete legal branches (Hernandez 2014; Leerkes and Broeders 2010; Sampson and Mitchell 2013). Today, all liberal democratic nations engage in immigration detention to varying degrees (Silverman and Massa 2012).

In Malaysia, incarceration is a widely deployed method for selectively punishing and containing the large number of irregular persons hailing predominantly from neighboring South and Southeast Asian countries.[10] Animus toward migrants and their descendants is part and parcel of Malaysia's ongoing racialized nation-building struggles, by which colonial-era ideologies of Malay indigeneity have been entrenched in the present day via policies that have stratified the country's political, economic, social, and intimate spheres along racial lines (Hirschman 1986). Since the 1970s, spurred on by the acceleration of Malaysia's industrial growth, rising immigration has created new rifts in the country's racial landscape (Yusof and Bhattasali

2008). Public anxieties about the incursion of migrants across the country's porous borders have been stoked by ruling elites in attempts to maintain the tenuous political bargain between the dominant Malays, Chinese, and Indians (Dannecker 2005; Neo 2006).

Today, Malaysia is a major migrant destination in the region, attracting foreign workers to its agricultural, construction, and service sectors (Kaur 2006). Sending countries include neighboring Indonesia, the Philippines, Bangladesh, India, Nepal, and Myanmar (International Organization for Migration 2021). Officially, there are an estimated 2.7 million noncitizens living in the country, making up almost 10 percent of the population (Malaysia Department of Statistics 2021). High antimigrant sentiment belies the reality that "illegal" migration has become an essential and normalized part of the domestic economy, with unauthorized workers occupying predominantly labor-intensive, low-skilled jobs in agriculture, construction, hospitality, and domestic service that Malaysian citizens have increasingly shunned (Chin 2003). The irregular population also includes people fleeing conflict and persecution from countries such as Myanmar, Sri Lanka, Pakistan, Somalia, Yemen, Syria, Iraq, Afghanistan, and Palestine (UNHCR 2019).

More than half of Malaysia's noncitizens reside in the state of Sabah on the northeastern part of Borneo, where an estimated one out of three residents is a noncitizen (Malaysia Department of Statistics 2021). This figure does not take into account the significant but unknown number of undocumented persons living in the state, the majority of whom came from the Philippines and Indonesia, or are descended from migrants from these countries. Irregular flows from the southern part of the Philippines were heightened during the 1970s by separatist conflicts in Mindanao, to which the Immigration Department responded by issuing Filipino refugees with annually renewable IMM13 cards, which provide their holders with temporary residence rights (Kassim 2009; Kurus 1998). While IMM13 eligibility can be passed to holders' children (with the exception of periods when IMM13 renewals are suspended),[11] there is no legal pathway to Malaysian citizenship from this status, resulting in the persistence of a long-standing ethnically Filipino stateless underclass in Sabah that has been joined by more recent labor migrants from the Philippines seeking work in industries such as construction and service.

By contrast, the route from Indonesia to Sabah is characterized by circular, temporary flows, though migrants' long-term goals of returning home after having achieved the means to sustain a higher standard of living are often disrupted or delayed by the precarious nature of the work they can obtain (Hugo 2009). Sabah, which is the state with the highest crude palm oil production in a country that is the second-largest producer of palm oil in the world, has a significant demand for cheap and flexible labor that is fulfilled mostly by migrants from Indonesia (Pye et al. 2012).[12] Given the high levies and bureaucratic burdens of foreign work permits, employers are incentivized to rely on undocumented migrants to perform the physically demanding and remotely located tasks involved in palm oil cultivation and harvesting. Palm oil plantations are thus obvious targets for authorities seeking to *tangkap* ("arrest") illegal migrants.

Since the 1990s, large-scale immigration crackdowns have been periodically carried out in a highly public and visible manner (Kudo 2013). These *operasi* ("operations") are arguably orchestrated in such a way as to serve not only legal and administrative ends but also ones that are political. Aggressive immigration enforcement "brightens" boundaries between Malaysians and foreign Others (Alba 2005), while providing opportunities for the Malaysian state to assert its territorial sovereignty. Beginning in July 2018, the Immigration Department launched "Op Mega 3.0," which, according to Director-General Datuk Seri Mustafar Ali, consisted of 473 operations conducted nationwide over the course of three days, which resulted in the arrest of more than 1,200 illegal immigrants among 5,038 foreigners who were swept up in the raids.[13] Op Mega 3.0 crackdowns amounted to just a few among a total of 9,449 operations the Immigration Department claimed to have carried out between January 1 and August 29 2018, during which 29,040 unauthorized persons were apprehended.[14] On July 29, Mustafar was quoted in the *New Straits Times* as encouraging Malaysians to "embrace the spirit of independence and help to flush out illegal immigrants."[15] Explicitly defining the hunting down of "illegals" as an act of nationalism, he stated, "We are celebrating National Day this August 31, so let us take this opportunity to embrace the spirit and make sure the country is free from illegal immigrants."[16]

Such calls to action are not unprecedented. In 2005, the *Ikatan Relawan*

Rakyat Malaysia (The People's Volunteer Corps of Malaysia, commonly known as RELA), a volunteer paramilitary force, was empowered with "the right to bear and use firearms, stop, search and demand documents, arrest without warrant, and enter premises without warrant when the RELA personnel has reasonable belief that any person is a terrorist, undesirable person, illegal immigrant or an occupier" (Equal Rights Trust 2010; International Federation for Human Rights and SUARAM 2008). From 2007 to 2009, RELA played a role in providing security inside immigration depots (International Federation for Human Rights and SUARAM 2008).

After their arrest, migrants become confined for indefinite periods of time—extending up to years—in Malaysia's detention system. Local and international observers have criticized Malaysian detention centers of multiple human rights abuses, including the deprivation of liberty, torture, and degrading treatment. Centers have been described as overcrowded and unsanitary, with detainees having inadequate access to clean water, food, and health care (Amnesty International 2010; Fortify Rights 2017; International Federation for Human Rights and SUARAM 2008). In its 2018 annual report, the National Human Rights Commission of Malaysia (SUHAKAM) concluded from monitoring missions that the existing infrastructure within detention centers was insufficient to support the detainee population (SUHAKAM 2019). The report raised concern about the use of bucket toilets in lieu of plumbing, the lack of proper ventilation, insufficient personnel, and crumbling physical infrastructure such as flooring, lighting, and ventilation (SUHAKAM 2019). Public scrutiny of immigration detention practices was heightened in 2016, when it was reported that 118 foreigners had died in the immigration detention system between 2015 and 2016.[17] Causes of death included sepsis, bacterial infection, pneumonia, lung infections, and heart-related conditions, with fifty of the deaths having no reported cause.[18]

Detainees in Malaysia include not just single adult male laborers but also women, children, and families. While immigration detention has deleterious physical and psychological impacts on all persons, mothers and children face particular risks and vulnerabilities, and pose an ongoing challenge to the practical operation of the detention system. The diversity of the detained population was apparent while conducting participant observation of visiting hours at a *rumah merah* (the colloquial term for immigration depot, literally translated to "red house" because of the red color of the compounds' roofs) in eastern Sabah on a hot and dry Tuesday afternoon in 2017. More than a hundred visitors waited in an outdoor shaded area just outside the detention center gates after being assigned a number indicating their turn to see a requested detainee. Many visitors carried large plastic bags full of provisions, which detainees relied on to supplement their sparse diets. The most common amenities were large bottles of mineral water, Coca-Cola and other kinds of soft drinks, packets of Maggi instant noodles, Milo powder, biscuits, bundles of clothing, and soap.

A Filipino woman with Malaysian permanent residence status who was in the waiting area remarked that she had come to see her husband's seventeen-year-old nephew, who had been arrested a month ago. He had only newly arrived in Sabah and had not yet even secured a job before he was picked up by immigration. Though she did not personally know the boy well, she dutifully was delivering amenities to him as a favor to his mother, who was back in the Philippines and had been crying every day out of worry for her son. She remarked, "*Operasi* these days have been *kuat*" (literally translated from Malay to mean "strong," but used in this context to mean "intensified"). The Filipino woman was in the first batch of visitors who were allowed to approach the visiting area, which consisted of a single long counter separated by thin metal caging with holes large enough for parcels of goods to be passed through—and, on occasion, small babies to be embraced. The detainees were brought out in an orderly line, wearing bright yellow bibs. They were men and women of all ages: teenaged boys, an old frail man, and young women, some carrying toddlers. The nephew impassively took the package from his aunt, and, after a brief exchange of words, she left.

More intimate exchanges play out in this public, regulated space, underscoring the distortions wrought on familial relationships by the practice of incarceration. After the first round of visitors were ushered out of the compound, it came time for Auntie Isabella, a middle-aged Malaysian-Filipino woman who routinely donated goods to detained mothers in need, and who invited me to accompany her on one of her weekly visits to the detention center, to get in line. Seated beside her on the crowded bench, I had my shoulder pressed up against the armpit of a young man, who was grasping the hand of a female detainee as they spoke to each other in Bahasa

Indonesia. On my other side was another woman, who was being visited by her husband, around whom hovered three impeccably groomed children dressed in formal wear. Next to them was a solitary teenager being visited by a crowd of adolescent boys who excitedly addressed him as *abang* ("big brother"), some of them piggybacked on one another to fit around the counter.

Babies and pregnant or nursing mothers are not exempt from detention. Despite evidence of the deleterious impact on children of even small amounts of time in detention (UN Human Rights 2016), the Malaysian Immigration Department has rationalized the detention of children by arguing that it is preferable to separating them from mothers who are rounded up for apprehension. That afternoon, Auntie Isabella had come to see one such mother, Murni, and her toddler, a boy aged one year and nine months who stood on the countertop, clutching the dividing bars. Murni, who was thin and missing a few of her teeth despite her young age, had been in detention for six weeks by then. She said she sleeps exposed on the floor on a *sarong* with her baby in the women's block, which she estimates to contain 150 people, though I could not verify the accuracy of this number. Water for bathing, according to her, is rationed to ten ladles per day. While the detention center provides baby formula, other amenities, such as diapers and medicine are in high demand. "It is not a proper place to raise a baby," Murni lamented, "but what choice do I have?" The women were responsible for cleaning the common space they shared, and they and their children often became sick. Her toddler was suffering from a bad cough, which she said was common among the babies in the block.

Murni's experience aligns with that of Nur, a woman on the other side of Sabah who had migrated from the Philippines more than three decades ago. In Sabah, she met and married an Indonesian man in 1990, and they have seven children between the two of them. Without valid legal status in Malaysia, she was caught and detained along with one of her daughters, who was around eight years old at the time. She described life in detention as wretched and tedious, with days consisting only of sitting on the floor ("One day felt like one year inside"). She recalled that many of her block mates had skin diseases and diarrhea. Nur attested that her child did not receive any special treatment and did not have access to education while inside, though Nur said that there were others who were worse off than them since her husband was able to bring them items such as food and soap on a regular basis. She observed that some mothers, after running out of soap, had to use laundry powder to bathe their children.

To summarize, Malaysia has continued to rely on mass-scale incarceration as a tool of immigration control. Migrants and those without legal status are constantly at risk of being swept up in *operasi*, including children and youth who are unaccompanied, or who are caught along with their parents. Once inside detention, children are kept alongside adults in overcrowded, dirty, poorly ventilated spaces, with no access to education or adequate health services. In the next section, I discuss the legal paradox that the Malaysian state is confronted with when "managing" the immigration statuses of stateless children.

Legal Pathways into Statelessness

Multiple generations of irregular migration to Malaysia, in which citizenship is predominantly inherited via the principle of jus sanguinis (with some jus soli conditions), have created what Shachar (2009) describes as "problems of under-inclusion"—the existence of populations that have an attachment to the country, but with no pathway to acquiring citizenship there. The children of irregular migrants are particularly at risk not only of being excluded from the polity in Malaysia but also may have difficulty acquiring the nationality of their ancestral country, rendering them stateless. Since stateless children's experiences with immigration control in Malaysia are the focus of this article, I first provide a brief overview of the major possible legal pathways into statelessness:[19]

Being born to irregular migrants. Citizenship is governed by the Federal Constitution of Malaysia. The most common way to obtain Malaysian nationality is to be born within official wedlock on Malaysian territory to at least one parent who is a Malaysian citizen or permanent resident. Descendants of irregular migrants are thus ineligible for citizenship, irrespective of the length of time or number of generations direct forebears have resided in the country. They may become stateless if they are unable to claim citizenship of their ancestral countries—for example, if their parents die and do not leave any documentary proof of their nationality.

Being born out of official wedlock. Children who are born out of wedlock—meaning that their parents' marriages were not officially registered at the National Registration Department—are assumed to follow the nationality of their mother. A child may find herself stateless when she is born in Malaysia to a Malaysian national father and a foreign mother who—for various reasons, such as death or abandonment—loses contact with the family, leaving the child unable to substantiate a relationship to her, and therefore lacking eligibility to inherit her nationality (provided that her country of nationality allows for the jus sanguinis transfer of citizenship to children born outside of the territory). Even when a child's foreign mother is still in the picture—for example, when a mixed-status couple undergoes a customary wedding without official recognition of its validity by civil authorities, or when a couple is separated but the mother's identity and whereabouts are still known—inheriting citizenship from her is likely to feel incongruous to the child's lived experience as a Malaysian, especially if it is the intention for the child to continue living in Malaysia.

Being an abandoned child/foundling. While a number of other countries practice the granting of citizenship to foundlings within their territory, children who are abandoned without documentation are not considered to be citizens of Malaysia by right. Even when they are formally adopted by Malaysian national parents, their citizenship status is typically labeled *belum ditentukan* ("not yet determined") (Ngin 2010).

The Federal Constitution provides one possible legal remedy for stateless children to acquire citizenship by registration. Article 15A of the Federal Constitution gives "special power to register children" to the Home Minister. Children younger than the age of twenty-one may apply for citizenship with the National Registration Department through this channel. Applications are forwarded to the Home Ministry, which has total discretion over the matter. The decision process, however, is a lengthy and nontransparent process, and no reason is given for why applications are rejected.

In the following section, I draw on ethnographic data to show how Malaysia's restrictive nationality policies, and the gaps that render certain categories of youth stateless, constrain the everyday lives and aspirations of those who find themselves "deportable to nowhere."

Deportable to Nowhere

> People tell me to go back to Indonesia and get a passport from there. But how can I "go back"? I've never been to Indonesia. I was born here in Malaysia. All of my family lives in Malaysia. I am a Malaysian!
> —Khoo (quoted from field notes)

Twenty-two-year-old Khoo's legal dilemma is representative of the liminal status that many stateless youths occupy in the nation-state system. Khoo was born in a small town in Sabah to a Malaysian-Chinese man and an Indonesian-Bugis woman. He lived with both of his parents, though they were not legally married because his father had not formally divorced from his first wife, a Malaysian-Chinese woman, after they had separated. Khoo's claim to citizenship was weakened as a consequence of his birth as an "illegitimate" child with a non-Malaysian mother. According to the federal constitution, children born out of wedlock on Malaysian soil are assumed to follow the citizenship of their mother. Because Khoo's mother was an undocumented Bugis woman, he was classified as *bukan warganegara* ("noncitizen") on his birth certificate. Being a noncitizen was at odds with Khoo's lived experience as a Malaysian. He grew up speaking not only the official language of Malay but also the commonly used languages of English and Chinese as well as, thanks to his enrollment in his town's Chinese vernacular government school. He did not find it unusual that he was of mixed descent, as many of his friends in the neighborhood had Indonesian or Filipino blood. The most common form of scrutiny he did attract from strangers, however, was the incongruity between his dark skin—which he inherited from his mother—and his Chinese name.

The consequences of his citizenship status only became perceptible to Khoo the day he went to the National Registration Department to apply for a MyKad (national identity card) at the age of twelve, which is a rite of passage that all Malaysian children typically undertake at that age. He was turned away from the counter because he did not have a copy of his parents' marriage certificate, since proof of marriage was required to inherit Malaysian citizenship from his father. Khoo's very biological connection to his father, who had passed away from an illness only two years prior, was questioned by the National Registration Department officers, despite his father's name appearing on Khoo's birth certificate, and Khoo's ability to furnish his father's death certificate. Similar forms of "erasure, invisibility, and denial" experienced by stateless persons at National Registration Department counters in Malaysia have been documented by Liew (2021: 83). Analyzing interviews with stateless persons and other stakeholders, including lawyers and NGO representatives, Liew (2021) argues that frontline bureaucrats and other agents charged with carrying out administrative tasks often end up making *substantive* legal decisions that have the potential to alter the citizenship fates of persons such as Khoo.

Without a MyKad, the transition from childhood to adolescence involves, as Gonzales (2011: 602) writes of undocumented migrant children growing up in the United States, a "move from protected to unprotected, from inclusion to exclusion, from de facto legal to illegal." At thirteen, Khoo was kicked out of school because he could not produce proof of his Malaysian citizenship. Shortly afterward, his mother passed away, and he was taken in by her relatives. In 2014, at the age of nineteen, with the help of his half-brother from father's first marriage, Khoo applied for citizenship at the National Registration Department under Article 15A, the clause in the constitution that endows the Home Minister with special powers to grant citizenship to children younger than the age of twenty-one, initiating a years-long process of uncertainty. While stateless youth wait for their fates to be decided, they remain at risk of arrest for not possessing identity documents, despite there being no country to which they can be deported. Working informally at various jobs obtained through social connections, including at a restaurant and an appliance installation company, Khoo has experienced three close calls during immigration raids at his work sites, during which he managed to hide or leave the premises on being warned by his boss that an *operasi* was rumored to be afoot.

When he sought legal advice from others, such as social workers and lawyers, regarding how to resolve his status, he would often receive the suggestion that he apply for an Indonesian passport and come back to Malaysia with a valid work permit. Such a notion frustrated Khoo, who did not possess any official documentation of his mother's nationality, save for her name and ethnicity (Bugis) on his birth certificate, which would make it technically impossible to establish his eligibility for Indonesian citizenship under the law. Moreover, the notion of becoming an Indonesian on paper was at odds with Khoo's self-understanding as a Malaysian person, even though "his" country refused to recognize him as belonging to it.

At a grassroots-organized public forum in which he and other stateless youth shared their stories, a girl in the audience—who was informally adopted into a middle-class Malaysian family with no knowledge of her biological parents' identities or whereabouts—told a similar story:

> I was caught by immigration because I'm like you [referring to Khoo]. I'm still stateless. So, I was detained for eighteen days in immigration, and they asked me, "Why don't you have an IC [identity card]?" I said, "I can't apply for one." I can't apply for anything. I walk in fear every time I step out the door. After I was caught and released, every day I cross my fingers that it doesn't happen again. That scared me a lot. I have no legitimate documents except for a receipt for my application [for citizenship, which is still pending], and a not legitimate birth certificate I'm bringing around with me. The police, when they stop me, they'll let me go because they want money. But Immigration? They don't know what to do with me.

Vulnerability to being ensnared within the immigration system in Malaysia does not attenuate with time, or even over generations. Mariam was born in Sabah to Filipino parents who had migrated from Zamboanga in 1983. They were given IMM13 passes, a renewable visa that allowed refugees fleeing conflict from the southern Philippines during the 1970s and 1980s to reside in Malaysia indefinitely. She and her husband, a Filipino migrant, have six children together, born between 1999 and 2014. Her children, all born at home, did not have any birth certificates or IMM13 passes to prove their ties to Malaysia. In 2016, two of her teenaged sons were caught in their home during an immigration raid and kept in detention for three months. Though they were still underage, they looked older than they were, and were kept in a block with adult men. Mariam recalled, "My children were arrested, but they didn't know where to send them to, because they were born here [in Malaysia]. The problem is, they didn't have birth certificates." For three months, Mariam went back and forth from the Immigration Department in Kota Kinabalu, a two-hour-long journey from the small town where she lived, to plead for them to be released under her sponsorship as an IMM13 pass holder. Her greatest worry was that her sons would be deported to the Philippines, a country they had never been to. Just as they did not have any documentary proof of their status as Malaysians, neither did her children have any evidence that conclusively condemned them for deportation to the Philippines. The situation was resolved, according to Mariam, when she received a phone call informing her that her sons would be released back into Sabah as directed by the Immigration Department.

In summary, stateless children in Malaysia were similar to illegal migrants in their vulnerability to becoming targets of immigration control. Unlike migrants, however, stateless children, who are by definition not considered nationals of any state, were simultaneously unwanted in Malaysia and deportable to no other country. In the following section, I discuss the consequences that arise when deportations do occur.

Transforming Stateless Children into Illegal Migrants

Ironically, Malaysia's citizenship and immigration policies served to produce illegal migrants from their "homegrown" stateless children (Liew 2019). Deportation from Malaysia (the country in which they were born and raised, and where the majority of their familial and social networks lie) to their ancestral countries (which is likely foreign to them) often constitutes stateless children's first cross-border experiences, and incentivizes eventual illicit return migration to Malaysia.

Aini, born at home in Sabah to IMM13 refugees from the southern Philippines, is one such youth who has undergone the cycle of detention, deportation, and return. Like other noncitizen children, Aini was ineligible to attend government school, but received an informal education from a former Christian missionary worker whom Aini's mother convinced to tutor her and her younger sister. As Aini progressed through her studies and the makeshift school grew in number from word of mouth, she eventually began to volunteer as an assistant teacher, helping other undocumented and stateless children in her community to learn how to read and write in English and do basic mathematics. At seventeen, she worked full-time as a housekeeper for a Malaysian family, but allotted two afternoons a week to teach at the school.

On the way to work one morning, Aini was stopped by the police and put in a detention center for a month. They eventually deported her to the Philippines, which she described less like being sent back home and more like being shipped away from it. Once in the Philippines, Aini was determined to return to her family, her work, and her students in Sabah through proper channels. She managed to raise money and entrusted it to an agent who promised to help process her Filipino passport. The agent, however, did not follow through with this commitment, and disappeared with her money. Describing the moment she realized that she had been taken advantage of, Aini recalled, "I lost my hope to come back here in Sabah where my family lived." With a year having elapsed since her deportation and desperate to return, she accepted a distant uncle's offer to take her across the Sulu Sea on his boat during one of his trips to ferry commercial goods from Malaysia to the Philippines. He dropped her off near Sandakan, a city on the eastern coast that serves as an entry point for many migrants arriving informally from the Philippines. There, she met up with her mother's younger brother, who helped her navigate the 300-kilometer journey back to her neighborhood and family, while successfully managing to evade roadblocks and other surprise encounters with the authorities.

Aini made sincere efforts to regularize her status in Malaysia by attempting to apply for a Filipino passport, but ultimately had to resort to taking the unauthorized yet commonly used route back home, which marked the second time in her life of crossing an international border—the first being her initial expulsion from Malaysia. Back in Sabah, Aini reflected on her uncertain future:

> So, I'm here in Sabah without any documents and working as a housekeeper while volunteering at the school to help my own community, who are also like me. What I mean is, we are an illegal people, although we've lived here in Sabah for a long time. Some of my community, which are called Suluks, have lived here for a few decades, and their children were

also born here, but don't have any documents. Sabahans say that Suluks are bad people, so maybe that's the reason why the government hasn't given us any documents to prove that we belong here.

Being an illegal is very hard. What's even worse is that, as an illegal, we cannot go anywhere we want to, or we can't work anywhere but being a housekeeper only. We must hide whenever we see police or an immigration officer because once we get caught by police or an officer they'll send us to the Philippines. Before they send us [to the Philippines], they'll put us in *rumah merah*. The hard thing for men is that they get caned once they are in the lockup.

Now I'm so confused about which country I belong to. I really don't know what I will do in the future. Shall I stay here in Sabah as an illegal or maybe I should just go back to the Philippines where my parents came from? If I stay here in Sabah, maybe I'll be an illegal for the rest of my life and that won't be good for me in the future. The only thing I really hope is the government will give me an IC [identity card] or PR [permanent residence] to stay forever here in Sabah. I love Sabah. That's why I was so brave to come back here without my passport.

Aini's reflections capture the anxiety that stateless youths have about their uncertain futures, and their internalization of an "illegal" identity. Aini was fully aware of the unsatisfactory options before her: attempting to stay in Malaysia would entail a life under constant fear of apprehension, with little hope of regularization. On the other hand, going to the Philippines meant being separated from her family, community, and means of livelihood. Aini, in making the choice to reenter Sabah informally, chose the former, and in effect became not only "an illegal" but also an immigrant—the very target of the Malaysian state's deportation apparatuses.

As a result of the peculiarities of the Malaysian federal system whereby Sabah and Sarawak have retained the right to monitor migration into their territories from West Malaysia, the transformation into an illegal migrant can occur not just across international borders but also internally as well. By 2017, when I first met Khoo, it had been three years since he had lodged his citizenship application. By then, he was twenty-two years old and no longer considered a child according to the law, meaning that he would be unable to lodge a second application should his initial one be rejected by the Home Ministry. He balanced working full-time and following up with the National Registration Department and Home Ministry regarding his case, making phone calls on a regular basis and taking expensive bus trips to Kota Kinabalu to inquire at the Sabah state government offices in person. Each time, he would simply be told that his application was *dalam proses* ("in process") at Putrajaya, the administrative capital of Malaysia, adjacent to the national capital of Kuala Lumpur on the Peninsular side of the country.

With the blessing of his adoptive family, Khoo made plans to fly to Kuala Lumpur so that he could personally monitor his case, and to unburden his aging adoptive parents from caring for him. Extended family members and friends in the Peninsula offered to assist Khoo in finding him a job and housing on his arrival. What Khoo soon discovered was that, despite the journey being a domestic one, he would need a *perlepasan* ("permit") in lieu of a MyKad from the Immigration Department of Sabah state, which would allow him to travel from Sabah to the Peninsula. The permit, issued in November shortly before his planned departure, authorized Khoo to travel to West Malaysia provided that he returned to Sabah within one month's time. Khoo's hope, though he recognized it was unlikely to occur, was that he would be able to receive a positive decision on his citizenship application before the permit expired, which would presumably nullify the directive to return within the specified time period. Unfortunately, this plan did not pan out as he had hoped because the Immigration Department national office reiterated the same message he had been told in previous years: that his application was *masih dalam proses* ("still in process"). After the permit expired, Khoo became a kind of illegal internal migrant within Malaysia, uncertain of the repercussions of attempting to return to his hometown in Sabah and more broadly without the right to reside in Malaysia given his noncitizen status.

In summary, the biographies of Malaysian-born stateless youth become shaped through encounters with immigration enforcement such that they are at risk of conforming to the profile of the illegal migrant that is the state's target of expulsion. Without proof of legal status in the form of a MyKad, valid passport and visa, or IMM13 card, stateless children become indistinguishable in the eyes of immigration authorities from illegal migrants.

Despite being deportable to nowhere in a strictly procedural sense because of their lack of formal citizenship in any country, they may end up being processed according to their ancestral heritage. Migratory flows between Sabah, the Philippines, and Indonesia are circular in nature, with migrants' movements structured by international labor market dynamics, conflict, social networks, and deliberate population "management" carried out by forces of immigration control. Deportation initiates the migration cycle for stateless youth like Aini, who are compelled to return by familial and lived connections to Malaysia, and the corresponding lack of acculturation to or viable future in their ancestral countries.

Discussion and Conclusion

This article examines how logics of immigration control are challenged by the figure of the stateless child. Drawing on the entanglements of stateless children and their families in Malaysia's punitive immigration system, I show how stateless children's deportability to nowhere defies the organizational principles of the nation-state system, which are built on the assumption that every person can be accounted for in at least one nation-state. Efforts to deter illegal migration through the widespread use of violent detention and deportation practices ironically serve to inadvertently transform stateless children into the illegal migrants that the state seeks to keep out: expulsion from their "home" country of Malaysia often constitutes the first time that stateless children cross an international border. This places them on the path of illicit cyclical migration undertaken by many irregular migrants circulating between Sabah and the Philippines or Indonesia.

In putting forth these arguments, this article deepens our empirical understanding of children's encounters with immigration detention and deportation, and provides qualitative accounts of the lived experiences of the "problems of under-inclusion" that emerge when people's substantive connections to a country are at odds with restrictive applications of jus sanguinis citizenship policies (Shachar 2009). In doing so, it reveals how the ideals embedded within the term *migration management* become realized on the ground as physical and emotional violence wrought by border enforcement practices on the most vulnerable among migrant and/or stateless populations, namely children and families. Focusing on the specific risks and vulnerabilities faced by this minority furthermore serves to denaturalize the institution of immigration control more broadly, which has traditionally been modeled on containing the figure of the lone male worker. The increasing diversification of the global migrant population and the ensnarement of nonmigrant stateless children into carceral systems will likely continue to challenge the defensibility of punitive immigration control in the name of territorial sovereignty.

Notes

1   See Objective 13(f) in the Global Compact for Safe, Orderly, and Regular Migration, Final Draft (2018), refugeesmigrants.un.org/sites/default/files/180711_final_draft_0.pdf (accessed December 8, 2021).

2   Some exceptions can be found, for example, in Bhabha (2016), a recent volume edited by Boehm and Terrio (2019), and a special issue edited by Menjivar and Perreira (2019). There is also a body of research that explores the experiences of children in mixed-status families whose relatives have been detained or deported, particularly in the US context (Allen, Cisneros, and Tellez 2015; Brabeck and Qingwen Xu 2010; Dreby 2012, 2015; Gulbas et al. 2016; Lovato et al. 2018; Rojas-Flores et al. 2017; Yoshikawa 2012; Zayas 2015).

3   I use the term *illegal* rather than a more politically neutral synonym such as *unauthorized* or *undocumented* in keeping with the language that is used in debates surrounding migration in the Malaysian context. The initial use of scare quotes around the term *illegal* gives nod to ongoing efforts to change the language that is used to talk about irregular migrants—namely, efforts to eliminate the use of the term *illegal* to describe humans who cross borders without authorization. The decision to deliberately use the term *illegal* in this article is not an endorsement of the dehumanizing and stigmatizing connotations that are attached to it.

4   Executive Office for Immigration Review (2019), "Adjudication Statistics, Current Representation Rates," www.justice.gov/eoir/page/file/1062991/download (accessed December 8, 2021).

5   Laila L. Hlass, "Defenseless Children," *Slate,* slate.com/news-and-politics/2018/07/children-detained -at-border-dont-have-lawyers-must-represent-themselves.html (accessed December 8, 2021).

6   TRAC Immigration, "Representation for Unaccompanied Children in Immigration Court," trac.syr.edu/immigration/reports/371/ (accessed December 8, 2021).

7   UN Refugee Agency, "UNHCR's Position Regarding the Detention of Refugee and Migrant Children in the Migration Context," www.refworld.org/pdfid/5885c2434.pdf (accessed December 8, 2021).

8 Department of Homeland Security (2019), "Management Alert—DHS Needs to Address Dangerous Overcrowding and Prolonged Detention of Children and Adults in the Rio Grande Valley (Redacted)," www.oig.dhs.gov/sites/default/files/assets/2019-07/OIG-19-51-Jul19_.pdf (accessed December 8, 2021).

9 International Organization for Migration, "Key Migration Terms," www.iom.int/key -migration-terms (accessed December 8, 2021).

10 Irregularly statused persons are by nature difficult to reliably quantify. As of 2021, the UN Refugee Agency in Malaysia has registered 179,830 refugees and asylum seekers in the country, 45,870 of whom are below the age of 18 years. See UNHCR (2021), "Figures at a Glance in Malaysia," www.unhcr.org/en-us/figures-at-a-glance-in-malaysia.html (accessed December 8, 2021).

11 *Daily Express*, "IMM13 Registration Suspended," October 13, 2018, dailyexpress.com.my /news.cfm?NewsID=127903.

12 Malaysian Palm Oil Board, "Production of Crude Palm Oil for the Month of December 2018," bepi.mpob.gov.my/index.php/en/statistics/production/186-production-2018/850-production -of-crude-oil-palm-2018.html. See also Malaysian Palm Oil Council, "Malaysian Palm Oil Industry," mpoc.org.my/malaysian-palm-oil-industry/.

13 Faris Fuad, "Over 1000 Illegal Immigrants Detained in Op Mega 3.0," *New Straits Times*, July 3, 2018, www.nst.com.my/news/nation/2018/07/386943/over-1000-illegal-immigrants-detained -op-mega-30.

14 "Immigration Set to Crack Down Hard on Illegals, Human Traffickers," *Star*, August 30, 2018, www.thestar.com.my/news/nation/2018/08/30/immigration-set-to-crack-down-hard -on-illegals-human-traffickers/.

15 Aliza Shah, "No Deadline Set for Op Mega 3.0," *New Straits Times*, July 28, 2018, www.nst .com.my/news/nation/2018/07/395567/no-deadline-set-op-mega-30.

16 Shah, "No Deadline Set for Op Mega 3.0."

17 A. Ananthalakshmi, "Exclusive: More Than 100 Die in Malaysian Immigration Detention Camps in Two Years," *Reuters*, March 30, 2017, www.reuters.com/article/us-malaysia-detention -deaths/exclusive-more-than-100-die-in-malaysian-immigration-detention-camps-in-two -years-idUSKBN1710GR.

18 Ananthalakshmi, "Exclusive."

19 For a more detailed overview of legal pathways into statelessness in Malaysia, see Liew 2019.

References

Alba, Richard. 2005. "Bright vs. Blurred Boundaries: Second-Generation Assimilation and Exclusion in France, Germany, and the United States." *Ethnic and Racial Studies* 28, no. 1: 20–49.

Allen, Brian, Erica M. Cisneros, and Alexandra Tellez. 2015. "The Children Left Behind: The Impact of Parental Deportation on Mental Health." *Journal of Child and Family Studies* 24, no. 2: 386–92. doi.org/10.1007/s10826-013-9848-5.

Allerton, Catherine. 2017. "Impossible Children: Illegality and Excluded Belonging among Children of Migrants in Sabah, East Malaysia." *Journal of Ethnic and Migration Studies* 44, no. 7: 1081–97.

Amnesty International. 2010. "There Is a Way Out: Stop Abuse of Migrants Detained in Malaysia." May 1. www.amnesty.org/en/documents/asa28/003/2010/en/.

Bennett, Colin, and David Lyon, eds. 2008. *Playing the Identity Card: Surveillance, Security, and Identification in Global Perspective*. London: Routledge.

Bhabha, Jacqueline. 1996. "Embodied Rights: Gender Persecution, State Sovereignty, and Refugees." *Public Culture* 9, no. 3: 3–32.

Bhabha, Jacqueline. 2009. "Arendt's Children: Do Today's Migrant Children Have a Right to Have Rights?" *Human Rights Quarterly* 31, no. 2: 410–51.

Bhabha, Jacqueline. 2016. *Child Migration and Human Rights in a Global Age*. Princeton, NJ: Princeton University Press.

Boehm, Deborah A., and Susan J. Terrio, eds. 2019. *Illegal Encounters: The Effect of Detention and Deportation on Young People*. New York: New York University Press.

Brabeck, Kalina, and Qingwen Xu. 2010. "The Impact of Detention and Deportation on Latino Immigrant Children and Families: A Quantitative Exploration." *Hispanic Journal of Behavioral Sciences* 32, no. 3: 341–61. doi.org/10.1177/0739986310374053.

Brané, Michelle, and Lee Wang. 2013. "Women: The Invisible Detainees." *Forced Migration Review* 44: 37–39.

Brettell, Caroline B., and Patricia A. de Berjeois. 1992. "Anthropology and the Study of Immigrant Women." In *Seeking Common Ground: Multidisciplinary Studies of Immigrant Women in the United States*, edited by Donna Gabaccia, 41–64. Westport, CT: Greenwood Press.

Broeders, Dennis. 2007. 'The New Digital Borders of Europe: EU Databases and the Surveillance of Irregular Migrants." *International Sociology* 22, no. 1: 71–92.

Chin, Christine B. N. 2003. "Visible Bodies, Invisible Work: State Practices toward Migrant Women Domestic Workers in Malaysia." *Asia and Pacific Migration Journal* 12, nos. 1–2: 49–73.

Constable, Nicole. 2014. *Born Out of Place: Migrant Mothers and the Politics of International Labor*. Berkeley: University of California Press.

Crawley, Heaven. 2000. "Gender, Persecution, and the Concept of Politics in the Asylum Determination Process." *Forced Migration Review* 9: 17–20.

Dannecker, Petra. 2005. "Bangladeshi Migrant Workers in Malaysia: The Construction of the 'Others' in a Multi-Ethnic Context." *Asian Journal of Social Science* 33, no. 2: 246–67.

Donato, Katharine M., and Donna Gabaccia. 2015. *Gender and International Migration*. New York: Russell Sage Foundation.

Dreby, Joanna. 2012. "The Burden of Deportation on Children in Mexican Immigrant Families." *Journal of Marriage and Family* 74, no. 4: 829–45. doi.org/10.1111/j.1741-3737.2012 .00989.x.

Dreby, Joanna . 2015. "US Immigration Policy and Family Separation: The Consequences for Children's Well-Being." *Social Science and Medicine* 132: 245–51. doi.org/10.1016/j .socscimed.2014.08.041.

Dudley, Michael, Zachary Steel, Sarah Mares, and Louise Newman. 2012. "Children and Young People in Immigration Detention." *Current Opinion in Psychiatry* 25, no. 4: 285–92.

Ehntholt, Kimberly A., David Trickey, Jean Harris Hendriks, Hannah Chambers, Mark Scott, and William Yule. 2018. "Mental Health of Unaccompanied Asylum-Seeking Adolescents Previously Held in British Detention Centres." *Clinical Child Psychology and Psychiatry* 23, no. 2: 238–57. doi.org/10.1177/1359104518758839.

Equal Rights Trust. 2010. "Trapped in a Cycle of Flight: Stateless Rohingya in Malaysia." January. www.equalrightstrust.org/files/Trapped%20in%20a%20cycle%20of%20flight%20 Stateless%20Rohingya%20in%20Malaysia.pdf.

Fazel, Mina, Unni Karunakara, and Elizabeth A. Newnham. 2014. "Detention, Denial, and Death: Migration Hazards for Refugee Children." *Lancet: Global Health* 2, no. 6: E313–14.

Fortify Rights. 2017. "Malaysia: Investigate Human Trafficking and Deaths in Immigration Detention Centers." News Release, April 4. www.fortifyrights.org/publication-20170404.html.

Galli, Chiara. 2020. "The Ambivalent US Context of Reception and the Dichotomous Legal Consciousness of Unaccompanied Minors." *Social Problems* 67, no. 4: 763–81. doi.org/10 .1093/socpro/spz041.

Garip, Filiz. 2017. *On the Move: Changing Mechanisms of Mexico-US Migration*. Princeton, NJ: Princeton University Press.

Gonzales, Roberto G. 2011. "Learning to Be Illegal: Undocumented Youth and Shifting Legal Contexts in the Transition to Adulthood." *American Sociological Review* 76, no. 4: 602–19.

Global Detention Project. 2018. "Malaysia: Submission to the Universal Periodic Review of the Human Rights Council 31st Session, November 2018." www.globaldetentionproject.org /submission-to-the-universal-periodic-review-malaysia (accessed December 8, 2021).

Gonzales, Roberto G., and Leo R. Chavez. 2012. "'Awakening to a Nightmare': Abjectivity and Illegality in the Lives of Undocumented 1.5-Generation Latino Immigrants in the United States." *Current Anthropology* 53, no. 3: 255–81.

Gros, Hanna, and Yolanda Song. 2016. "'No Life for a Child': A Roadmap to End Immigration Detention of Children and Family Separation." University of Toronto Faculty of Law International Human Rights Program. ihrp.law.utoronto.ca/sites/default/files/PUBLICATIONS /Report-NoLifeForAChild.pdf (accessed December 8, 2021).

Gulbas, Lauren E., L. H. Zayas, Hyunwoo Yoon, Hannah Szlyk, Sergio Aguilar-Gaxiola, and G. Natera. 2016. "Deportation Experiences and Depression among U.S. Citizen-Children with Undocumented Mexican Parents: Citizen-Children and Depression." *Child Care Health and Development* 42, no. 2: 220–30. doi.org/10.1111/cch.12307.

Hernandez, Cesar Cuauhtemoc Garcia. 2014. "Immigration Detention as Punishment." *UCLA Law Review* 61, no. 5: 1346–1414.

Hirschman, Charles. 1986. "The Making of Race in Colonial Malaya: Political Economy and Racial Ideology." *Sociological Forum* 1, no. 2: 330–61.

Hugo, Graeme. 2009. "Circular Migration and Development: An Asia-Pacific Perspective." migrationonline.cz, September. aa.ecn.cz/img_upload/6334c0c7298d6b396d213ccd19be5999 /GHugo_CircularMigrationAndDevelopment.pdf.

Human Rights Watch. 2009. "Detained and Dismissed: Women's Struggles to Obtain Health Care in United States Immigration Detention." March 17. www.hrw.org/report/2009/03/17 /detained-and-dismissed/womens-struggles-obtain-health-care-united-states#6f55ef.

Inter-Agency Working Group to End Child Immigration Detention. 2016. "Ending Child Immigration Detention." endchilddetention.org/wp-content/uploads/2016/09/IAWG_Advocacy -Brochure_Aug-2016_FINAL-web.pdf (accessed December 8, 2021).

International Federation for Human Rights and SUARAM. 2008. "Undocumented Migrants and Refugees in Malaysia: Raids, Detention, and Discrimination." March. www.fidh.org /IMG/pdf/MalaisieCONJ489eng.pdf.

International Organization for Migration. 2021. "Malaysia." www.iom.int/countries/malaysia (accessed December 8, 2021).

Kassim, Azizah. 2009. "Filipino Refugees in Sabah: State Responses, Public Stereotypes, and the Dilemma over Their Future." *Southeast Asian Studies* 47, no. 1: 52–88.

Kaur, Amarjit. 2006. "Indian Labour, Labour Standards, and Workers' Health in Burma and Malaya, 1900–1940." *Modern Asian Studies* 40, no. 2: 425–75.

Kelly, Nancy. 1993. "Gender-Related Persecution: Assessing the Asylum Claims of Women." *Cornell International Law Journal* 26, no. 3: 625–74.

Kronick, Rachel, Cecile Rousseau, and Janet Cleveland. 2011. "Mandatory Detention of Refugee Children: A Public Health Issue?" *Paediatrics and Child Health* 16, no. 8: e65–67.

Kudo, Sasagu. 2013. "Securitization of Undocumented Migrants and the Politics of Insecurity in Malaysia." *Procedia Environmental Sciences* 17: 947–56.

Kurus, Bilson. 1998. "Migrant Labor: The Sabah Experience." *Asian and Pacific Migration Journal* 7, nos. 2–3: 281–95.

Kyaw, Nyi Nyi. 2017. "Unpacking the Presumed Statelessness of Rohingyas." *Journal of Immigrant and Refugee Studies* 15, no. 3: 269–86.

Leerkes, Arjen, and Dennis Broeders. 2010. "A Case of Mixed Motives? Formal and Informal Functions of Administrative Immigration Detention." *British Journal of Criminology* 50, no. 5: 830–50.

Liew, Jamie Chai Yun. 2019. "Homegrown Statelessness in Malaysia and the Promise of the Principle of Genuine and Effective Link." *Statelessness and Citizenship Review* 1, no. 1: 95–135.

Liew, Jamie Chai Yun . 2021. "Statelessness and the Administrative State: The Legal Prowess of the First-Line Bureaucrat in Malaysia." In *Statelessness, Governance, and the Problem of Citizenship*, edited by Tendayi Bloom and Lindsey N. Kingston, 76–86. Manchester, UK: Manchester University Press.

Linton, Julie, Marsha Griffin, and Alan Shapiro. 2017. "Detention of Immigrant Children." *American Academy of Pediatrics* 139, no. 5. doi.org/10.1542/peds.2017-0483.

Lorek, Ann, Kimberly Ehntholt, Anne Nesbitt, Emmanuel Wey, Chipo Githinji, Eve Rossor, and Rush Wickramasinghe. 2009. "The Mental and Physical Health Difficulties of Children Held within a British Immigration Detention Center: A Pilot Study." *Child Abuse and Neglect* 33, no. 9: 573–85.

Lovato, Kristina, Corina Lopez, Leyla Karimli, and Laura S. Abrams. 2018. "The Impact of Deportation-Related Family Separations on the Well-Being of Latinx Children and Youth: A Review of the Literature." *Children and Youth Services Review* 95: 109–16. doi.org/10.1016/j.childyouth.2018.10.011.

Malaysia Department of Statistics. 2018. "Population." Population Quick Info. www.dosm.gov.my/v1/index.php?r=column/cone&menu_id=Nk1JZnJBMm1TdmRFSoxaTXZnanIrQT09 (accessed 8 December 2021).

Malkki, Liisa H. 2002. "News from Nowhere: Mass Displacement and Globalized 'Problems of Organization.'" *Ethnography* 3, no. 3: 351–60.

Mares, Sarah, and Jon Jureidini. 2004. "Psychiatric Assessment of Children and Families in Immigration Detention—Clinical, Administrative, and Ethical Issues." *Australian and New Zealand Journal of Public Health* 28, no. 6: 520–26.

Massey, Douglas S., Jorge Durand, and Nolan Malone. 2002. *Beyond Smoke and Mirrors: Mexican Immigration in an Era of Economic Integration*. New York: Russell Sage Foundation.

Menjívar, Cecilia, and Krista M. Perreira. 2019. "Undocumented and Unaccompanied: Children of Migration in the European Union and the United States." *Journal of Ethnic and Migration Studies* 45, no. 2: 197–217.

Morokvasic, Mirjana. 1984. "Birds of Passage Are Also Women . . ." *International Migration Review* 18, no. 4: 886–907.

Neo, Jaclyn Ling-Chien. 2006. "Malay Nationalism, Islamic Supremacy, and the Constitutional Bargain in the Multi-Ethnic Composition of Malaysia." *International Journal on Minority and Group Rights* 13, no. 1: 95–118.

Ngai, Mae N. 2014. *Impossible Subjects: Illegal Aliens and the Making of Modern America*. Princeton, NJ: Princeton University Press.

Ngin, ChorSwang. 2010. "Illegal Birth and the Dilemma of Color, Culture, and Citizenship in Malaysia." *Women's Studies Quarterly* 38, nos. 1–2: 201–17.

Ong, Aihwa. 1991. "The Gender and Labor Politics of Postmodernity." *Annual Review of Anthropology* 20: 279–309.

Pedraza, Silvia. 1991. "Women and Migration: The Social Consequences of Gender." *Annual Review of Sociology* 17: 303–25.

Pessar, Patricia R. 1986. "The Role of Gender in Dominican Settlement in the United States." In *Women and Change in Latin America*, edited by June Nash and Helen I. Safa, 173–94. South Hadley, MA: Bergin and Garvey.

Pessar, Patricia R., and Sarah J. Mahler. 2003. "Transnational Migration: Bringing Gender In." *International Migration Review* 37, no. 3: 812–46.

Pye, Oliver, Ramlah Daud, Yuyun Harmono, and Tatat. 2012. "Precarious Lives: Transnational Biographies of Migrant Oil Palm Workers." *Asia Pacific Viewpoint* 53, no. 3: 330–42.

Rabin, Nin. 2009. "Unseen Prisoners: Women in Immigration Detention Facilities in Arizona." *Georgetown Immigration Law Journal* 23, no. 4: 695–764.

Rojas-Flores, Lisseth, Mari L. Clements, J. Hwang Koo, and Judy London. 2017. "Trauma and Psychological Distress in Latino Citizen Children Following Parental Detention and Deportation." *Psychological Trauma: Theory, Research, Practice, and Policy* 9, no. 3: 352–61. doi.org/10.1037/tra0000177.

Sampson, Robyn, and Grant Mitchell. 2013. "Global Trends in Immigration Detention and Alternatives to Detention: Practical, Political, and Symbolic Rationales." *Journal on Migration and Human Security* 1, no. 3: 97–121.

Shachar, Ayelet. 2009. *The Birthright Lottery: Citizenship and Global Inequality*. Cambridge, MA: Harvard University Press.

Shields, Linda, Stephen Stathis, Heather Mohay, Alison van Haeringen, Hanne Williams, David Wood, and Elizabeth Bennett. 2004. "The Health of Children in Immigration Detention: How Does Australia Compare?" *Australian and New Zealand Journal of Public Health* 28, no. 6: 514–19.

Silverman, Stephanie J., and Evelyne Massa. 2012. "Why Immigration Detention Is Unique." *Population, Space, and Place* 18, no. 6: 677–86.

SUHAKAM (Human Rights Commission of Malaysia). 2019. "Annual Report 2018." drive .google.com/file/d/1fvvmlSqXJ2ysTdhRrYnSws6Bwz6FQiaG/view (accessed December 8, 2021).

UNHCR (United Nations High Commissioner for Refugees). 2014. "Handbook on Protection of Stateless Persons." www.unhcr.org/dach/wp-content/uploads/sites/27/2017/04/CH -UNHCR_Handbook-on-Protection-of-Stateless-Persons.pdf (accessed December 8, 2021).

UNHCR. 2018. "Update on UNHCR's Operations in Asia and the Pacific." www.unhcr .org/6141c5d74.pdf (accessed December 8, 2021).

UNHCR. 2019. "Figures at a Glance in Malaysia." 2019. www.unhcr.org/figures-at-a-glance -in-malaysia.html (accessed December 8, 2021).

UNHCR. 2021. "Fleeing Unaccompanied." www.unhcr.org/hk/en/unaccompanied-children (accessed December 8 ,2021).

UN Human Rights. 2016. "Children and Families Should Never Be in Immigration Detention." December 18. www.ohchr.org/EN/NewsEvents/Pages/DisplayNews.aspx?NewsID=21026 &LangID=E.

UNICEF. 2021a. "Child Migration." April. data.unicef.org/topic/child-migration-and-displacement /migration/.

UNICEF. 2021b. "Child Displacement." September. data.unicef.org/topic/child-migration-and -displacement/displacement/.

Vlieks, Caia. 2017. "Contexts of Statelessness: The Concepts 'Statelessness in Situ' and 'Statelessness in the Migratory Context.'" In *Understanding Statelessness*, edited by Tendayi Bloom, Katherine Tonkiss, and Phillip Cole, 35–52. London: Routledge.

Yoshikawa, Hirokazu. 2012. *Immigrants Raising Citizens: Undocumented Parents and Their Young Children*. New York: Russell Sage Foundation.

Yusof, Zainal Aznam, and Deepak Bhattasali. 2008. "Economic Growth and Development in Malaysia: Policy Making and Leadership." Commission on Growth and Development, Working Paper No. 27. openknowledge.worldbank.org/bitstream/handle/10986/28046/577 260NWP0Box353766B01PUBLIC10gcwp027web.pdf?sequence=1&isAllowed=y (accessed December 8, 2021).

Zayas, Luis H. 2015. *Forgotten Citizens: Deportation, Children, and the Making of American Exiles and Orphans.* Oxford: Oxford University Press.

"I Can't Do Anything but Wait": The Lived Experiences of Children of Transnational Migrants in Lombok, Indonesia

Harriot Beazley and Jessica Ball

> Waiting is not something that takes place in suspended time or outside of doing things. Instead it is an active and intentional process . . . and a significant shaping of the lived life.
> —Conlon 2011: 356

Over the last two decades neoliberal economic forces have led to a rise in transnational labor from Indonesia, with an accompanying surge in family fragmentation. In this era of intensified geographical mobility, however, there have also been increased and sustained experiences of immobility. In particular, children and young people who have been "left behind" by their migrating parents are expected to wait for them to return home, sometimes for years at a time.[1] The fact that these stay-behind children are compelled to wait for their parents, often with no contact, has become an acceptable social norm and aspect of family relations in many Indonesian communi-

positions 30:2 DOI 10.1215/10679847-9573344
Copyright 2022 by Duke University Press

ties. This article first summarizes the context of transnational migration in Indonesia, before providing an overview of the literature related to children left behind by their migrant parents, and recent scholarship on the temporalities of migration. The analysis of stay-behind children's lived experiences draws on child-focused research with children and young people living in out-migration communities in rural Lombok, Eastern Indonesia. The findings reveal the unpredictability of the temporality of migration, especially for children of parents who follow informal transnational flows, and the enduring temporal uncertainties that are produced. The analysis explores the ways that children respond to their parents' protracted absences and how the experience of waiting has become a significant aspect of their everyday lives.

Elsewhere research has explored children's emotional responses to parental migration in Lombok and how enmeshed they are in communal emotional economies of transnational migration, specifically the embodied, collectively shared and socialized emotion of *malu*, or shame (Beazley, Butt, and Ball 2018). In this article the analysis of communal emotional economies is continued by focusing on children's responses to their parents' sustained absence for unspecified periods of time, and the associated everyday temporalities of waiting that are mediated by family and community obligations. By concentrating on the lived experiences of the children who stay behind in high migration communities the article contributes to debates about the temporal implications of migration and the micropolitics of immobility for the youngest members of migrant societies.

Transnational Migration from Indonesia

The lives of children in migrant-sending communities in Indonesia are significantly shaped by a rapid growth in transnational labor migration. In the past two decades, the numbers of Indonesian workers migrating overseas has risen sharply (World Bank 2015). Approximately 700,000 documented male and female migrants left Indonesia in 2012, the majority of whom went to work on plantations or factories in Malaysia, or as construction workers or maids in the Middle East (ILO 2013). Many people secure false travel documents to complete the journey through official channels (Ball, Butt, and Beazley 2017). It is also widely recognized that labor migration without legal work documents is up to four times higher than official migration figures (ILO 2013).

Prior to the 1970s, overseas Indonesian migrants were mostly men, leaving to work in palm oil plantations in Malaysia. Increasingly there has been a feminization of transnational migration, and women now make up 76 percent of overseas migrants, working as domestic servants in Saudi Arabia and Hong Kong, or in factories in Malaysia (Andrevski and Lyneham 2014). Migration is not a single event, as migrants renew short-term (two year) contracts, perhaps several times. This ongoing practice of repeated transnational migration has been described by Graham and Jordan (2011) as "serial migration." For undocumented migrants, however, the physical distance, expense, and legal risks are overwhelming obstacles for those wishing to return home to see their families. In other cases, migrants renew their contracts while overseas or stay on without formal contracts. Many others have their passports taken from them by their employers and are unable to leave. All these experiences can result in migrants having limited contact with their families and children for many years, even decades, at a time (Beazley, Butt, and Ball 2018; Zentgraf and Stoltz Chinchilla 2012).

The Indonesian government actively promotes and facilitates temporary overseas migration by both men and women workers through agreements with foreign governments and recruitment agencies (Graham and Jordan 2011; World Bank 2015). Migrants traveling from Indonesia to Malaysia make up the second largest stream of transnational migrants globally (after Mexico-USA), and Indonesia is the third highest remittance-receiving country in Southeast Asia (World Bank 2017). Indonesian women are particularly encouraged to migrate overseas and are celebrated nationally as "heroes of development" because of the remittances they send home to pay for their children's education, to build concrete houses, and to improve their families' living conditions (Beazley, Butt, and Ball 2018; Chan 2014). As a result of the official support for temporary overseas migration a culture of migration has evolved in many low-income communities. Mothers and fathers feel compelled to work overseas to enhance the education and well-being of their children, while new generations also aspire to seek employment abroad (Beazley 2007, 2015; Beazley, Butt, and Ball 2018; Graham and Jordan 2011).

A consequence of accelerated migration flows is that approximately one million children stay behind in Indonesia while one or both parents work overseas (SMERU Research Institute 2014). The mother and father of a child in Lombok will typically work in separate countries; the husband in Malaysia and the wife in Saudi Arabia. It is assumed that local communities will take on responsibility for the care of migrant's children, although families receive no support from the government for the care of the children while their parents are away (Butt, Ball, and Beazley 2017; SMERU Research Institute 2014). Consequently, established traditions of fostering by grandparents and other family members are elicited, with older siblings, grandparents, extended family members, and neighbors caring for the children, often for years at a time (Butt, Ball, and Beazley 2017). This is because the migrant parents often-undocumented legal status does not allow them to freely travel to and from Indonesia, to visit their children left behind.

Theoretical Context: Temporalities of Migration and Waiting

This study is situated within the subdiscipline of children's geographies and the intersection between children's geographies, migration and mobility studies, and the temporalities of migration (Acedera and Yeoh 2019; Barker et al. 2009; Cresswell and Merriman 2011). Within children's geographies, migration has predominantly been viewed as a spatial process, with more recent research focusing on the agency, identity, and emotions of the migrant or stay-behind child (Beazley 2015; Beazley, Butt, and Ball 2018; McKay 2007; Punch 2012). Theoretically, the study follows Dobson (2009: 356), who renounces portrayals of children as "objects" and "non-persons lacking both feelings and agency of their own" within migration studies, and contributes to discussions concerning children's agency and how that agency is cast within migration literature (Beazley 2015; Beazley, Butt, and Ball 2018; Hashim and Thorsen 2011; Punch 2007; van Blerk and Ansell 2007). The article explores children's everyday lives while they wait for their parents to return to illustrate how such experiences need to figure more prominently in explanations about the impact of transnational migration in local communities (Graham et al. 2012; Hoang et al. 2014; Parreñas 2005).

Studies of children of migrants elsewhere in Southeast Asia have examined the economic impact of transnational migration on children's lives, arguing that the material benefits from migrant parent's remittances have a positive bearing on families, with many children experiencing an improved quality of life (Lam, Hoang, and Yeoh 2013; McKay, 2007). Within this literature, children of migrant parents are often portrayed as resilient, well looked after, and better off when cared for by others than living in poverty with their unemployed parents (McKay 2007). Studies in Indonesia, however, have revealed the risks connected with out-migration in low-income families and single-parent or no-parent households, including high rates of infant mortality, domestic violence, early school leaving, child neglect, and child abandonment (Allerton 2014; Graham and Jordan 2011; SMERU Research Institute 2014). A recent study has revealed how children in Indonesia who stay behind when their mothers migrate for work are more likely to be neglected in terms of physical and mental health and access to education than when their fathers migrate (SMERU Research Institute 2014). Behavioral problems and increased risk-taking behavior are also found to be more likely when both parents are working overseas (Beazley, Butt, and Ball 2018; Graham and Jordan 2011: 769).

Building on the above research, the aim of this article is to contribute to current discussions focused on the agency and well-being of children of transnational migrants, by interrogating the temporalities of migration as experienced by stay-behind children. The article discusses how children who stay behind are caught up in the geopolitics of migration by being static, immobile, and in a state of "protracted motility" (Gray 2011). It then explores how these children spend their time, while "stuck" in remote rural areas, waiting for their parents to return (Allerton 2016).

The relationship between time and space has been theorized by many prominent social scientists (D. Harvey 1990; Lefebvre 2004; Massey 1992; May and Thrift 2003), including children's geographers (Ansell et al. 2014; Harker 2005). Furthermore, the sociologist Eviatar Zerubavel (1977) has argued that time is intersubjective and felt at the individual level as well as at the community level. As Daina Cheyenne Harvey (2015) points out, however, there have been very few attempts to document how different communities make sense of, or how they spend, their time. Specifically, waiting as a topic for social analysis within studies of time has remained undertheorized in different social contexts. According to Harvey (2015: 541), this may be because the experience of waiting as a social phenomenon is considered so mundane and banal that it has gone largely unnoticed: "The remarkable inattention to waiting . . . is most likely due to the perception that waiting is empty time; that it is void of meaning, wasted, like negative space."

Recent research, however, has started to explore how people experience the temporalities of migration across different cultural contexts (Acedera and Yeoh 2018; Griffiths 2014; Griffiths, Rogers, and Anderson 2013). This new research includes a focus on the experiences of waiting and immobilities, especially for refugees in the Global South and asylum seekers in the Global North (Conlon 2011). Griffiths (2014), for example, suggests time is a social phenomenon that offers valuable insights into migration practices, including for refugees who are forced to wait for extended periods of time (see also Olson 2015). Alison Mountz (2011) has also theorized how temporality is often conceptualized as waiting and being in limbo for asylum seekers held in detention. Associated with the concept of time, therefore, a specific focus on the experience of waiting has begun to gain attention in the mobility literature and to be viewed as a crucial feature of migrant (im)mobility (Hee Kwon 2015). In particular, Conlon's (2011) edited special issue of *Gender, Place, and Culture* on migration and waiting has drawn our attention to the "various spatial and temporal dimensions of migrants' encounters with waiting as a significant facet of (im)mobility [that is] actively produced, embodied, experienced, encountered and resisted in everyday migrant spaces" (355).

Conlon argues that waiting is socially produced and can be understood as a "distinct spatial and temporal dimension of *statis* for migrants" (355). As in the literature on time and mobility, however, waiting is theorized in a diversity of ways. Specifically, the social and political implications of waiting, and being forced to wait, have been explored, including the ways space and waiting come together to produce and maintain potentially abusive arrangements of power and inequalities (Auyero 2012; D. C. Harvey 2015; Jeffrey 2008; Mountz 2011; Olson 2015). This literature claims that the significance of waiting has increased within different societies in response to the development of neoliberal economies, especially for those who are considered to be "surplus" to the system (Olson 2015: 518). Asylum seekers, for example, wait endlessly in limbo, longing for an end to the waiting and temporal uncertainty enforced on them by the techniques of power (Griffiths 2014; Griffiths, Rogers, and Anderson 2013; Mountz 2011). Javier Auyero (2012: 9) describes how waiting in Argentina is a modal experience for the destitute living in shanty towns, who suffer as they wait to "prove their worth." Similarly, Hee Kwon (2015: 495) explores the "work of waiting" in China by people whose spouses who have migrated to Korea for work, and how such "spousal waiting" is often unappreciated and largely unrewarded affective work.

Gray (2011) also interrogates the socially produced spaces created by waiting, claiming that to understand the temporality and experience of waiting in migrant communities, it is important to consider how it has been shaped by traditions and cultural norms. In her research with men and women who remained behind in 1950s Ireland, Gray identifies how waiting for migrant family members provoked disharmony between the lived experiences and the individual expectations associated with the passing of time. She describes waiting as an "in between experience," pervaded by anticipation, uncertainty, and hope, and how "waiting can be experienced as an extended or suspended present, thus significantly shaping the lived life" (421).

There are distinct parallels in early twenty-first-century Lombok with Gray's study of 1950s Ireland, where emigration was also an economic necessity, and waiting for the return of family members was also constructed as a social norm. For these reasons, her study is very useful in helping us to analyze migrant (im)mobility in rural Lombok. In particular, Gray (2011: 421) developed three functional and distinct modes of active waiting to understand the experiences of those who stayed behind: waiting for opportunity; waiting for return; waiting for an absence to be filled. In each of these modes of waiting, Gray sees waiting as being integrated into everyday life, and as an active and intentional process experienced by everyone in the community. Below the method of data collection for this study is described before turning to the research findings, which are framed within Gray's three types of waiting. The article ends with some brief conclusions about the importance of understanding the temporalities of migration for children within children's geographies and migration studies.

Method

The research for this article adopted a child-focused approach recognizing child participants as active agents, respecting children's opinions throughout the research process, and using appropriate methods so children could express themselves (Bessell, Beazley, and Waterson 2016). Research was conducted in two poor high out-migration villages in East Lombok, in 2014 and 2016. One objective of the research—part of a larger study on birth registration of children of overseas migrants in rural Lombok—was to explore the lived experiences of children after one or both parents had migrated for work (Beazley, Butt, and Ball 2018).

The research team conducted semistructured interviews with eight family groups consisting of adult caregivers and their children, and seven focus groups with young people aged twelve to seventeen years. Interviews were in Indonesian with local translators providing translations of the local Sasak dialect when required. Focus groups were held with groups of young people whose parents had migrated overseas, including adolescent girls, a mix of adolescent girls and boys, and a group of boys. During discussions participants were asked to talk about (1) their experiences of their parents' migration including the impact it had on them; (2) their coping strategies during the absence of parents; and (3) their aspirations for the future. Participants' accounts were contextualized through observation and informal unstructured interviews with young people in the villages. Local government officials, teachers in a primary school, and adult caregivers—including grandmothers, aunts, fathers, other family members, and neighbors—were also interviewed. The names of respondents have been changed to protect their identity.

The research location, East Lombok, was identified as an ideal site for the research as it has a strong local culture of migration and is one of the highest "sending areas" of overseas migrants in Indonesia (Beazley 2007; Khoo et al. 2014; Lindquist 2010). The research sites and many of the adult research participants were also known to the first author, who has had a relationship with the community for more than a decade. The sites of this study are not identified because of the vulnerability of the children and the sensitivities of some cases discussed.

Findings

East Lombok is a parched and impoverished district on the island of Lombok in Eastern Indonesia. It is characterized by high population growth, low wages, low education and employment, food insecurity, falling agricultural productivity, poor communications, and poor health, including much higher rates of infant mortality than the national average (Ball, Butt, and Beazley 2017). The villages where the research took place are extremely isolated, situated in the foothills of the volcano Mount Rinjani, and next to dense forest. The area is subject to flash floods and is characterized by poverty, low education, poor community access to health and other services, no public transport, and no secondary school. The villages lack sanitation and have only recently been provided with access to clean running water and electricity. There is no internet, and no one has a television or a computer. Mobile phone coverage has recently been provided, and most adults have basic mobile phones, which they use to communicate with family members overseas. The people in this area call themselves *orang-hutan* ("people of the forest"), as that is where they spend most of their time, gathering resources (firewood, leaves, grass, birds, fruit, and wild plants) to survive.

An estimated 100,000 people per year migrate overseas from Lombok through formal routes, and at least 200,000 through irregular, undocumented channels, especially from low income families (ILO 2013). The cultural tradition of *merantau* (wandering) is important in Lombok when traditionally young men migrate to other islands to find work and return as a "success," which means being able to build a concrete house and provide for their families on their return. In the locations where the research was conducted, communities are highly transient, with adults constantly moving to other islands and overseas in search of work. In the past two decades, overseas migration has particularly been seen as a reliable source of income in the research locations, for both men and women, as a result of the lack of income earning opportunities elsewhere and high levels of poverty. Almost every household had a family member who had worked or was currently working abroad. These mobile practices have led to high rates of divorce and fragmented families, with children being separated from their parents for extended periods of time (Beazley 2007; Beazley, Butt, and Ball 2018).

In the villages where the research was conducted, so many adults were away that child-parent separation was socially constructed as normal and family fragmentation seen as a necessary and unavoidable part of the migration process. During interviews provincial and local government officials made light of the impact that parental migration had on children, saying they were "tough" and "they will be fine." Local government officials interviewed said children were well cared for by a remaining parent or the extended family, and that parents' remittances ensured their children's survival. It was assumed that the children had the same desires as their parents, whom they were expected to obey.

The true benefits of parental migration, however, depended on many intersecting factors, including whether one or both parents had migrated; whether the child could be properly cared for while the parent(s) were away; whether a child had a birth certificate to enroll in school and access welfare supplements; if the parent(s) had migrated through official channels; whether parent(s) had skilled or low-skilled employment; whether remittances were reliable; whether the family was able pay off recruitment debts; how long the parent(s) were away; and whether the parent(s) were able to communicate with their child(ren) during their separation (Beazley, Butt, and Ball 2018).

During focus group discussions and individual interviews, the main difficulties faced by children and young people as a result of their parents' absence were articulated as an increase in household tasks and other responsibilities; pressure to earn an income, especially on the part of boys; an increase in school dropouts, especially in the case of girls; and a decline in health. Children also reported feelings of loneliness and of missing their parents and other family members. A prominent concern that emerged were feelings of having to continually wait in some sort of limbo, feeling that one did not belong anywhere or to anyone.

Waiting for Return

Within the social context described above, the experience of protracted waiting is an active and intentional practice that is negotiated and incorporated into everyday lives by everyone in the community. Some children explained how their parents migrated with a plan for a specific time away and a scheduled return. Once gone, however, the time was often extended beyond initial expectations. Short-term seasonal migration became long-term, or a regular occurrence instead of a one-time occasion, while longer-term stays became indefinite or permanent. Other children said that their parents did not tell them how long they were going to be away, or when they were coming back.

> "I don't know how long my parents have gone for or when they will come back." (Adi, aged thirteen).
>
> "I don't know when my mother is coming home. I can't do anything but wait. I am always waiting (*tunggu terus*)." (Rini, fifteen).

One child told how she did not know her mother was going away, and only found out from her grandmother when she woke up to find she had left for *Saudi* (Saudi Arabia).

In spite of the intense uncertainty that such ambiguous absence creates, strong cultural values shape children's affective experiences, enforcing norm-compliant behavior when they are expected to respond in a particular way to the sustained absence of their parents. While they wait for their parents to return, children are expected to perform resilience, hiding their negative emotions about their parents' absence (see also Beazley, Butt, and Ball 2018). They are socialized to suppress intense emotions of anger, sadness, resentment, or abandonment, and thus to wait for extended periods of time without complaining (Beazley, Butt, and Ball 2018).

> "Like it, don't like it, you have to like it." (Tuti, fourteen)
>
> "I do mind my parents have left but I have to agree. I don't show that I mind." (Ratna, thirteen)

In spite of the necessary suppression of the children's feelings, however, the collective experience of waiting in the village is palpable. Everybody is waiting. They are waiting for a phone call or a text, waiting for money to arrive, waiting for a loved one to return, waiting for an absence to be filled, waiting for something to happen. A form of emotional support during this waiting time is regular communication with migrant loved ones via mobile phones and texting. As Acedera and Yeoh (2019: 250) have noted in their research with Filipino migrant workers in Singapore: "'Doing family' across distance is centrally facilitated through the affordances of communication technologies to create rhythms and manage ruptures. These technologies are crucial in (re)making domestic family time in the transnational household."

In recent years, since the introduction of mobile phones, long-distance communication has become a normalized feature of migration and transnational relationships in rural Lombok. It has greatly facilitated the sending of remittances via Western Union or direct bank transfers, whereas in the past remittances were sent home via letter to the village head (Beazley 2007). However, the frequency of contact that the children in this study had with their migrant parents varied considerably, and long-distance communication between different family members was not always smooth or equal. For example, one child never spoke with his parents who were both working overseas, while another spoke with her mother by phone every week.

Unlike other studies (Acedera and Yeoh 2018; McKay 2007; Peng and Wong 2013) of transnational relationships in which regular communication has enabled emotional ties and kept absent loved ones "virtually present," in this study most children had inadequate or erratic communication with their absent parent(s). With no internet available in the study location, children were not able to Skype or Facebook their parents and instead relied on mobile phones (cf. McKay 2016). However, none of the children owned mobile phones, which were regarded in the community as "tools of power" (Acedera and Yeoh 2019: 251). Instead, they were required to communicate with their absent parents using a relative or the village headman's mobile phone, resulting in the children's channels of communication with their absent parents being "embedded in power geometries" (251). The children were therefore forced to rely on another person, and to wait for their parents to text or call them, seeking emotional validation via distance, and "displays of caring from abroad" (McKay 2007: 178).

Waiting for an Absence to Be Filled

Children in this study were often forced to wait in a transitional liminal state, between separation and reunification, a lived experience that Allerton (2016) has characterized as "stuckness." Many children who participated in the research had not seen one or both of their parents for years, and they longed to see them again. They were excited about their return and the anticipation of what gifts they would bring when they came: "I felt happy when he came home and brought me gifts, including a towel" (Dewi,14).

As well as learning to express culturally appropriate emotions about their parents' absence, children have been socialized to have strong feelings of obligation toward their absent parents. Some boys talked about learning how to recite the Quran, and girls talked about having to do well at school while their parents were away. They knew their parents were working to pay for their schooling, and they had intense feelings of obligation and "duty" to work hard and learn the Quran while they waited for the return of their parents. Boys also talked about the pressure they felt to earn money to supplement the family income while their parents were away. Some children explained how they could not wait to see their parents to show them how responsible they had been and what they had learned while they were away, and how good they had been during their parents' absence. As well as fulfilling feelings of obligation, these activities helped to fill the children's time while they waited. As Gray (2011: 425) has noted: "Waiting is also structured by affect and morally inflected familial relations, so that personal longings and desires . . . are ultimately shaped by affective relationships to family 'home' and security."

Other children were not able to fill their parents' absence with study. This was particularly true of girls who had to help with household tasks, helping their mothers while the father was away, or performing their mothers' household duties while she was away. In East Lombok, girls whose mother or both parents were overseas often drop out of school at the end of primary school (at age eleven) to care for their younger siblings, and boys drop out to seek work to bring money home for the family. One local income activity that boys engaged in was collecting sand and rocks from the riverbed and carrying it up the road to sell to construction companies, which bought these materials to use for cement. Girls were also engaged in this activity, and one ten-year-old girl had dropped out of school to collect sand with her mother, as her father was away and never sent money home.

Other boys reported that they felt *malas* (unmotivated) to go to school because of their parents' absence. This feeling of apathy was also reported by teachers in the local primary school who said that children of parents who had both migrated were often "sluggish," less attentive, and emotionally disturbed as a result of prolonged parental absence. Responses to parental absence also included very high nonattendance, high volatility, and suddenly crying or shouting out in class. One boy, aged nine, started screaming in class for no apparent reason. When asked why he was screaming, he replied, "I miss my mother and I want to see her." These children were also described by the teachers as socially isolated "daydreamers" who failed to engage with other children at playtime.

This form of "daydreaming" can be understood as a way of passing time (escaping the present, coping with the negative aspects of parental absence) and as a mode of waiting. In their study exploring how daydreaming and happiness relate, Mar, Mason, and Litvack (2012: 406) found a negative relation between daydreaming and happiness, with daydreaming providing a helpful means to ease boredom and pass the time, as well as to alleviate emotional stress, conflict, and pain (402). The study also found that daydreaming about people with whom one cannot be close has a negative relation to well-being, often characterized by loneliness and less social support, with child loneliness predicting a proneness to daydreaming (402). Furthermore, when exploring the links between imagination and waiting in young children, Singer (1961: 399) found that "an important behavioral consequence of the development of daydreaming tendencies in children may manifest in their waiting ability."

Waiting for Opportunity

During these acutely uncertain periods of waiting for their parents to return and an absence to be filled, children described how they negotiated their immobility by waiting for an opportunity or until they were old enough to be independently mobile themselves. While they wait, the children of transnational migrants are therefore in an enforced state of statis—"a state of protracted motility" (Gray 2011).

Sasak culture, the dominant culture in Lombok, is a male-dominated society and the experience of statis and protracted motility is highly gendered in the villages, with unmarried girls having much less opportunity to be mobile than boys. In Lombok being skilled in housework is considered a benefit to girls when they marry (Bennett 2005). Girls are also responsible for working in the fields, looking after younger siblings and cooking and cleaning at home. They are not permitted to go far from home. Boys' tasks include looking after livestock, hoeing in the gardens, cutting grass, and collecting firewood, grass, and birds from the forest. They also look for opportunities to go to the village center, to earn money, to visit friends or holy graves on the island, or to visit the seaside resort town of Senggigi for the weekend. These are all activities that girls are not permitted to do.

The research found that stay-behind boys actively respond to their marginalized and restricted position by developing a repertoire of strategies to survive and fill their time. One strategy involves dropping out of school and roaming around the village and in the forest with other children, looking for food to eat and things to do. These children were described by teachers and other adults as having been "neglected" by their parents and caregivers and as running "wild" (liar) in the forest. The village head said these children faced discrimination and social stigma in the community, and some left the village to go to the local market to scavenge, beg, busk, or shine shoes, which is acceptable for boys, but not for girls. Others go farther afield and live on the streets in the provincial capital city of Mataram, or they travel to the nearby islands of Sumbawa, Bali, or Java. In 2006 a street children NGO in Lombok conducted a study of two hundred street children who had dropped out of school and left home. Most of the children were boys aged nine to fifteen years old, whose parents had migrated overseas (Fetter 2006). An additional reason for leaving home was that the boy's mother had remarried because his father had not returned from overseas, but the child was not accepted by the stepfather and was subsequently rejected or neglected.

Focus group discussions with adolescent girls revealed that some had been forced to drop out of school to care for their siblings, and to help at home with household chores, especially if their mother was overseas. These girls talked about feelings of boredom in the village, particularly once they had completed primary school and there was no nearby secondary school to go to. Once they reached puberty these girls were not permitted to leave the family compound unless they were accompanied by a male sibling or family member. Girls reported how they felt bored with nothing to do, and they found it hard to fill their time. Their restricted mobility had further decreased since water had been piped into the village a few years before, which meant that they no longer had a reason to walk down to the river four times a day to collect water, and to combine play with work (Punch 2007).

The promise of an increased income and material well-being meant that most children we spoke to considered overseas migration as a life option, and many articulated their aspiration to migrate overseas as soon as they could or were old enough. A group of adolescent boys described their overseas migration plans, saying it was necessary because of the lack of income opportunities in Indonesia: "We can get jobs in Sumatra, Bali or Kalimantan, but it is not much money" (Agus, sixteen). The boys were motivated by a desire to build a concrete house, to start a family, and to improve their lives: "But we have to build a house first before we can marry," which would mean working overseas, Untung (seventeen) explained.

Some girls also aspired to go overseas and talked about their plans of going: "I can't wait until I am old enough to go overseas and earn money for my family. I want to go to Taiwan." Feelings of filial duty therefore also contributed to their desire to migrate. For example, fifteen-year-old Witri was raised by her mother, while her father worked overseas. When he did not return, her mother also went away to work, and Witri stayed with a neighbor. Witri said that soon she would also seek work overseas: "Our family is very poor. We need to go away to save enough money to build a concrete house and to pay for better food and for school for my little brothers. It is my duty to go. I am just waiting until I have enough money to leave." Given her age, Witri would need to pay an agent to falsify the necessary documents. However, recent Indonesian government policy aiming to tighten migration legislation to prevent undocumented migration has resulted in it becoming harder (and more expensive) for underage children to go overseas to work.

A reported unexpected consequence of the tighter legislation, however, has been an increase in early marriage for adolescent girls. Since the laws on migration were enforced, making it harder to migrate overseas for work without genuine documents, it was reported by provincial government officials in Lombok that in some districts girls and young women are getting married and having children instead. This may be because they see marriage and having babies as a better option to school, or migration, and because there was "nothing else to do." During discussions with grandparents about adolescent girls, it was also reported that girls of migrant parents were often married off young, sometimes as young as fifteen, since with no parents around there was "no one responsible to take care of her." It was felt by these grandparents that they could not manage to look after their female grandchildren, as they were too old to control their behavior while the parents were away. It was considered safer to marry a girl into an arranged marriage than try and protect her honor, which if lost would bring shame on the whole family (Bennett 2005).

These experiences of raising a family by young girls whose parents have gone can also be understood as a mode of waiting by occupying the space of the village through relationships to people and place, thus remaking the self, place, and feelings of belonging (Gray 2011: 426). Such a way of negotiating their own motility may also be understood as a form of compensation for the loss of loved ones and the impact of migration on their lives. This situation is similar to what Gray found in 1950s Ireland: "The temporalities of family and reproductive life are sometimes in tension with the temporalities of productive life . . . as for many women at the time the capitalist separation of domesticity and paid labor time meant a stark choice between one and the other" (426). The difference between 1950s Ireland and Lombok in the early twenty-first century, however, is that once the young women are old enough, they may also leave their babies with family members and migrate overseas themselves, to earn money to pay for a home and the child's future. In recent years, however, the option to migrate overseas has been regarded as less appealing for some young people in Indonesia, especially young educated women, with more women opting to stay behind rather than migrate for work (Chan 2017; Somaiah, Yeoh, and Arlini 2019). This has been the result of tighter legislation and control on undocumented migration, a recent ban by the Indonesian government on transnational migration to the Middle East (Chan 2016), and as an "informed resistance" to the "social risks" that transnational migration has brought to families (Somaiah, Yeoh, and Arlini 2019).

Similar to what Somaiah, Yeoh, and Arlini (2019) observed in East Java, a reduction in transnational migration by young women in East Lombok has been the result of stigma that is attached to migrant women when they return home from Saudi Arabia, and the negative experiences (of sexual abuse and mistreatment) reported by the Indonesian press and migrant women who have returned home to their village. During our research, one fifteen-year-old girl, Mutiara, said she had heard these stories and did not want to migrate away from her family; instead, she wanted to stay in school and become a teacher to make her parents happy. Most of the girls who participated in the research knew their parents went overseas to pay for their schooling and improve their lives. They were content to go to school and had intense feelings of obligation and "duty" to work hard at school, to make their parents happy. These findings align with those of Somaiah, Yeoh, and Arlini (2019: 7), who determined that young women were choosing to stay behind to make something of their education, so that their parents' sacrifices to put them through school were not wasted. The problem for young educated women in East Lombok, however, is the lack of opportunities to find well-paid work after finishing school without leaving home. On a return trip to the research site eighteen months later, we learned that Mutiara had dropped out of school, got married, and had a baby. She was living with her mother-in-law, taking care of her baby and her husband's younger siblings, while her husband had left to work in the plantations in Malaysia.

Conclusion

This article offers a response to Auyero's (2012) appeal for further exploration of the temporal experience of marginalized people; what D. C. Harvey (2015) terms the "tempography of hyper-marginalization." The research location for this study was an impoverished and hyper-marginalized community in East Lombok, characterized by low wages, low education and employment, food insecurity, and high levels of out migration. The research findings contribute to a deeper understanding of the impact of transnational migration on the well-being of children who stay behind, and to debates on the temporalities of migration and immobility. In particular, the article has explored how children who stay behind while their parents are overseas make use of their time, and how waiting is a lived experience that is integrated into every aspect of their lives.

As described by Auyero (2012) and D. C. Harvey (2015), waiting is often a shared social experience among the poor, but it is not a homogeneous experience. In rural Lombok, waiting is a shared social experience because everyone is waiting for a loved one to return and, as has been found elsewhere, for remittances to be sent (Hee Kwon 2015). Children, however, have different trajectories than adults while they wait, which are influenced by their gender and household responsibilities as well as which parent is away (which impacts their lived experience). Lombok is an Islamic and patriarchal society, and the gendered patterns of mobility in rural East Lombok lead to different opportunities for girls and boys, including experiences of protracted motility, especially for unmarried girls.

The research has revealed that within migrant communities the experiences of immobility and waiting are just as important to survival as migration and mobility. Waiting is actively experienced in the villages of East Lombok, as young people wait years for their parents to return, while many simultaneously aspire to migrate as soon as they are old enough to do so. Children waiting for their migrant parents to return are thus caught up in the geopolitics of migration precisely because of their age. The findings highlight how the micropolitics and practices of migration create movement and statis (Gray 2011; Hannam, Sheller, and Urry 2006), with the focus of this study on children who are "*moored*" within an otherwise highly mobile society (Conlon 2011). The article has, therefore, explored the lived experiences of the children of migrants in Lombok and contributes to debates about the micropolitics of mobility and immobility that impact most on the youngest members of society. Results of the research provide new data about a population of children who have received less attention in the literature regarding transnational migration in Indonesia.

In impoverished rural Lombok, transnational migration and the protracted periods of waiting for those left behind has become a social norm, which is collectively shared and shaped by customs and cultural practices. Furthermore, the cultural norm of transnational migration in rural Lombok has been both shaped and reproduced by gendered expectations of family obligations, work, and care. For the children in East Lombok, waiting has become an active community practice, embodied and experienced, and sometimes resisted, either by choosing to leave the village to seek work and survive elsewhere, or by falsifying documents so they can migrate overseas themselves. Early marriage and having a baby were also identified by some adolescent girls as ways of alleviating monotony and negotiating their motility.

Finally, the research validates claims by a growing number of scholars within migration studies that child-centered research is vital to understanding how children respond to their parents' sustained absence, instead of believing the positive discourse that is imbued in government rhetoric about the impact of migration of local communities in Indonesia. It is imperative that the specific social and cultural conditions that shape children's circumstances are considered in all policy formation and child protection strategies, and that children's views are included in policies of migration, to ensure policies are implemented in the best interests of the child.

Note

1   The "children" who participated in this research were between twelve and seventeen years of age. Their names have been changed to protect their identities.

References

Acedera, Kristel Anne, and Brenda Yeoh. 2019. "'Making Time': Long-Distance Marriages and the Temporalities of the Transnational Family." *Current Sociology* 67, no. 2: 250–72. www.ncbi.nlm.nih.gov/pmc/articles/PMC6402049/.

Allerton, Catherine. 2014. "Statelessness and the Lives of the Children of Migrants in Sabah, East Malaysia." *Tilburg Law Review* 19, nos. 1–2: 26–34.

Allerton, Catherine. 2016. "Rural Mobility and Urban Immobility: Comparative Perspectives on Migration, Movements, and Children's Lives in Flores and Sabah." Paper presented at the Children, Families, and Mobility in Southeast Asia Panel of the Association for Southeast Asian Studies in the United Kingdom (ASEASUK) Conference, University of London, September 17.

Andreveski, Hannah, and Samantha Lyneham. 2014. "Experiences of Exploitation and Human Trafficking among a Sample of Indonesian Migrant Domestic Workers." *Trends and Issues in Crime and Criminal Justice*, no. 471: 1–11.

Ansell, Nicola, Flora Hadju, Lorraine van Blerk, and Elsbeth Robson. 2014. "Reconceptualising Temporality in Young Lives: Exploring Young People's Current and Future Livelihoods in AIDS-Affected Southern Africa." *Transactions of the Institute of British Geographers* 39, no. 3: 387–401.

Auyero, Javier. 2012. *Patients of the State: The Politics of Waiting in Argentina*. Durham, NC: Duke University Press.

Ball, Jessica, Leslie Butt, and Harriot Beazley. 2017. "Birth Registration and Protection for Children of Transnational Labor Migrants in Indonesia." *Journal of Immigrant and Refugee Studies* 15, no. 3: 305–25.

Barker, John, Peter Kraftl, John Horton, and Faith Tucker. 2009. "The Road Less Travelled—New Directions in Children's and Young People's Mobility." *Mobilities* 4, no. 1: 1–10.

Beazley, Harriot. 2007. "The 'Malaysian Orphans' of Lombok: Children and Young People's Livelihood Responses to Out-Migration in Eastern Indonesia." In *Global Perspectives on Rural Childhood and Youth: Young Rural Lives*, edited by Ruth Panelli, Samantha Punch, and Elsbeth Robson, 107–20. London: Routledge.

Beazley, Harriot. 2015. "Multiple Identities, Multiple Realities: Children Who Migrate Independently for Work in Southeast Asia." *Children's Geographies,* 13, no. 3: 296–309.

Beazley, Harriot, Leslie Butt, and Jessica Ball. 2018. "'Like It, Don't Like It, You Have to Like It': Children's Emotional Responses to the Absence of Transnational Migrant Parents in Lombok, Indonesia." *Children's Geographies* 16, no. 6: 591–603.

Bennett, Linda Rae. 2005. *Women, Islam, and Modernity: Single Women, Sexuality, and Reproductive Health in Contemporary Indonesia*. London: Routledge Curzon.

Bessell, Sharon, Harriot Beazley, and Roxana Waterson. 2016. "Methodology and Ethics of Child-Rights-Oriented Research and Practice." In *"Children Out of Place" and Human Rights*, edited by Antonella Invernizzi, Manfred Liebel, Brian Milne, and Rebecca Budde, 211–32. Basel, Switzerland: Springer.

Butt, Leslie, Jessica Ball, and Harriot Beazley. 2017. "Migrant Mothers and the Sedentary Child Bias: Constraints on Child Circulation in Indonesia." *Asia Pacific Journal of Anthropology* 18, no. 4: 372–88.

Chan, Carol. 2014. "Gendered Morality and Development Narratives: The Case of Female Labor Migration from Indonesia." *Sustainability* 6, no. 10: 6949–72.

Chan, Carol. 2017. "Not Always 'Left-Behind': Indonesian Adolescent Women Negotiating Transnational Mobility, Filial Piety, and Care." *Asia Pacific Journal of Anthropology* 18, no. 3: 246–63.

Coe, Cati, Rachel Reynolds, Deborah Boehm, Julia Meredith Hess, and Heather Rae-Espinoza, eds. 2011. *Everyday Ruptures: Children, Youth, and Migration in Global Perspective*. Nashville, TN: Vanderbilt University Press.

Conlon, Deirdre. 2011. "Waiting for Feminist Perspectives on the Spacings/Timings of Migrant Mobility." *Gender, Place, and Culture* 18, no. 3: 353–60.

Cresswell, Tim, and Peter Merriman. 2011. *Geographies of Mobilities: Practices, Spaces, Subjects.* Farnham, UK: Ashgate Publishing.

Dobson, Madeleine. 2009. "Unpacking Children in Migration Research." *Children's Geographies* 7, no. 3: 355–60.

Fetter, Chaim. 2006. *The Research Study of Street Children, Lombok, Indonesia.* Mataram, Indonesia: Peduli Anak Foundation.

Graham, Elsbeth, and Lucy Jordan. 2011. "Migrant Parents and the Psychological Well-Being of Left-Behind Children in Southeast Asia." *Journal of Marriage and the Family* 73, no. 4: 763–87.

Graham, Elsbeth, Lucy Jordan, Brenda Yeoh, Theodora Lam, Maria Asis, and Su-Kamdi. 2012. "Transnational Families and the Family Nexus: Perspectives of Indonesian and Filipino Children Left Behind by Migrant Parents." *Environment and Planning A: Economy and Space* 44, no. 4: 793–815.

Gray, Brenda. 2011. "Becoming Non-Migrant: Lives Worth Waiting For." *Gender, Place, and Culture* 18, no. 3: 417–32.

Griffiths, Melanie. 2014. "Out of Time: The Temporal Uncertainties of Refused Asylum Seekers and Immigration Detainees." *Journal of Ethnic and Migration Studies* 40, no. 12: 1991–2009.

Griffiths, Melanie, Ali Rogers, and Bridget Anderson. 2013. *Migration, Time, and Temporalities: Review and Prospect.* COMPAS Resources Paper, March. www.compas.ox.ac.uk/2013/migration-time-and-temporalities-review-and-prospect/.

Hannam, Kevin, Mimi Sheller, and John Urry. 2006. "Editorial: Mobilities, Immobilities, and Moorings." *Mobilities* 1, no. 1: 1–22.

Harker, Christopher. 2005. "Playing and Affective Time-Spaces." *Children's Geographies* 3, no. 1: 47–62.

Harvey, Daina Cheyenne. 2015. "Waiting in the Lower Ninth Ward in New Orleans: A Case Study of the Tempography of Hyper-Marginalization." *Symbolic Interaction* 38, no. 4: 539–56.

Harvey, David. 1990. "Between Space and Time: Reflections on the Geographical Imagination." *Annals of the Association of American Geographers* 80, no. 3: 418–34.

Hashim, Imam, and Dorte Thorsen. 2011. *Child Migration in Africa.* London: Zed Books.

Hee Kwon, June. 2015. "The Work of Waiting: Love and Money in Korean Chinese Transnational Migration." *Cultural Anthropology* 30, no. 3: 477–500.

Hoang, Lan Anh, Theodora Lam, Brenda Yeoh, and Elsbeth Graham. 2014. "Transnational Migration, Changing Care Arrangements, and Left-Behind Children's Responses in South-East Asia." *Children's Geographies* 13, no. 3: 263–77.

ILO (International Labour Organisation). 2013. "Better Protecting Indonesian Migrant Workers through Bilateral and Multilateral Agreements." Press release, May 8. www.ilo.org/jakarta /info/public/pr/WCMS_212738/lang--en/index.htm.

Jeffrey, Craig. 2008. "Waiting." *Environment and Planning D: Society and Space* 26, no. 6: 954–58.

Khoo, Chen Yen, Maria Platt, Brenda Yeoh, and Theodora Lam. 2014. *Structural Conditions and Agency in Migrant Decision-Making: A Case of Domestic and Construction Workers from Java, Indonesia.* Working paper, eSocialSciences. econpapers.repec.org/paper/esswpaper/id _3a7084.htm (accessed November 22, 2021).

Khoo, Chen Yen, and Brenda Yeoh. 2017. "Responsible Adults-in-the-Making: Intergenerational Impact of Parental Migration on Indonesian Young Women's Aspirational Capacity." *Geoforum* 85: 280–89.

Lam, Theodora, Lan Anh Hoang, and Brenda Yeoh. 2013. "Securing a Better Living Environment for Left-Behind Children: Implications and Challenges for Policies." *Asian and Pacific Migration Journal* 22, no. 3: 421–45.

Lefebvre, Henri. 2004. *Rhythmanalysis: Space, Time, and Everyday Life,* translated by Stuart Elden and Gerald Moore. New York: Continuum.

Lindquist, Johan. 2004. "Veils and Ecstasy: Negotiating Shame in the Indonesian Borderlands." *Ethnos* 69, no. 4: 487–508.

Lindquist, Johan. 2010. "Labour Recruitment, Circuits of Capital, and Gendered Mobility: Reconceptualizing the Indonesian Migration Industry." *Pacific Affairs* 83, no. 1: 115–32.

Mar, Raymond, Malia Mason, and Aubrey Litvack. 2012. "How Daydreaming Relates to Life Satisfaction, Loneliness, and Social Support: The Importance of Gender and Daydream Content." *Consciousness and Cognition* 21, no. 1: 401–7.

May, Jon, and Nigel Thrift. 2003. *Timespace: Geographies of Temporality.* London: Routledge.

McKay, Deirdre. 2007. "'Sending Dollars Shows Feeling'—Emotions and Economics in Filipino Migration." *Mobilities* 2, no. 2: 175–94.

McKay, Deidre. 2016. *An Archipelago of Care: Filipino Migrants and Global Networks.* Bloomington: Indiana University Press.

Mountz, Alison. 2011. "Where Asylum-Seekers Wait: Feminist Counter-Topographies of Sites between States." *Gender, Place, and Culture* 18, no. 3: 381–99.

Olson, Elizabeth. 2015. "Geography and Ethics 1: Waiting and Urgency." *Progress in Human Geography* 39, no. 4: 517–26.

Parreñas, Rhacel Salazar. 2005. *Children of Global Migration: Transnational Families and Gendered Woes.* Stanford, CA: Stanford University Press.

Peng, Yinni, and Odalia M. H. Wong. 2013. "Diversified Transnational Mothering via Telecommunication: Intensive, Collaborative, and Passive." *Gender and Society* 27, no. 4: 491–513.

Punch, Samantha. 2007. "Migration Projects: Children on the Move for Work and Education." Paper presented at the Workshop on Independent Child Migrants: Policy Debates and Dilemma, University of Sussex, Westminster, London, September 12.

Punch, Samantha. 2012. "Studying Transnational Children: A Multi-Sited, Longitudinal, Ethnographic Approach." *Journal of Ethnic and Migration Studies* 38, no. 6, 1007–23.

Schwartz, Barry. 1975. *Queuing and Waiting: Studies in the Social Organization of Access and Delay.* Chicago: University of Chicago Press.

Singer, Jerome L. 1961. "Imagination and Waiting Ability in Young Children." *Journal of Personality* 29, no. 4: 396–413.

SMERU Research Institute. 2014. *The Well-Being of Children Left by Their Mothers Who Become Migrant Workers: Study Case in Two Districts in Indonesia.* Jakarta, Indonesia: SMERU.

Somaiah, Bittiandra Chand, Brenda Yeoh, and Silvia Mila Arlini. 2019. "'*Cukup* for Me to Be Successful in This Country': 'Staying' among Left-Behind Young Women in Indonesia's Migrant-Sending Villages." *Global Networks: A Journal of Transnational Affairs*, April 29. doi.org/10.1111/glob.12238.

van Blerk, Lorraine, and Nicola Ansell. 2007. "Participatory Feedback and Dissemination with and for Children: Reflections from Research with Young Migrants in Southern Africa." *Children's Geographies* 5, no. 3: 313–24.

Whitehead, Ann, and Imam Hashim. 2005. *Children and Migration: Background Paper for DFID Migration Team.* London: Department for International Development.

World Bank. 2015. "Migration and Remittances: Recent Developments and Outlook Special Topic: Financing for Development." Migration and Development Brief 24, April 13. www.knomad.org/sites/default/files/2017-08/MigrationandDevelopmentBrief24.pdf.

World Bank. 2017. "Personal Remittances, Received (% of GDP)." data.worldbank.org/indicator/BX.TRF.PWKR.DT.GD.ZS?name_desc=true (accessed November 22, 2021).

Zentgraf, Kristine, and Norma Stoltz Chinchilla. 2012. "Transnational Family Separation: A Framework for Analysis." *Journal of Ethnic and Migration Studies* 38, no. 2: 345–66.

Zerubavel, Eviatar. 1977. "The French Republican Calendar: A Case Study in the Sociology of Time." *American Sociological Review* 42, no. 4: 868–77.

Barriers Faced by Returning Migrant Children in Vietnam:

The Case of the Mekong Delta Region

Misaki Iwai

As many researchers have pointed out, inter-Asian marriages have mostly been focused on "marriage-scapes" or global hypergamy from southern underdeveloped countries to northern developed countries. Such research has examined gender mobility or geographies of power (Constable 2005; Williams 2010) and the migration-development nexus (Chung, Kim, and Piper 2016). The primary theme has been related to family relations in host countries, mainly the multimarginalized status of marriage migrants and foreign brides and their social adaptation to (or integration into) families-in-law in destination countries. For example, foreign brides face assimilation pressures from the traditional patriarchal values of parents-in-law. This often leads brides to experience alienation within their families and build "hidden spaces" to escape pressures enforced by mothers-in-law (Wang 2007).

positions 30:2 DOI 10.1215/10679847-9573357
Copyright 2022 by Duke University Press

Since the mid-2000s, local nongovernmental organizations (NGOs) in Taiwan and Korea have attempted to empower marriage migrants through financial support from the central government. Foreign brides began to be regarded as "new citizens" with diverse values and foreign backgrounds, not as "immigrants" (Iwai 2013; M. Kim 2013). They are no longer the "weak" who lurk in "hidden spaces." Instead, they are regarded as actors who manage to establish their places and improve their positions by overcoming social stigma and discrimination (Phạm and Iwai 2014a, 2014b). Meanwhile, responding to an imbalanced multiculturalism policy from the top, grassroots multiculturalism at both the individual and community levels have been established for foreign wives, their husbands, and their in-laws (Bélanger and Wang 2012; A. Kim 2017; M. Kim 2018).

Despite these efforts, the number of transnational divorces has increased rapidly since the mid-2000s. This is because various conflicts caused by language barriers and cultural differences may still result in the dissolution of marriages, leading some women to return to their home countries. This article explores the fate of children upon the dissolution of transnational marriages between Vietnamese mothers and foreign fathers. It focuses on children who are sent or taken to Vietnam by their mothers. In recent years, there has been a noticeable presence of children known as "unrecognized" (*không được thừa nhận*) in the Vietnamese media (Cửu Long 2016a, 2016b; Hoàng and Trần 2014; Hoài Đăng 2016; Phạm Tâm 2015; Phương Nguyên and Yên Trinh 2016; Phương Nguyên, Yên Trinh, and Ngọc Diện 2016; Viễn Sự and Sơn Lâm 2018a, 2018b, 2018c). These children are the offspring of Vietnamese women who married Korean or Taiwanese men and who have returned to Vietnam following divorce or separation. However, since the media reports on them only fragmentarily, little is known about their everyday lives and experiences.

Various studies have explored the disadvantages that the dissolution of international marriages brings children and women. Returning "home" prior to the finalization of one's divorce is said to result in the denial of a women's full citizenship in her country of origin (Kim, Park, and Shukhertei 2016). The poverty of children is aggravated, as can be seen in the case of Korean-Vietnamese children (Le 2016), Japanese-Filipino children (Suzuki 2010), and Japanese-Thai children (Ishii 2016), and even when they maintain the citizenship of the father, if he is Japanese (Ishii 2016; Suzuki 2010). This article adds to these discussions by focusing on children from Vietnamese and Korean unions who are sent to Vietnam upon the dissolution of their parent's marriage and examines the politics of their integration. It establishes that the gender marginalization of their mothers and the discrimination against them as mixed-nationality children will lead to their receiving limited state benefits and being socially ostracized.

This article highlights the legal ambiguity of these children's citizenship in Vietnam as well as their social marginalization as "foreigners." The legal ambiguity of these children arises from their not having a birth certificate, as many were born in Korea, and their ineligibility to secure Vietnamese nationality because the continuing legal rights that their fathers have over them. In turn, the absence of Vietnamese nationality, which often manifests itself in their non-Vietnamese names, results in their social marginalization and treatment as outcasts in the community. This article identifies and examines the effects of such legal ambiguity, which include limited access to public provision of education, financial hardships aggravated by the absence of paternal support, and social stigma in the community.

The Legal Landscape of Citizenship in Inter-Asian Marriage Migration: The Case of Vietnam

In what Constable (2005) calls the gendered geographies of power, poor and low-educated women who cannot achieve social-economic mobility in their countries marry men from wealthier countries to provide economic support for families back home and to change their own lives in the host countries (Constable 2005: 5–7; Yang and Lu 2010: 20–21). The most visible cases of these marriages are between Southeast Asian women and East Asian men, particularly Vietnamese, Thai, or Filipino women and Japanese, Korean, and Taiwanese partners (Bélanger, Khuất Thu Hồng, and Tran Giang Linh 2010; Hugo and Nguyen 2007; Ishii 2016; Nguyen and Tran 2010; Phan 2005; Suzuki 2005). According to Statistics Bureau data in Taiwan and Korea, about 108,000 Vietnamese brides have been married in Taiwan (National Immigration Agency 2021) and about 87,000 in Korea (Vũ Thị Trang 2018). It can be said that foreign brides have two identities: on the one hand, they are "the weak" and suffer significantly in relationships with families-in-law, but, on the other hand, they are "the strong" who provide financial support to their own families.

Illustrating this paradox, the majority suffer communication failures because of language differences with their husbands and their families-in-law. However, the fiduciary relationship with their biological families that is maintained through remittances to their home countries and the desire to have children who would give them stability in their host countries are extremely important motivations for their migration. Emigrant daughters who find jobs send monetary remittances to their own families. This changes the power relationships with their parents and siblings in their home countries and allows them to exert a certain influence on the local community (Bélanger, Khuất Thu Hồng, and Tran Giang Linh 2010, 2013; Suzuki 2005).

However, pathways to citizenship present various hurdles for foreign brides and their children. Foreign brides are usually conditional residents whose legal status is contingent on their continuing to be married. Obtaining citizenship then requires the cooperation of their spouses. This becomes a barrier when marriages dissolve, which affects a growing number of women. What happens to their children is partially addressed in this article with its focus on the fate of children who return to Vietnam.

According to the Consulate General of the Republic of Korea in Hồ Chí Minh City, the rate of international divorce in South Korea has soared, and the rate of divorce between Vietnamese women and Korean men has reached 15 to 20 percent (Viễn Sự and Sơn Lâm 2018d). This statistic does not include rates of nonlegal separation. Those fleeing domestic violence usually escape to Vietnam without having completed divorce proceedings or securing the Vietnamese citizenship of their children, which in turn leaves these children with a legally ambiguous status in Vietnam.

Divorce usually leaves foreign women legally vulnerable. If the marriage breaks down (even if the husband is responsible), the wife is not allowed to stay in South Korea, and must return home prior to the expiration of her visa. Those who wish to bring their children to Vietnam cannot easily do so because the nationality of the child is the same as that of the father, which in turn places the child in a very complex situation on their return to the mother's home country. Minor citizens who gain a second passport at birth are allowed to maintain both nationalities, but in Vietnam at a certain age they must relinquish one of them.

Vietnamese citizenship is not extended immediately to the child of the Vietnamese mother born in a foreign country as obtaining it requires the agreement of both parents and the application for citizenship within a particular period after the birth of the child (National Assembly 2008). However, most of Vietnamese mothers in foreign countries such as Taiwan and Korea do not know how to secure their children's dual citizenship or are not interested in pursuing the matter. As a result, in many cases, the children are not citizens in their mothers' home country and are socially excluded in the local community. The numbers at the national level are unknown, but according to its Public Security Bureau, Cần Thơ City in 2017 had 1,306 mixed children, of whom 402 were not able to attend school (Cửu Long and Hữu Công 2017).

Research Methodology and Field Site

This discussion is based on the results of nonconsecutive fieldwork conducted in the Vị Thắng commune in Hậu Giang Province in the Meking Delta, which, as of August and December 2017, produced Vietnam's second highest number of married migrant women. Vị Thắng is a specialty agricultural commune located 200 kilometers southwest of Hồ Chí Minh City and 50 kilometers southwest of the Cần Thơ city center. As of April 2017, the commune had a population of 9,559 people, with 2,351 households residing in seven hamlets. Vị Thắng was chosen because Vietnamese newspaper articles reported that elementary schools in the commune had accepted children without birth certificates as a humanitarian effort. These children attend classes as "nonenrollment students" (*học gửi*), meaning that they are not included in student lists and do not enjoy the same rights as their classmates (Hoài Thanh 2016; Ngọc Tài 2016; Văn Vĩnh 2016). The commune was chosen as a community model after consultation with the Vietnam Ministry of Labor, Invalids, and Social Affairs and in cooperation with the Office of the United Nations High Commissioner for Refugees (UNHCR) (UBND xã Vị Thắng 2017).

This study is based on observations conducted in sixteen households and interviews with various stakeholders including mothers, other caregivers, and children.[1] The perspectives of eighteen returning migrant children from dissolved marriages are represented in the discussion. The author identified and obtained access to research participants with the assistance of local NGOs as well as schools. Prior to the field research, executives of the Vietnamese Women's Union (VWU) in Hậu Giang province were contacted, and general information was obtained from them concerning returning migrant women and their children. The VWU is an NGO in Vietnam that provides legal support regarding international marriage and divorce (Hội liên hiệp Phụ nữ tỉnh Hậu Giang 2017). Full-time social workers belonging to the VWU regularly visit the homes of returning families who are facing difficulties. Two VWU workers attended each family interview visit, as they had a good grasp of the individual cases and were in a position to provide advice on legal procedures. All interviews were conducted with their cooperation. In addition, the vice president in the Vị Thủy district (the former president of Vị Thắng) and the present president in the Vị Thắng commune, both of whom knew the local situation well, assisted with interviews and family visits. The VWU was responsible for requesting and scheduling family interviews during the field research. Most families agreed, though some refused.

A visit was also made to the Korea Center for United Nations Human Rights Policy (KOCUN), a South Korean NGO responsible for supporting divorced or separated women and their children. In 2011, KOCUN had offices in Cần Thơ and Hà Nội to provide support to women who had married Koreans and later left Korea and educated their children in Vietnam. The organization had also begun to cooperate with the VWU to provide service to the Mekong Delta region. Three local schools (Vị Thắng kindergarten, elementary school, and junior high school) were also visited to investigate the children's school enrollment situation, academic ability, and relationships with classmates.

Returning migrant children who are foreign nationals in the Vị Thắng commune can be divided into three types of households. Of those three types, the second and third will be discussed because these cases concern fatherless families and the focus of the larger research project from which this article draws is on the fate of children who return to Vietnam following the dissolution of their parent's marriage.

> Type 1: *Two-parent transnational households*: Children are born in a foreign country and migrate to Vietnam temporarily while parents reside abroad.

> Type 2: *Single-mother proximate households*: Children are born in a foreign country and return to Vietnam accompanied by their mother following the latter's divorce or separation. Mothers temporarily care for children in proximity but eventually remigrate to the city to pursue work.

> Type 3: *Single-mother transnational households*: Children return to Vietnam while their mothers live in a foreign country as a result of the absence of labor market opportunities.

In each type of household, including type 3, mothers and children do not live together or near each other, thus challenging traditional gender notions of the family. The mothers maintain the family via regular remittances. The children are raised by maternal relatives.

Overview of Returning Migrant Children in Vị Thắng

According to statistics of Vị Thắng commune in December 2017 (see fig. 1), twenty-seven mixed children were registered temporarily:[2] eleven Korean nationals, twelve Taiwanese nationals, two Malaysian nationals, one (mainland) Chinese national, and one Vietnamese national.

However, these data indicate only the time at which returning migrant children were registered as temporary residents of the commune and do not reflect the actual number of children living in the commune. According to the chairperson of VWU, there were eighteen returning migrant children living in the commune as of August 2017. The reason for the difference in the numbers is that when the children left the commune, their maternal relatives did not notify the commune government. The commune chairperson stated that foreign nationals have to apply for temporary residence registration, but they are not obligated to provide notification when they leave.

The author obtained a list of children temporarily residing in the com-

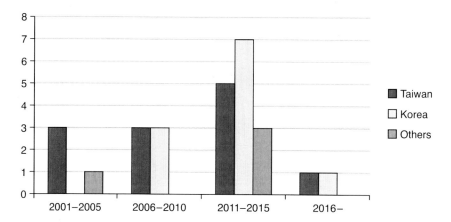

Figure 1 Returning migrant children with temporary registration in the Vị Thắng commune. Unit: person.
Source Created by the author with data from UBND xã Vị Thắng 2017.

mune as of 2017 from the VWU's chairperson at the commune level and carried out a survey of all the children. The author visited sixteen households and met eighteen children: thirteen Korean-Vietnamese children and five Taiwanese-Vietnamese children. With regard to resident patterns, out of sixteen mothers of eighteen children, the author could meet only three mothers (one married, two divorced/separated) who live at home with their children. The rest of the mothers were absent from their homes and lived in other countries or the urban center.

Given the field survey results (see table 1), the characteristics of the eighteen children with foreign roots are as follows. First, nearly all of the children returned to Vietnam during infancy (at younger than four years of age, or even in utero). This means that the length of time they have spent in Vietnam is often longer than the time they spent in the country in which they were born. Four children were brought to Vietnam in utero and were born in Vietnam; three of them are Korean-Vietnamese children, and one is Taiwanese-Vietnamese. Most of the returning migrant children have been raised by extended family, either maternal grandparents or maternal aunts. Only five children have been raised by their mothers.

Second, a significant number of the children (eleven of eighteen, 61 per-

Table 1 Characteristics of mixed children living in the Vị Thắng commune (n = 18).

Characteristics				*Results*
Present age	7	Younger than 6 years	8	Between 7 and 11 years
	3	Older than 12 years		
Gender	5	Male	13	Female
Age in months or years	4	In utero	2	Younger than 12 months
upon returning home	7	1–2 years old	2	3–4 years old
	2	Older than 5 years old	1	Unknown
Place of birth	10	Korea	4	Taiwan
	4	Vietnam		
Length of stay	1	Less than 1 year	8	1–5 years
	8	6–10 years	0	More than 11 years
	1	Unknown		
Main caretaker	8	Maternal grandparents	5	Aunt (mother's sister)
	5	Mother		
Nationality	7	Korean only	1	Both Korean and Vietnamese
	5	Taiwanese only	2	Vietnamese only
	3	Stateless		
Name usage	11	Korean/Taiwanese names only		
	4	Both Vietnamese and Korean/Taiwanese names		
	3	Vietnamese name only		

Source Created with data collected during the author's fieldwork.

cent) do not have Vietnamese names and still use their Chinese or Korean names in daily life. As will be discussed later, their foreign names are the cause of bullying at school.

Third, of the eighteen children, five are of Taiwanese nationality, eight are of Korean nationality, two are of Vietnamese nationality, three are stateless,[3] and one has dual nationality (Korean-Vietnamese). Of the two children with Vietnamese nationality who are both Vietnamese-Korean, one is a boy who was adopted by a maternal aunt living in Hồ Chí Minh City, while his divorced mother still stays in Korea because she obtained Korean nationality. The other one is a girl who came from Korea to Vietnam in utero and was registered as a member of her grandfather's family while her mother left home for Hồ Chí Minh City for work. Before 2010, when children were sent to their mothers' homes from abroad, in many communes of the Mekong Delta the procedure for changing their nationality was relatively loose; so, these two children easily obtained Vietnamese nationality. Since then, regulations have become stricter, rendering the looser measures illegal.

Fourth, the majority of the children (twelve of eighteen, 67 percent) are girls of elementary school age or younger.

The Structural Barriers Preventing Social Integration

The structural barriers faced by returning migrant children mainly concern problems with their legal status because citizenship in Vietnam is not automatically extended to them despite the nationality of their mother. Barriers to citizenship include gender and the rights extended to the "foreign" father, who must acknowledge his children in order for them to be formally recognized by the Vietnamese state. Not considered is the likelihood that the father will not wish to cooperate, especially if the mother fled the marriage because of domestic abuse and violence.

Another potential barrier is Vietnam's requirement that a "birth certificate" (*giấy khai sinh*) be provided to prove a child's legal status as a Vietnamese citizen. To obtain this document, it is necessary to register one's birth notification (*giấy chứng sinh*) along with the mother's identification card and marriage certificate with the local government. The birth notification is issued by the hospital.[4] As a result of their foreign nationality, returning migrant children are unable to secure citizenship as many had not had their birth registered in Vietnam. Moreover, most mothers who return to Vietnam from Korea only have their children's passports, which is insufficient to obtain citizenship in Vietnam regardless of where they were born.

Only those who have had their birth formally registered can attend school. Returning migrant women can bypass this hurdle by registering the birth of their child on their return to Vietnam. However, this requires the cooperation of the father and his family. In most cases, the mothers have lost contact with their husbands after returning to Vietnam, which makes obtaining their children's birth registrations nearly impossible. Until 2016, many returning migrant children were not allowed to attend school in the rural areas of the Mekong Delta, and the press often reported on this issue. After 2017, "nonregular enrollment" came to be recognized as a humanitarian issue. However, since this is an interim relief measure, many returning migrant children are still not listed in school registries.

Let me provide two such cases of returning migrant children whose parents' marriage had dissolved prior to their migration to Vietnam. The first case is that of H. D. Jun, a Korean-Vietnamese ten-year-old boy who "returned" at the age of eighteen months with his mother. His mother, Muội, stayed with him for only a few months as she had to migrate to seek employment to support him. Creating barriers to his citizenship were first his expired passport and second the expiration of his visitor visa. He now lives illegally in Vietnam because he never managed to change his status from a "visitor" to a "resident" (citizen) despite the Vietnamese nationality of his mother.

According to Jun's aunt, Loan, who takes care of him, Jun's mother hopes to live with him permanently in Vietnam, but she has not secured his legal residency. One reason for this is her continuing absence from home as she works in a factory in Hồ Chí Minh City. This has deterred her from following the formal procedures in local government offices that she alone, as his mother, can do to change his legal status. For this reason, Jun did not attend school until he was nine years old.

The second case is P. T. Vy, who was conceived in South Korea in 2015 but was born in Vietnam in 2016. Her mother returned to Vietnam at the end of 2015, when she was five months pregnant. She gave birth to Vy in the Hậu Giang provincial hospital in 2016 and was issued a birth notification at the hospital. The surname on her birth notification was her mother's, P. T. Ngoan. However, the authority of the Vị Thắng commune refused to accept her birth notification because the mother had not yet officially divorced her Korean husband and the authority requires the provision of a marriage certificate. In other words, if the mother's formal divorce had been completed, Vy's birth could have been registered in her mother's home commune. This would have allowed Vy to obtain a resident card similar to those of other local children. Vy's grandmother said that her father in Korea knew about her birth but never contacted Ngoan after she returned home. As a result, Vy's status is made legally ambiguous by the absence of a registration card. For this reason, she cannot avail herself of various citizenship benefits including easily obtaining medical care and attending school. Compounding the alienation of Vy is her lack of citizenship in Korea, as her father has yet to register her birth in his family's registry. This renders Vy technically stateless.

Vietnamese nationality policies define citizenship by bilateral jus sanguinis. In other words, a child with a parent who is a Vietnamese citizen is also Vietnamese. Nevertheless, in practice, many governments at the commune level are likely to apply domestic paternalistic measures. In other words, local authorities insist that since the child's legal status is identified by the father, the legal procedure for birth registration of the mixed child should not be performed in Vietnam but in the father's country. Otherwise, the mother must legally dissolve the marriage before registering the child's birth. This practice has severe consequences for the well-being of not only the women but also their children, whose legal rights as Vietnamese nationals are denied. This results in the denial of children's welfare rights, including access to government-assisted medical insurance and education.

The Social Barriers Preventing Mixed Children from Social Inclusion

It is not only structural but also social barriers that result in the marginalization of returning migrant, mixed-nationality children who come to Vietnam. They are also likely to confront various social barriers that hinder their inclusion, such as prejudice, discrimination, and isolation. The marginalization of these children is best exemplified by the bullying they experience both at home and in school. They are often taunted as being "fatherless" once the children learn of their "mixed" identity from their foreign surnames.

Providing a vivid example, K. H. In, an eleven-year-old Korean-Vietnamese girl, was bullied at school for being "a child without a father" and came home crying repeatedly until she managed to transfer to another school. Her mother resents how adults often enabled the bullying. As she claims,

> The problem of child bullying is in adults. As adults say, children would tease. My daughter was being bullied by a male teacher's child. Since the teacher protected him and never scolded, other children followed up.

Children do not know anything. Because adults discriminate, children also discriminate.

Another child who faced severe bullying at school is Nhi, a girl of mixed Korean and Vietnamese heritage who was conceived in South Korea and born in Vietnam. Despite being one of the few who obtained Vietnamese citizenship, Nhi was not spared incessant discrimination and bullying.

It is not only in school but also at "home" where children may feel bullied. Maternal family members who care for returning migrant children may unconsciously contribute to the social stigma of the children. This occurs when they use the phrase "go back to your country" while scolding them or when they consciously conceal the mixed-ethnicity origins of the child from their neighbors. Neighbors often stare at Vy and make a remark such as the following: "What a similarity between her and her mother, though she is a child of South Korea." Yet her grandmother, who lives next door, refuses to tell Vy about her Korean heritage.

Interviewer: What will you do if your granddaughter asks you where her father is?

Grandmother: At that time, I will tell her that her father has been in Saigon, but he has gone away because her mother got divorced from her father.

Interviewer: You do not tell her that her father is Korean?

Grandmother: Yeah.

Interviewer: However, maybe the neighbors may talk someday?

Grandmother: I will leave it alone. Whoever wants to say something, let them say it. Is it obvious that the granddaughter should believe us?

The grandmother might have the best intentions for hiding her granddaughter's ethnic identity—for instance, to shield her from bullying—but doing so, even as a protective measure, may unintentionally send the message that the child has the "wrong" identity. Moreover, hiding the identity of the child is sometimes impossible. A significant number of the children do not have Vietnamese names but still use their Chinese or Korean names in daily life.

Measures Taken by the Local Government, Schools, and NGOs

Local organizations have taken note of the struggles that children from cross-border marriages face on their return to Vietnam. For this reason, they have extended support on both an individual and an institutional level. On an individual level, KOCUN offers one-on-one assistance to women and their families. They try to assist women in processing their divorces and contacting their husbands in Korea to mediate the divorce proceedings amicably (Ngô Thị Vân Phượng 2018: 110–24). This process is a key step that women need to undertake to secure the citizenship rights of their children in Vietnam. Concomitantly, these organizations also assist women in securing custody of their children when husbands go to Vietnam with the intention of forcibly bringing their children back to South Korea.

On an institutional level, the central government has begun to consider ways to solve the educational issues confronted by returning migrant children with foreign nationality. Many citizens and organizations in the rural Mekong Delta have raised issues with the government, such as children's inability to attend school if they lack a birth registration. The central government is also deciding on the possibility of giving exempt status to children from international marriages and granting them citizenship despite not meeting the birth registration period. Some local governments have also spearheaded efforts to extend legal recognition to children. This is the case in Hậu Giang Province. In contrast to other provinces in the Mekong Delta, such as Cần Thơ or Vĩnh Long, it permits children who have no birth certificates to attend local public schools. Since the end of 2014, the Vị Thắng commune's government has issued temporary birth certificates to children with passports and has begun to implement educational support for these children. Local schools allow some form of nonregular enrollment, accepting so-called nonenrollment students (*học gửi*), awarding graduation certificates, and providing opportunities for children to learn in the classroom without being separated from their Vietnamese citizen counterparts.

Yet legal support alone does not address all the issues faced by families from failed cross-border marriages. Unfortunately, according to the women and families interviewed in Vị Thắng, women will not seek access to legal support—for example, an international divorce application to a provincial court—if they are burdened by the trauma and psychological pressure of having a failed marriage. The mental suffering and despair that mothers experience in unfamiliar countries and their feelings of inferiority and loneliness after returning home cannot be immediately healed. As a result, although there are documents to support their children's applications for Vietnamese citizenship, some mothers are reluctant to comply with the formalities because of their sense of inferiority. As the above case of Ngoan has shown, if mothers are not helped to regain their dignity and self-confidence, then their children's citizenship is not made a priority. This suggests a need to have programs in place that prioritize psychological services to women returning from failed cross-border marriages.

Conclusion

This article focuses on an understudied set of children of migration in Asia: the children who return to their maternal country of origin after the dissolution of their parent's marriage. It looks specifically at the case of children in Vietnam, one of the largest source countries of "foreign brides" in Asia. The high rates of divorce among international marriages suggests that this is a large group of children. As discussed in this article, the Vietnamese government has increasingly paid attention to their plight.

There are, as described above, several types of citizenship status among these children. Some manage to obtain Vietnamese citizenship; some hold the citizenship of their father but at the risk of becoming undocumented in Vietnam; and, finally, some are rendered stateless and are citizens of neither Vietnam or Korea/Taiwan. That last type results from their fathers "abandoning" them: for example, the father fails to register the child in, say, Korea and then refuses to cooperate or be available to assist the mother in processing the child's legal residence in Vietnam. This article documents two salient challenges confronted by such children, the first concerning the structural barriers they confront in Vietnam (e.g., the challenge of obtaining legal status) and the second pertaining to their social ostracization not as just ethnic foreigners but also as children in single-parent households.

External organizations have in recent years begun to recognize the plight of these children. For instance, the local government of Hậu Giang Province has issued provisional birth certificates and allowed local school authorities to accept nonenrollment students (*học gửi*). International NGOs, such as KOCUN, also collaborate with local organizations such as the VWU to provide support for mixed mother-child families, actively advocating to extend educational support to these children and vocational training to mothers who wish to reside with their children in the local community. In addition, these organizations play an important role in connecting children's paternal families in Korea with their maternal families in Vietnam. They help facilitate the process by which children can obtain Vietnamese citizenship. While humanitarian efforts have now been extended by both government and nongovernmental organizations in Vietnam, the marginalization of such children continues. This is because of the stigma that haunts these children in Vietnamese society. The families of children from dissolved mixed-nationality marriages are considered nonnormative. For this reason, they are seen as deviant, resulting in their being incessantly bullied. Aggravating the negative perception is the absence of *both* the father and the mother. To build a tolerant society, it seems necessary to create a mechanism to integrate such nonnormative mother-child families into Vietnamese society. Additional state assistance is urgently required to find solutions to the barriers faced by them in Vietnam.

Notes

This work was supported by the Japan Society for the Promotion of Science (JSPS) under grant # 16H02737.

1   Because mothers are often absent from the commune, researchers managed to conduct interviews with only three mothers, all of whom usually worked in the city but had been visiting during the time of the research. To capture the perspective of guardians, interviews were conducted with the children's grandparents or aunts (mothers' sisters). The bulk of interviews were conducted with children; however, efforts to triangulate yielded different information from adult informants, indicating that it was perhaps a challenge for children

to describe their complex feelings and sentiments regarding their family. This must be acknowledged as a limitation of this study.

2 Children with parents who are foreign nationals have to register for temporary residence once every three months because they are not Vietnamese citizens.

3 Of the three stateless children, one Vietnamese-Korean boy and one Vietnamese-Taiwanese boy were identified as stateless because their passports expired after returning to their mothers' homes, and one Korean-Vietnamese girl was stateless because her birth registration had not yet been completed by the local government.

4 If a mother has a child's birth registration in a foreign language, she must have the document translated into Vietnamese by a notary office.

References

Bélanger, Danièle, Khuất Thu Hồng, and Tran Giang Linh. 2010. "From Farmers' Daughters to Foreign Wives: Marriage, Migration, and Gender in Sending Communities of Vietnam." In *Asian Gender under Construction: Global Reconfiguration of Human Reproduction*, edited by Emiko Ochiai, 157–80. Kyoto, Japan: International Research Center for Japanese Studies.

Bélanger, Danièle, Khuất Thu Hồng, and Tran Giang Linh. 2013. "Transnational Marriages between Vietnamese Women and Asian Men in Vietnamese Online Media." *Journal of Vietnamese Studies* 8, no. 2: 81–114.

Bélanger, Danièle, and Hong-Zen Wang. 2012. "Transnationalism from Below: Evidence from Vietnam-Taiwan Cross-Border Marriages." *Asian and Pacific Migration Journal* 21, no. 3: 291–315.

Chung, Chinsung, Keuntae Kim, and Nicola Piper. 2016. "Marriage Migration in Southeast and East Asia Revisited through a Migration-Development Nexus Lens." *Critical Asian Studies* 48, no. 4: 463–72. doi.org/10.1080/14672715.2016.1226600.

Constable, Nicola. 2005. "Introduction: Cross-Border Marriages, Gendered Mobility, and Global Hypergamy." In *Cross-Border Marriages: Gender and Mobility in Transnational Asia*, edited by Nicola Constable, 1–16. Philadelphia: University of Pennsylvania Press.

Cửu, Long. 2016a. "Nhiều cô dâu miền Tây tháo chạy khỏi chồng ngoại" ("Many Brides of the Mekong Delta Origin Run Away from Their Foreign Husbands"). *VN Express*, October 4. vnexpress.net/thoi-su/nhieu-co-dau-mien-tay-thao-chay-khoi-chong-ngoai-3413294.html.

Cửu, Long. 2016b. "Những đứa con lai 'vô thừa nhận' ở quê ngoại miền Tây" ("The 'Unrecognized' Mixed-Race Children in Their Mothers' Home of the Mekong Delta"). *VN Express*, October 5. vnexpress.net/nhung-dua-con-lai-vo-thua-nhan-o-que-ngoai-mien-tay-3413320.html.

Cửu, Long, and Hữu Công. 2017. "Chủ tịch Quốc hội: Hơn 400 con lai ở Cần Thơ phải được đi học ngay" ("President of the National Assembly: More than 400 Mixed-Race Children in Can Tho Must Go to School Right Away"). *VN Express*, September 27. vnexpress.net /chu-tich-quoc-hoi-hon-400-con-lai-o-can-tho-phai-duoc-di-hoc-ngay-3647492.html.

Hoài, Đặng. 2016. "Số phận của 2 đứa trẻ không cha từ hôn nhân xứ người đầy nước mắt" ("Destinies of Two Fatherless Children from Tearful Cross-Border Marriages"). *YAN NEWS*, June 6. www.yan.vn/cuoc-song-cua-hai-dua-tre-vo-thua-nhan-o-cu-lao-han-quoc -92913.html.

Hoài, Thanh. 2016. "Chuyện 'học gửi' của những đứa con lai" ("'Nonenrollment Studies' of Some Mixed Children"). *Vietnamnet*, October 7. vietnamnet.vn/vn/giao-duc/goc-phu -huynh/chuyen-hoc-gui-cua-nhung-dua-con-lai-o-truong-lang-332614.html.

Hoàng, Văn Minh, and Trần Lưu. 2014. "Đỏ-đen lấy chồng xa xứ: Những đứa trẻ 'vô thừa nhận'" ("Risky Cross-Border Marriages: Unrecognized Children"). *Lao Động*, December 16. laodong.vn/phong-su/do-den-lay-chong-xa-xu-nhung-dua-tre-vo-thua-nhan-526780.ldo.

Hội liên hiệp Phụ nữ tỉnh Hậu Giang (Hau Giang Women's Union). 2017. "Báo cáo hoạt động tư vấn, hỗ trợ hôn nhân và gia đình có yếu tố nước ngoài" ("A Report on Consulting, Supporting Marriage, and Families Related to Foreign Countries"). Unpublished report.

Hugo, Graeme, and Nguyen Thi Hong Xoan. 2007. "Marriage Migration between Vietnam and Taiwan: A View from Vietnam." In *Watering the Neighbour's Garden: The Growing Demographic Female Deficit in Asia,* edited by Isabelle Attané and Christophe Z. Guilmoto, 365–91. Paris: Committee for International Cooperation in National Research in Demography.

Ishii, Sari K. 2016. "Child Return Migration from Japan to Thailand." In *Marriage Migration in Asia: Emerging Minorities at the Frontiers of Nation-States*, edited by Sari K. Ishii, 118–34. Singapore: NUS Press.

Iwai, Misaki. 2013. "'Global Householding' between Rural Vietnam and Taiwan." In *Dynamics of Marriage Migration in Asia*, edited by Sari K. Ishii, 139–62. Tokyo: Tokyo University of Foreign Studies.

Kim, Aekyoung. 2017. "Kankoku ni okeru kokusai kekkon no zouka to shien seisaku" ("Increasing Cross-Border Marriages and National Policies for Support in South Korea"). *Nagoya Gakuin daigaku ronshu Shakaikagaku hen* (*Journal of Nagoya Gakuin University: Social Science*) 54, no. 1: 13–28.

Kim, Hyun Mee, Shinhye Park, and Ariun Shukhertei. 2017. "Returning Home: Marriage Migrants' Legal Precarity and the Experience of Divorce." *Critical Asian Studies* 49, no. 1: 38–53. doi.org/10.1080/14672715.2016.1266679.

Kim, Minjeong. 2013. "Citizenship Projects for Marriage Migrants in South Korea: Intersecting Motherhood with Ethnicity and Class." *Social Politics* 20, no. 4: 456–81.

Kim, Minjeong. 2018. *Elusive Belonging: Marriage Immigrants and "Multiculturalism" in Rural South Korea.* Honolulu: University of Hawai'i Press.

Le, Hien Anh. 2016. "Lives of Mixed Vietnamese-Korean Children in Vietnam." In *Marriage Migration in Asia: Emerging Minorities at the Frontiers of Nation-States*, edited by Sari K. Ishii, 175–86. Singapore: NUS Press.

National Assembly. 2008. "Law on Vietnamese Nationality." Socialist Republic of Vietnam, November 13. thuvienphapluat.vn/van-ban/quyen-dan-su/Luat-quoc-tich-Viet-Nam-2008 -24-2008-QH12-82204.aspx.

National Immigration Agency. 2021. "Statistical Data: Number of Foreign Spouses by Nationality from 1987 to September 2019." Ministry of the Interior, Republic of China (Taiwan), October 25. www.immigration.gov.tw/5382/5385/7344/7350/8887/?alias=settledown.

Ngô Thị Vân Phượng. 2018. "Giới thiệu tình hình tư vấn và các trường hợp cụ thể tại KOCUN Cần Thơ" ("Introduction of the Consulting Situation and Specific Cases in KOCUN, Can Tho City"). Paper presented at the Hội thảo thực trạng và giải pháp hỗ trợ phụ nữ hồi hương và trẻ em Việt-Hàn cư trú tại Việt Nam (Conference on the Situation and Solutions to Support Return Migrant Women and Vietnamese-Korean Children Residing in Vietnam), Trung tâm Việt-Hàn Chung tay Chăm sóc (Vietnam-Korea Center for Joint Care), Can Tho, January 25.

Ngọc, Tài. 2016. "Chuyện học 'gửi' ở làng ngoại kiều" ("'Nonenrollment Studies' in Some Villages Related to Cross-Border Marriages"). *Tuổi Trẻ Online*, December 1. tuoitre.vn/chuyen -hoc-gui-o-lang-ngoai-kieu-1228285.htm.

Nguyễn, Viễn Sự. 2014. "Những đứa trẻ không tổ quốc" ("Children without a Fatherland"). *Tuổi Trẻ Online*, August 5. tuoitre.vn/nhung-dua-tre-khong-to-quoc-630571.htm.

Nguyen, Xoan, and Xuyen Tran. 2010. "Vietnamese-Taiwanese Marriages." In *Asian Cross-Border Marriage Migration: Demographic Patterns and Social Issues*, edited by Wen-Shan Yang and Melody Chia-Wen Lu, 157–78. Amsterdam: Amsterdam University Press.

Phạm, Tâm. 2015. "Những ông bố ngoại quốc và những đứa trẻ 'vô thừa nhận'" ("Foreign Fathers and 'Unrecognized' Children"). *Dân Trí*, June 5. dantri.com.vn/xa-hoi/nhung-ong -bo-ngoai-quoc-va-nhung-dua-tre-vo-thua-nhan-1434095368.htm.

Phạm, Văn Bích, and Misaki Iwai. 2014a. "Cô dâu Việt Nam thành công ở Đài Loan: Hai nghiên cứu trường hợp" ("Successful Vietnamese Brides in Taiwan: Based on Two Case Studies"). *Nghiên cứu gia đình và giới* (*Journal of Family and Gender Studies*) 24, no. 1: 43–53.

Phạm, Văn Bích, and Misaki Iwai. 2014b. "Cô dâu Việt Nam thành công ở Đài Loan: Hai nghiên cứu trường hợp" ("Successful Vietnamese Brides in Taiwan: Based on Two Case Studies"). *Nghiên cứu gia đình và giới* (*Journal of Family and Gender Studies*) 24, no. 2: 28–43.

Phan, An. 2005. *Hiện Tượng Phụ Nữ Việt Nam Lấy Chồng Đài Loan* (*Phenomenon of Vietnamese Women Who Are Married to Taiwanese Men*). Ho Chi Minh City, Vietnam: Nhà xuất bản tre.

Phương, Nguyên, and Yên Trinh. 2016. "Con lai Đài Loan (kỳ 1): 'Sóng ngầm' ngày đi" ("Mixed Taiwanese (Episode 1): 'Underground Waves' Date"). *Tuổi Trẻ Online*, July 29. tuoitre.vn/con-lai-dai-loan-ky-1-song-ngam-ngay-di-152990.htm.

Phương, Nguyên, Yên Trinh, and Ngọc Diện. 2016. "Đường về với những đứa con lai" ("The Way Back for Mixed Children"). *Tuổi Trẻ Online*, July 30. tuoitre.vn/duong-ve-voi-nhung-dua-con-lai-153118.htm.

Suzuki, Nobue. 2005. "Tripartite Desires: Filipina-Japanese Marriages and Fantasies of Transnational Traversal." In *Cross-Border Marriages: Gender and Mobility in Transnational Asia,* edited by Nicola Constable, 124–44. Philadelphia: University of Pennsylvania Press.

Suzuki, Nobue. 2010. "Outlawed Children: Japanese Filipino Children, Legal Defiance, and Ambivalent Citizenships." *Pacific Affairs* 83, no. 1: 31–50.

UBND xã Vị Thắng. 2017. "Báo cáo tình hình thực hiện công tác bình đẳng giới và hôn nhân gia đình trên địa bàn xã Vị Thắng" ("Vi Thang Commune People's Committee. A Report on the Implementation of Gender, Marital, and Family Issues in Vi Thang Commune"). Unpublished report.

Văn, Vĩnh. 2016a. "Hỗ trợ cô dâu Việt và con lai hồi hương" ("Supporting Vietnamese Brides and Mixed-Race Children to Repatriate"). *Công an Nhân Dân Online*, October 28. cand.com.vn/doi-song/Ho-tro-co-dau-Viet-va-con-lai-hoi-huong-414358/.

Văn, Vĩnh. 2016b. "Hàng chục ngàn cô dâu miền Tây khốn đốn sau làn sóng lấy chồng ngoại" ("Tens of Thousands of Miserable Brides in the Mekong Delta after a Wave of Cross-Border Marriages"). *Công an Nhân Dân Online*, October 30. cand.com.vn/doi-song/Hang-chuc-ngan-co-dau-mien-Tay-khon-don-sau-lan-song-lay-chong-ngoai-414673/.

Viễn, Sự, and Sơn Lâm. 2018a. "Trẻ con lai ở miền Tây: Con không cha như nhà không nóc" ("Mixed Children in the Mekong Delta: A Child without a Father Is Like a House without a Roof"). *Tuổi Trẻ Online*, January 22. tuoitre.vn/tre-con-lai-o-mien-tay-con-khong-cha-nhu-nha-khong-noc-20180122101058204.htm.

Viễn, Sự, and Sơn Lâm. 2018b. "Trẻ con lai ở miền Tây: Không khai sinh được cho con vì lỡ . . . lấy chồng ngoại" ("A Mixed-Race Child in the Mekong Delta: Unable to Register a Child's Birth because She . . . Got Married to a Foreign Husband"). *Tuổi Trẻ Online*, January 23. tuoitre.vn/tre-con-lai-o-mien-tay-khong-khai-sinh-duoc-cho-con-vi-lo-lay-chong-ngoai-20180123100733271.htm.

Viễn, Sự, and Sơn Lâm. 2018c. "Trẻ con lai ở miền Tây: Cắt đứt máu mủ" ("Mixed Children in the Mekong Delta: Cut Off Blood and Blood"). *Tuổi Trẻ Online*, January 24. tuoitre.vn/tre-con-lai-o-mien-tay-cat-dut-mau-mu-20180124093828376.htm.

Viễn, Sự, and Sơn Lâm. 2018d. "Cần một chính sách cho trẻ con lai miền Tây" ("Need a Policy for Mixed Children in the Mekong Delta"). *Tuổi Trẻ Online*, January 25. tuoitre.vn/can -mot-chinh-sach-cho-tre-con-lai-mien-tay-20180125120659988.htm.

Vũ, Thị Trang. 2018. "Kết quả khảo sát thực trạng phụ nữ hồi hương và trẻ em Việt-Hàn cư trú tại Việt Nam" ("Survey Results on the Situation of Returning Migrant Women and Vietnamese-Korean Children Residing in Vietnam"). Paper presented at the Hội thảo thực trạng và giải pháp hỗ trợ phụ nữ hồi hương và trẻ em Việt-Hàn cư trú tại Việt Nam (Conference on the Situation and Solutions to Support Returning Migrant Women and Vietnamese-Korean Children Residing in Vietnam), Trung tâm Việt-Hàn Chung tay Chăm sóc (Vietnam-Korea Center for Joint Care), Can Tho, January 25.

Wang, Hong-Zen. 2007. "Hidden Spaces of Resistance of the Subordinated: Case Studies from Vietnamese Female Migrant Partners in Taiwan." *International Migration Review* 41, no. 3: 706–27.

Williams, Lucy. 2010. *Global Marriage: Cross-Border Marriage Migration in Global Context.* Basingstoke, UK: Palgrave Macmillan.

Yang, Wen-Shan, and Melody Chia-Wen Lu, eds. 2010. *Asian Cross-Border Marriage Migration: Demographic Patterns and Social Issues.* Amsterdam: Amsterdam University Press.

Children's Experience and Practice of Belonging: The Realities of Integration among De Facto Stateless Vietnamese Children in Cambodia

Charlie Rumsby

In Southeast Asia, the prioritization of economics and security over rights (Nishikawa 2009: 226) by states manifests in the plight of stateless children, meaning "children without a state" (J. Bhabha 2011: 1). As a strand of research that explores how "contexts of reception" shape migrant experiences, most of the literature on the legal exclusion of migrants has focused on the experiences of adult immigrants in the United States (Akinwumi 2006; Kleifgen and Le 2007; Menjivar 2006; Rumbaut 1994, 2005), but some of it has begun to explore the legal displacements of children raised in "mixed-status" families (Dreby 2015) and the "collateral consequences" for the American children of deported parents (Golash-Boza 2019). I focus on statelessness as a salient context of reception defining the integration of children of Vietnamese descent in Cambodia. A focus on de facto statelessness diverges from the literature on children of migration in Southeast Asia,

positions 30:2 DOI 10.1215/10679847-9573370
Copyright 2022 by Duke University Press

where discussions on children have focused mostly on those "left behind" (Beazley 2015; Orellana 2016; Parreñas 2005) and builds on recent ethnographic studies of children's lived realities of statelessness (Allerton 2014, 2017; Beazley, Butt, and Ball 2018; Rumsby 2021).

Article 1 of the 1954 Statelessness Convention defines a stateless person as one "who is not considered a national by any state under the operation of its law." This is legally defined as de jure stateless. The causes of statelessness lie both within and outside the state as sovereignties draw boundaries of inclusion and exclusion according to changing power relations across international and domestic boundaries (Sperfeldt 2020). As a result, there is a lack of international agreement over who is to be considered "stateless," especially so when considering populations unable to prove their nationality, or notwithstanding having documentation, are denied access to human rights (Malischewski 2013).

The definition of de jure stateless becomes rather narrow considering that there are no universal standards for citizenship or nationality. Furthermore, because discriminatory policies, laws, and practices can mean that citizenship is experienced unequally, even among citizens, citizenship can be experienced in such an ineffective manner that the experience of legal citizens can mirror that of those who are de jure stateless. The term *de facto stateless*, therefore, exists to describe the situation of those who fall within the large range of people whose lived experiences are "effectively" those of statelessness (Bhabha 2011) but who do not satisfy the de jure definition. While it is difficult to clarify the position of de facto statelessness, this does not mean it should be omitted as a focus of research. An appreciation of the phenomenon of statelessness as "plural and diverse" (Sigona 2016) gives proper attention to the social conditions of statelessness, with regard to its historical specificities as well as its close connection with citizenship and ethno-nationalism.

This article examines the integration of stateless Vietnamese children in Cambodia and exposes feelings of dislocation that arise in this process. Integration is a chaotic concept. Definitions differ depending on the context and actor using it, be it the researcher, the policy maker, or the third sector practitioner (Ager and Strang 2008). Migration scholars recognize the contradiction embedded in using a term that is criticized as being highly normative and teleological in nature, yet it continues to be central in many studies and academic debates (Penninx and Garcés-Mascareñas 2016). While the opaque condition of de facto statelessness does not easily lend itself to a critical analysis of integration models (and such an analysis is beyond the scope of this article),[1] I argue that the understandings of integration and assimilation developed in the migration literature are useful for grasping the context in which de facto stateless children in Cambodia negotiate "place belonging" (Antonsich 2010).

Cambodia's state practice of ethno-cultural political exclusion, for example, requires a cultural assimilation model of integration (Esser 2003) that contrasts with pluralistic models of integration often found in liberal democracies, whereby immigrants can—in theory—maintain their own cultural and religious identities while taking on a new citizenship status (e.g., African American) (Ager and Strang 2008). In Cambodia's nationality law, cultural adjustment and positive positioning toward "Khmerness" has to be proven for someone to be naturalized. This usually means that being accepted as Khmer is predicated on being seen to adopt and live out key elements of Khmer culture and religion, along with having a command of the Cambodian language. The wording of Cambodia's 1993 constitution suggests an ethnicity-based conception of citizenship. All rights involved in the constitution are provided to "Khmer citizens" only. In contrast to the multiculturalist and civic understandings of "Khmer citizenship," the constitution, "taken at its most literal reading, baldly denies basic human rights to anyone so unfortunate as to be labelled non-Khmer" (Ehrentraut 2011: 788).

Even children of mixed Vietnamese and Khmer heritage, or those who have learned Cambodian as a first language, did not experience straightforward integration. Why is this the case? What causes the fractious positioning of Vietnamese children who live among the Khmer majority while speaking their language? How is belonging lived and negotiated within and beyond discursive practices that seek to exclude along ethno-national lines? Concentrating on an analysis of children's experiences of place belonging exposes the paradox of integration and feelings of dislocation. This dislocation: an extreme feeling of ethnic exclusion born from ethnocentric views of the Vietnamese, propagated by Cambodian nationalism, hinders children's integration into Cambodian society despite their acculturation.

Children's accounts reveal the ways that ethnic discrimination can alter their assimilation trajectory; children respond to the discrimination wielded against them by either crystallizing their minority identity, rejecting identification with the majority, or seeking to conform.[2] The empirical sections of this article make apparent that socioeconomic factors play a significant part in children being incorporated (or not) into the core institutions of the host society—what Heckmann (2005) calls "structural integration"—and in their ability to resist expected behaviors linked to "assimilation" (such as speaking Cambodian in public spaces).

The first section briefly details the historical backdrop that frames the hostility that ethnic Vietnamese communities face in Cambodia, highlighting the context that has produced a risk of statelessness within the community. Given that work with children often raises important ethical and methodological questions, the second section addresses these issues.

Section three identifies the mechanisms by which exclusion is established, namely, through poverty, violence, and language. By comparing the lives of Cammy with sisters Huong and Hung, I demonstrate that children experience feelings of dislocation in different ways but often with similar results. A dislocation from place, rooted in negative experiences of living in Cambodia, gives rise to cross-border affiliations among children.[3]

Despite the experience of dislocation, children did not or could not afford to fully disengage from society. Instead, as shown in section four, they became aware of ways to minimize the feelings of marginalization by coexisting in society. The need to coexist was not just motivated by a desire for peace; coexistence was also a tactically considered practice that secured residence, education, and sometimes economic security. To secure these things, children at times performed alternative "Khmer" identities that enabled some degree of coexistence among the majority.

Ethnographic Context

Ethno-nationalism in Southeast Asia has played a large role in imagining communities (Anderson 1991) that are categorized by common ancestry, history, and culture (Lamont and Molnar 2002). Thus, it is usually nationalism and not race that centrally determines ethnic relations in the context of Asia (Ho 2019). The significance of ethno-nationalism in building the Khmer Kingdom from the time of its being a French protectorate (1863–1954) to date is well documented (Edwards 2007). Cambodia's citizenship laws from the protectorate era to the postcolonial (1954–1970), postwar period onward[4] contain obvious biases as to what was and is considered to be "pure Khmer": for instance, one has to speak Khmer "fluently" and to exhibit a "sufficient cultural assimilation" of Khmer manners, customs, and traditions to naturalize (Amer 1994: 214).

Scholarship that traces the long-standing habitation of communities of Vietnamese descent in Cambodia since the period of the French protectorate demonstrates how the country's citizenship laws have fostered their legal exclusion (Canzutti 2019; Berman 1996; Ehrentraut 2011; Nguyen and Sperfeldt 2012; Sperfeldt 2017), and how political elites have encouraged racist and violent rhetoric against the minority group (Metzl 1995; Oesterheld 2014). Territorial disputes, "invasions," and the attempted "Vietnamization" of Cambodia have driven historical depictions of the Vietnamese as "immoral," "untrustworthy," and "illegal" and frame how they are perceived in Cambodia today (Edwards 1996, 2007; Goscha 2012). The continued hostility toward communities of Vietnamese descent has been termed Cambodia's "anti-Vietnamese obsession" (Frewer 2016). Despite their long-term residence, people of Vietnamese descent living in Cambodia have been characterized as unable to assimilate into Cambodian society (Ehrentraut 2011). Many live without valid citizenship papers and do not qualify for any government assistance (United Nations 2019). Such communities are denied basic rights such as education, decent wages, and political legitimacy, leaving them on the margins of Cambodian society (Brown 2007).

In her research on the reasons, modalities, and consequences of the Cambodian and Vietnamese governments' engagement with the Vietnamese diaspora in Cambodia, Lucrezia Canzutti (2018) brings a new interpretation to the continued liminality and ambiguity concerning the status and guarantors of the Vietnamese. She shows the Vietnamese to be "inconvenient subjects" (115), whose presence is of decreasing value to the Cambodian state. Nevertheless, despite the heightened political tension among the Khmer populace pertaining to the presence of the Vietnamese on Cambodian soil, the Cambodian People's Party are sensitively managing their presence at the request of the Vietnamese regime.[5] Canzutti calls this the "bounded exclusion" of the Vietnamese, who are symbolically kept outside the Cambodian nation and citizenry but allowed inside the territory of the Cambodian state (118). As an example of how this works, at the time of conducting this research Vietnamese people born in Cambodia but without citizenship in Cambodia or Vietnam were often allowed to travel into Vietnam for short periods of time—on the condition they returned to Cambodia.

Children in this study may have legitimate claim to Cambodian or Vietnamese nationality but currently do not have access to legal protections from either country and are prevented from doing so as a result of the interplay of exclusionary institutional and economic factors. For children, their parents' inability to prove their own identity, after losing key documents in periods of war (Ang, Weill, and Chan 2014) or having their documents confiscated at random by officials (Canzutti 2019), together with lack of a birth certificate, is what puts them at risk of statelessness (Nguyen and Sperfeldt 2012).

The focus on the realities of integration among ethnic Vietnamese children into Cambodian society is important because the literature that addresses the stateless Vietnamese in Cambodia has focused to date on the experience of adults. Research has provided a thorough analysis of the legal context of exclusion (Sperfeldt 2017) and the varied influences beyond documentation and legal status that combine to impact interaction between communities and the state (Parsons and Lawreniuk 2018). Nevertheless, children's in-depth accounts of being "Vietnamese" in Khmer society and their experience and practice of belonging are notably absent. These accounts underscore the complexity of integration, and it is important to note that cultural assimilation, even when "successful," can produce its own problems.

In the empirical sections to follow, the realities of integration are viewed through the lens of a child's sense of place belongingness (Antonsich 2010). That sense emerges from several sources:

> *autobiographical accounts*—children's personal experiences, elations, and memories that attach person to place [Dixon and Durrheim 2004; hooks 2009])

relationships—the personal and social ties that enhance life in a given place

environmental factors—that is, how people invest everyday environments with richly symbolic, aesthetic, moral, and, above all, identity-relevant meanings (Stokols 1990)

culture—language, traditions, habits and religion (Buonfino and Thomson 2007; Esser 2003; hooks 2009)

economic opportunities—being able to get a job, build a professional life and look after one's family (Yuval-Davis and Kaptani 2008; Chow 2007).

Place belongingness is a vital part of understanding how de facto stateless children experience integration beyond state-implemented mechanisms. Such an analysis is especially important among children who live on the margins of society without the protection of state citizenship. As will be shown in the empirical sections that follow, an examination of place belonging reveals the transferability of understandings of integration and assimilation, as developed in the migration literature, to an analysis of how stateless populations belong.

Methodology

The data presented in this article were derived from a nine-month ethnographic study undertaken in Cambodia from October 2015 to July 2016. The research focused on issues having to do with identity, belonging, potential statelessness, education, and faith. Over the course of the research, I conducted 144 semi-structured interviews with thirty-seven children aged six to seventeen years old—thirteen boys and twenty-four girls. Interviews were only one part of the research. I built relationships with interviewees and other adult participants and community members by hanging out with them, eating meals, and having conversations about daily life. While I could thus have used thirty-seven participants' interview data, only eleven participants are directly referenced in this article because of the limitation of space. I gained access to the group of participants involved in this research through

Table 1 Interviewed children's age, first language, and country of birth

Age group, years	Number of children interviewees		Language	Children interviewees' first language
6–8	4		Cambodian	10
9–11	6		Vietnamese	23
12–14	16		Both	
15–17	11		Unassigned	4

Country of birth	Number of children interviewees	Father's birth country	Mother's birth country	
Cambodia	29	9	21	
Vietnam	8	17	8	
Khmer Krom		1		
Unassigned		10	8	

a school, known locally as the "God School," that provided education to excluded Vietnamese communities in and around the area I call Preah Thnov.[6] The children I interviewed were the most consistent school attendees, which granted me the opportunity to get to know them very well and see the research journey through with them from inception to completion. In addition, the children represented the different demographics within the community as shown in table 1.

This research drew on participatory research methods enabling greater exploration of place belonging and the cultural contexts that structure children's lives (Hart and Tyrer 2006). Past and future time lines (Bagnoli 2009) and self-portraits were used to aid consideration of participants' lives to date and how they envisaged their futures. To explore family history and heritage, each participant drew their family tree. To understand in what places participants spent their time, children drew maps of the places where they hung out. Identity flowers (Rumsby 2019) were used to elicit what constitutes participants' sense of self and belonging (fig. 1). For example,

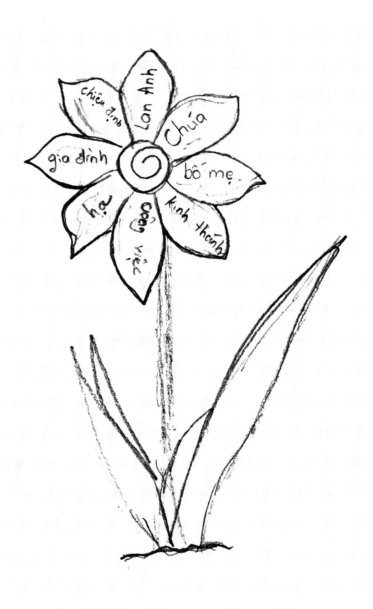

Figure 1 Example of an identity flower. This one represents Lucy, aged fifteen.

participants had to think and write down in each petal of the flower what made them who they are. The point of the exercise was to understand how participants constructed their identity and how they experienced belonging. Each petal represented an element of the participants' perception of themselves.

Poverty, Violence, and Local Experiences of Integration

By contrasting the experiences of Cammy, aged fifteen, with the experiences of sisters Hung, fourteen, and Huong, twelve, this section draws attention to the factors that contributed to feelings of dislocation. These included the village a child lived in and the sense of safety they had living there, the strength of local relationships, and a child's experience of poverty and violence. We see that dislocation from place can occur even when a child has a strong experience of place belonging. For instance, dislocation can be provoked directly because of integration, highlighting what is known as the "paradox of integration" (Ghorashi 2010).

The God School was made up of a mix of children from three villages: Preah Thnov, Preah Rotn Phon, and Preah Amnr Sabbay. The assortment of young people included families who had been in Cambodia for generations, those who had migrated from Vietnam soon after their birth, and mixed marriage (Khmer and Vietnamese) households. The villages that children lived in varied in terms of housing, income, and the strength of local relationships. The physical layout of each village was fundamentally different. Preah Thnov was relatively clean. The community was mainly made up of Vietnamese who had lived two or three generations in Cambodia, and Cambodian was spoken broadly there. In stark contrast to Preah Thnov, the villages of Preah Rotn Phon and Preah Amnr Sabbay appeared more impoverished, given the cramped housing with narrow walkways, excessive amounts of trash, and wooden stilt housing. While poverty was probably worse in these villages, many families in Preah Thnov also experienced debt, insecure employment, and de facto statelessness.

Cammy

Cammy, a resident of Preah Thnov, had a different experience of poverty and violence compared with participants from other villages. Reflecting on the village she is from, she explains to me the differences as she sees them: "I live in this village [Preah Thnov], which is different from Preah Rehab and Preah Rotn Phon. My village is quite quiet, not much gambling, fighting or arguing. In the other villages, when I went there, I saw they gamble a lot, and swear" (Cammy, female, 15 years old).

During her self-portrait exercise, Cammy talked about her house, family, and parents being important to who she is. Her home is secure: "No strangers can come in." She saw her ethnic identity as mixed; she said that she "felt Khmer despite her parents being Vietnamese." Unlike most of the other students, Cammy did not face a risk of statelessness. Her parents had managed to secure a birth certificate for her, which enabled her to go a local Cambodian school (referred to here as "Khmer School," as was the term used by participants) before she attended the God School. Cammy shared how her experience at Khmer School, playing with Khmer friends and speaking Cambodian, made her feel Khmer. To some extent Cammy's experience of belonging should tick the boxes of the "cultural assimilation" integration model (Esser 2003). She can speak Cambodian fluently, and this made it easier for her to interact with Khmer people. Yet, ironically, it became apparent that it was precisely her deeper integration and daily interaction with the Khmer majority that eventually stoked a feeling of being an "outsider." This experience reflects what has been described as the "integration paradox": the more one is involved in society, the more sensitive to feelings of unfair treatment one becomes (Buijs, Demant, and Hamdy 2006, cited in Rouvoet, Eijberts, and Ghorashi 2017: 107).

As one of the more economically secure students, Cammy had the means to pay the bribes required for her to attend Khmer School. Yet her experience of Khmer School provoked a degree of dislocation, since she was more exposed to the historical charges against the Vietnamese taught in the curriculum than other, less structurally integrated Vietnamese children. She learned an antagonistic history of Vietnam and Cambodia's relationship at Khmer School, leaving her feeling out of place in Cambodia and, as expressed in her future timeline exercise, having a desire to be in Vietnam:

> When I am older, I will live in Vietnam. I don't like living in Cambodia because Khmer people tell us it is not good that we live here, and they always say we [Vietnamese] are the ones who take their land. They said this from grade one to grade seven—any grade. Every grade they always talked about it. Especially in grade six it was in the history books. The books said Vietnamese came to their country and then put the camp in Udon place. It made me feel sad. I didn't tell my parents. They work and live in Cambodia; they know the Khmer talk about this story. In Vietnam, I don't have to think about these things. (Cammy, female, 15 years old)

Cammy's opinion demonstrates empathy with the Vietnamese who live under the stigma of being "othered" and a desire to avoid the marginalization that results from accusatory rhetoric. For Vietnamese-heritage children who are born in Cambodia and want to identify as Khmer, the process of integration is disrupted by their being rejected by the society in which they live. While this does not dissolve the "longing to belong" (Probyn 1996), the internalization of hostile discourse and the experience of being "othered" highlights Said's (2003) notion of "in-betweenness." The tension of in-betweenness—being and feeling part of the society but experiencing an internal feeling of dislocation—acts as a catalyst for children's construction of the Khmer as morally inferior, as will be seen later in this article.

Environmental Factors, Social Bonds, and Place Belongingness

Feelings of dislocation are not produced in isolation from the environment. In my research, children's accounts often included a consideration of the physical surroundings they lived in. Common among the comparisons that participants would make between Cambodia and Vietnam was the influence the physical environment had in generating different degrees of dislocation.

Dixon and Durrheim (2004) argue that in treating the environment as an insignificant setting for, or container of, social relations, or as a behav-

ioral setting that inhibits or encourages interaction, researchers have overlooked what Stokols (1990) refers to as the "spiritual" dimension of human-
environment relationships. That is, how people invest everyday environments with richly symbolic, aesthetic, moral, and, above all, identity-relevant
meanings. This is evidenced in the ways that the children in my study spoke
of their preference for Vietnam as a place over Cambodia and of the Vietnamese as morally superior people.

The physical environment could have contributed to Cammy's expressed
desire to live in Vietnam. Her village was experiencing noisy ongoing road
development all around it, and the record-breaking oppressive heat in Cambodia during the research period made the fringes of the village akin to a
sweltering dust bowl. When discussing her opinions of Vietnam and the
Vietnamese, Cammy highlighted the differences she noticed:

> In my place in Vietnam there are not many people, the roads are quiet,
> there is green nature and it's cool, and in Cambodia it is always so noisy.
> There are differences in people too. Khmer [have] dark skin, Vietnamese
> fair skin. Vietnamese know how to love, to help, and they are kinder.
> This is because of the education in the school. I hope that it [Cambo-
> dian education] would be better, that teachers will not take bribes from
> pupils. The teachers do not focus on teaching but are drunk, and gossip.
> (Cammy, female, 15 years old)

It might seem that the desire to live in Vietnam, the descriptions of its
greenness, and the perception of Vietnamese people as being "more loving"
evidence a longing to exit. On the other hand, it could be indicative of a
longing for change in the home environment. Children often responded to
what they thought were incorrect representations of the Vietnamese with
counternarratives about the Khmer as shown here, and in the accounts to
come later in this article.

In short, there are differing degrees of dislocation that result from an
underlying nationalism based on ethnocentric views of the Vietnamese.
Cammy's experience of this kind of dislocation was less extreme. Her
example shows she was able to experience a connection with the majority
Khmer as she felt a sense of community, home, and safety in Preah Thnov.
The space in which she lived—the coffee shop—was popular, and much

of community life took place around it. Cammy's immediate family, her parents, and siblings, lived peacefully and securely, and she spoke positively about her future prospects. For instance, she was confident that her mother would secure her a passport at the age of eighteen, and rumor had it among the other children that her parents knew the right "middlemen." Contrary to this, Cammy told me her parents would buy a passport for $125 from the police. Because of space limitations, this article does not focus on the quest for documentation and legitimacy. This information is inserted here to contrast Cammy's experience with that of Huong, aged twelve, and her sister Hung, aged fourteen, who lived with their parents in Preah Amnr Sabbay; they had a very different personal sense of poverty and violence compared with Cammy, who did not share any experiences of physical violence. In the next section I demonstrate how even if a child in the study had one Khmer parent, their Vietnamese heritage produced social ostracization and a fractured sense of place belonging.

Hung and Huong

Hung and Huong spoke both Vietnamese and Cambodian as a result of their parent's mixed marriage and their living among many Khmer in Preah Amnr Sabbay. Huong was born in Vietnam, Hung in Cambodia. Neither has a birth certificate. The autobiographical rendering of their lives told through their self-portrait and timeline exercises unraveled complications and negative experiences associated with their Vietnamese heritage. As true of Cammy, this encouraged them to feel cross-border affiliations with Vietnam. The sisters' stories were embedded with elaborate details and characters that were illustrated with moral and aesthetic comparisons between the place and people in their current environment and what they perceived of place and people in Vietnam. These stories are important. They support research that has argued that positive "two-way exchanges" between majority and minority groups are necessary to generate feelings of acceptance among those who are "othered" (Penninx and Garcés-Mascareñas 2016). In the absence of strong relational ties with the Khmer community, family becomes a significant maker of home.

During her self-portrait exercise, Hung did not draw herself, as she found it difficult to do so. As I encouraged Hung to say what she would have drawn if she could, she explained: "I wanted to draw that I really want to study at this school because I really love this school [the God School] and I want to stay here always, because I like my teachers and love God; I believe in God" (Hung, female, 14 years old). Given the overt preference for the God School, I wanted to know whether Hung had attended Khmer School and, if so, what her experience there was. Hung had had two experiences of school. She told me that she and her sister previously attend an NGO school for the homeless and orphaned as a result of their parents' inability to pay school fees; but because she left to visit Vietnam, they were not allowed back in that school on their return. Prior to that Hung had been to Khmer School although she did not enjoy her experience: "It was difficult. Because Cambodian is difficult. When I answered the questions, it was difficult. I can read but when I am asked it is difficult. My teacher was strict and would scold us. They would say, 'You are a dog, no one [can] teach you'" (Hung, female, 14 years old). To call a person a dog is a big insult to Vietnamese children and their parents, as the role of parents in teaching their children is pivotal (Rydstrøm 2001). It was not clear whether the harsh treatment was related to Hung's Vietnamese heritage, given that Hung said she spoke Cambodian at school. However, the feelings of exclusion were remembered and came to frame how Hung saw herself in the present, as illustrated by her preference for the God School. This story was directly followed by another. Hung explained why she does not speak Vietnamese outside:

> I do not speak Vietnamese outside as they will call me "Yuon" [Vietnamese]. It has happened before. My uncle is a Vietnamese soldier and came to visit my house, and some Khmer people came and talked with him, and swore at him, and he got out a gun in front of the village chief's nephew, and then from that day they drew on the walls of people's houses and said some words that are not good about the Vietnamese. They used charcoal to write on the wall. They wrote in Cambodian: "If Vietnamese people want to remain alive, they need to say sorry." This happened a long time ago. Sometimes for two or three days they threw stones at all the Vietnamese houses, not just mine. (Hung, female, 14 years old)

The house Hung's family lived in was built by her maternal Khmer grandparents, and she spoke fondly about how they planted various trees, including a coconut tree, outside the house. Hung would water the trees and help her grandmother buy rice in the mornings and go to school in the afternoons. Hung starkly contrasted her home, once a place of happiness, status, and protection afforded by her Khmer grandparents, with the more recent experience of violence as described above. Unfortunately, that experience of violence was not an isolated instance for Hung. During the identity flower exercise, her younger sister Huong wrote, "I love Vietnam." It transpired that she did not want to go and live there, but her experience of violence negatively influenced her opinion of Cambodians. She explained why she loves Vietnam:

> I have friends in Vietnam, they are really good, they never swear or argue with me. When I live here, I play with Vietnamese because there is this Cambodian who always swears at me and their mum said she will kill me and chop me up. I don't know why, they always say I am "Yuon," and I got angry and I said, "I am Vietnamese and that's none of your business," and they went to tell their mum because Phum [the owner of the land] is their uncle. (Huong, female, 12 years old)

Despite their house having been built by her maternal grandparents, the land the family lived on was rented. This brings to life the emphasis placed on the growing of trees by Hung. The description of planting trees, watering them, and marveling at their growth points to a symbolic rootedness, an ability to control the land, and a season of life in which her belonging was not challenged.

Family as Home

Huong and Hung's fractious relationships within their village had the effect of influencing the extent to which the sisters felt a sense of place belonging. Both girls strongly convey that their belonging is connected to their family. Huong moved to Cambodia when she was three years old. When I asked her if she remembered Vietnam, she said: "I remember it being peaceful, no one argued together. They had green grass and it has storks. Khmer argue and some of them gamble and Khmer people, when they fight together, they use a knife. There is not much peace here" (Huong, female, 12 years old). While the comparison alluded to a homelier feel in Vietnam, Huong did not have a sense of home there either: "[In Vietnam] I did not feel at home, I just stayed in Vietnam to play with my friend and to visit my grandma and grandpa. Whenever I go hang out with my family, I feel like I'm at home." However, it was clear that Huong thought of the Vietnamese as less confrontational. For example, in discussing Huong's future I asked her what she wanted her husband to be like. She replied that she wanted him to be "a good man, so we can live and love each other and not argue." I asked her where her husband would be from. She answered, "From Vietnam."

In contrast, the older sister, Hung, overtly expressed a desire to live in Vietnam. She wanted to go to Vietnam because it is "happy and funny," but she was not sure if her father would let her go. Yet, in her interviews about her future, Hung was invested in remaining with her family and working to provide for them. In the same interview about her future, I asked Hung if she has any dreams: "Yes, I have a wish that my parents always stay with me, live with me in my house and that they will love us more, me and my siblings." Discussing her self-portrait, I asked Hung whether anything other than her family is important to her. She replied, "I don't want to separate from my parents." Given her experiences, it is no wonder Hung wanted to be somewhere "happy and funny." Much like Cammy's view of Vietnam, perhaps Hung's aligns with how she wanted her present circumstances to be. Notwithstanding negative experiences, their accounts of their past and how they see their present and future contained a strong sense of familial responsibility.

This section has demonstrated the complexity of integration. The paradox of integration is that integration can expose children to situations that make them feel disconnected, which increases feelings of dislocation. The negative portrayals and acts of violence aimed at the ethnic Vietnamese are also felt by children. In response, they (re)frame the Khmer as morally inferior and imagine a Vietnam that represents a desire for a more settled experience in Cambodia. In their everyday lives, children negotiated the difficult terrain of exclusion and their presence in specific spaces. The next section will focus on what could be (mistakenly) conceived as mundane, minor everyday happenings in participants' daily lives, yet they are in fact tactics (Certeau 1984) employed to secure a degree of integration.

Coexistence: The Practice of Belonging

This section illustrates how children of Vietnamese heritage—and their parents—were acutely aware of the need to publicly perform "Khmerness" to belong to the Khmer majority, particularly in public spaces.[7] While this performance is at times a strained effort when a child does not speak much Cambodian, at other times young people's "Vietnamese-ness" would go completely unnoticed. Children were actively processing what they needed to do to gain access to essential services such as education and employment, although some young people refused to speak Cambodian to the Khmer as a tactic of resistance (Certeau 1984). Others, meanwhile, wanted to assimilate as "Khmer." These identity-relevant performances were not fixed, supporting the notion in other research on self-identification and integration that "identities are never fully and finally 'established'; instead they are seen always in process, always in a relative state of formation" (Rattansi and Phoenix 2005: 105). They do hint at children's "selective acculturation"—that is, learning majority culture while remaining embedded, in part, in the ethnic community (Waters et al. 2010: 2).

During the fieldwork period, I noticed during a break between lessons and chatting with participants informally that having a Khmer name and speaking Cambodian outside was necessary to not be harassed. When I asked why, the class members shared the same reasoning: "Because when we go outside, we need a Khmer name, so no one will know we are Vietnamese. If you tell them your Vietnamese name, they will know you are Vietnamese. People don't always ask our name, but we must use it if the police come or the 'paper people.'"[8] Khmer names were given to students by different people, mostly Khmer relatives or friends. The importance and reason for being able to speak and act Khmer in public was widely understood. As Zara, aged sixteen, told me: "If they [Vietnamese children] live here and go outside, you need to know how to speak Cambodian. Here in Cambodia some love Vietnamese, they understand, but most of them [the Khmer] hate Vietnamese more than love so it's not good for you if you don't know how to ask and you just point. They will not understand you; they hate you" (Zara, female, 16 years old).

The excerpts below from Trang, Hung and Huong, and Hien elaborate further on the use of language as a tactic to assert belonging in a space and acting within it, whether that be to secure the sale of a house, to trade in the market, or gain a desired education.

Trang, aged thirteen, lived with her Khmer mother and siblings in a houseboat that was paid for and built by her deceased Vietnamese father. The houseboats that floated on the section of the Tonlé Sap that Trang lived on were mostly occupied by communities of Vietnamese descent. There were growing fears in the community that Vietnamese residents would be evicted from the waterways, in the name of development, leaving them homeless. Trang's mother wanted to rid herself of any connection to her daughter's Vietnamese heritage, and thus she planned to sell the houseboat to avoid this situation. Yet, the houseboat would be sold to Vietnamese buyers, so the paperwork needed to be processed in Vietnamese. This encouraged Trang to attend the God School to learn Vietnamese. While it is true that I heard more cases of participants playing up their Khmer identity, in the case of Trang we see an example of the tactic of performing two identities to achieve belonging and economic security. Trang was able to articulate the rationale for undertaking two identities.

During the flower petal exercise, Trang wrote, "I am Cambodian." When I asked her to explain what she meant by this, she said: "I know that I am Cambodian. I came to the God School so I can study Vietnamese so when my mum makes the paper to sell the house, because they do it in Vietnamese, I will know how to read it for my mum to make sure that the one who buys the house will not trick us" (Trang, female, 13 years old).

Trang told me that when her father was alive people would say she was Vietnamese. However, now she says she is Cambodian. She explains how she is lucky because she is dark skinned, which means the Vietnamese think she is Khmer, but Trang also described how suppressing her Vietnamese identity is hard for her:

Vietnamese people say I am Cambodian because I have dark skin which is okay because I am Cambodian not Vietnamese . . . I'm afraid. Khmer talk about the Vietnamese taking the land. That's why they, Khmer, hate the Vietnamese. When I am outside, I speak Cambodian. My mother wants to sell the house because she heard that the government would expel the ones who live on the houseboats, so she wants to live on the land. I want to be Vietnamese more because Vietnamese people have helped Cambodians. But if they [the Khmer people] say a bad word about Vietnamese people, they talk badly about me and my parents because my parents are Vietnamese. (Trang, female, 13 years old)

Trang is one of the few participants in the research who had documentation confirming that she was Cambodian. However, she still faced stigma and experienced the fear associated with her father's Vietnamese identity. Despite this, she was ready to reidentify as Vietnamese (the God School was overtly seen as a school for Vietnamese children) and to learn how to read and write Vietnamese for her family's benefit. Yet, like the other children, she understood the need to speak Cambodian outside.

Hung told me that when she is outside, she speaks Cambodian because the "ones who sell are Khmer." Like her sister, Huong told me that she wanted to make and sell clothes to Khmer people to provide money for her mother. The sisters saw a need to interact in the market space as their "Khmer" selves as this was the accepted norm. They understood that speaking in Cambodian provided the opportunity of trade. However, this did not pave the way for full acceptance by the majority at the time of my research, as is evidenced by their accounts of violence noted earlier.

Other participants were aware of the need to speak Cambodian to integrate into the national education system. Hien, aged fourteen, lived in Preah Rotn Phon and did not have a birth certificate even though her mother is Khmer. Hien's mother gave birth to her children at home and was not able to afford the documents. Her husband was Vietnamese, which brought specific complications. Hien's mother was told she was herself "Vietnamese" and must pay $100 for a birth certificate for each of her six children. Having lost her Cambodian identity documents during the time of the Khmer Rouge regime, Hien's mother could not prove her Khmer identity. Hien understood that to receive a preferable education she would need to speak Cambodian. Discussing a school near her grandmother's house she wanted to attend, Hien explained, "I want to speak Cambodian because at that place they do not speak Vietnamese, so I need to speak Cambodian to go there." From Hien's point of view, language was necessary to interact and integrate into new spaces. However, for other participants in my study, refraining from speaking Cambodian was a statement of affinity to the Vietnamese, who were seen to be more industrious and collectively capable of survival in a hostile world. Special conditions were necessary for someone who could speak Cambodian and Vietnamese to decide to behave in such a way, as the case of Minh illustrates.

A Language of Resistance

Minh, aged fifteen, one of the older research participants, was born in Cambodia. His mother is Vietnamese, and he lived with her Vietnamese parents on a houseboat in Preah Rehab (fig. 2). Minh's Khmer father had died a few years before the research. The circumstances of his death were only spoken of in passing, and Minh did not refer to his father at all in interviews. Minh worked extremely hard for his aunt on her fish farm, which also served as a residence. His village was a community mainly made up of river residents. This organized network was open, less cramped, and more connected compared to Preah Rotn Phon and Preah Amnr Sabbay.

Judging from his accounts of the business, Minh's family was relatively successful. He would regularly be out of school assisting with the work that needed to be done. When not attending school, Minh would work around the clock beginning at 3:00 a.m. to prepare the fish to dry, then working on until 6:00 p.m. and going to bed at 10:00 p.m., before beginning the next workday. Previously, Minh had been to a school run by Vietnamese in Cambodia who employed a Khmer teacher. This school was also a Christian school, so going to the God School where I met him was a preference of his family, all of whom were Christians except his mother.

When talking about his village and home life, Minh explained that despite people in his village speaking both languages he preferred to speak Vietnamese. Seeing himself as Vietnamese, he did not see a reason why he should speak Cambodian and said he would only do so if "absolutely necessary." It was clear from interviews with Minh that he saw himself living

Figure 2 Preah Rehab. Photo taken by Kevin, aged fifteen.

in a foreign country despite having been born in Cambodia. For instance, when discussing his recent baptism, I asked Minh what it is like being a Christian living in Cambodia: "In Cambodia, most people are Buddhists, but I follow God. When you're living in another person's country you should believe what they believe, which is Buddhism, but because a lot of people in my family are Christian, I have listened to what they have said" (Minh, male, 15 years old).

In discussing his opinions about the Khmer, Minh used the phrase "not very nice at all." This is because he thought they "easily get mad or angry, like when I or some others just walk past the house, they get mad, and yell at us not to speak Vietnamese." This kind of behavior evidently annoyed Minh and encouraged his "reactive ethnicity" (Portes and Rumbaut 2001)—that is, his determination to not speak Cambodian outside, in reaction to the exclusion and ethnic discrimination he had experienced.

Minh was in a privileged position compared to others without identity papers. His family made relatively good money in the fishing business and had recently bought a house in Vietnam. In discussing his future, Minh had plans to start his own business after learning a trade and building his own house. He told me he would prefer to live in Cambodia when he was older, but his grandmother wanted him to go to Vietnam. He had a clear view of his social mobility and told me he preferred being an adult so he could work. Minh had planned how much he wanted to earn each month: $300, so he could give $100 to the family members he lived with and provide an additional $100 for food. He would save $100 for his building project. Minh explained that the reason he had thought about his future so much was because when he was five years old, he had experienced poverty. He remembers his family not having enough money to buy rice, and he wished at that time he could grow up to earn money for his family.

The simplicity of Cambodia's "cultural assimilation" model omits some of the complexities of language use, especially why people may choose to refuse to speak a language or what economic and structural conditions enable such resistance. In Minh's case, his family's financial security afforded him some linguistic freedom of choice. In asking his opinions of the future of students at the God School whose families, unlike his, did not have a profitable fishing business and could not speak Cambodian, Minh acknowledged the need for communities to work together to improve their life in common. He said: "I think if they work together their life will be good. If they don't swear, steal, fight, or yell at each other, then gradually they will be alright. Because when young [Vietnamese] people come to a village, get angry and fight, they fight so much that the locals hate them. So, when they come to their village, the villagers hate them" (Minh, male, 15 years old). Minh's description of the behaviors that would provoke villagers demonstrates that even though he decided not to speak Cambodian, and from time to time was reprimanded for not doing so, he also advocated living peaceably along with engaging in a degree of linguistic resistance. This tactic enabled Minh to be rooted in a community locally, away from the majority group but still able to function daily. As was true of most participants in the study, Minh conveyed to me a strong sense that the relationship between the Vietnamese and Khmer was embedded in a historical identity politics characterized by land disputes. However, for the sake of living peacefully he did not broadcast his opinions in public, although it was clear he had considered at great length the relationship between the two peoples. Toward the end of the research period, Minh explained why he thought there would be continued hostility: "I think if Khmer people are more yielding, then Vietnamese people would do the same. Because when the land was shared, they [Khmer] would not even yield one little bit, like if you are a little bit late, you will be driven out" (Minh, male, 15 years old). Minh's reasoning that there was a compromise to be had among the Khmer and Vietnamese alluded to a contestation over land. It was not clear whether this was a discussion about local land or national border lines, yet the feeling that the Khmer were less willing to be accommodating added to the narrative of "them" being the problem.

Conclusion

This article demonstrates the varied responses of children to the experience of ethno-nationalism in Cambodia and how experiences of dislocation impacted on their integration. Interactions among people within communities of difference can be characterized by positive and affirming or, conversely, fractured relationships. This article has emphasized the latter, showing how experiences of exclusion influenced participants' sense of belonging.

I argue that despite the slipperiness of terms such as *de facto statelessness* and *integration*, scholarship that has theorized integration and assimilation can help to clarify children's experience and practice of belonging when looking at statelessness as a salient context of reception defining the integration of children of Vietnamese descent in Cambodia. Children's accounts of their lives show how negative experiences of ethnicity gave rise to cross-border affiliations and reinforced their ethnic Vietnamese identities. Socioeconomic conditions were evidently important factors that set the conditions of integration for communities of Vietnamese descent living in Cambodia. They offered children a degree of agency to selectively assimilate. Despite strong feelings of dislocation and experiences of poverty, participants in the study were willing to perform "Khmerness" by tactically utilizing language to coexist in certain spaces, structurally integrate, or avoid further discrimination.

Notes

Previous versions of this article have been presented at a panel titled "The Vietnamese Question: Multidisciplinary Perspectives on the Vietnamese Minority in Cambodia," which was held at the 2017 European Association of Southeast Asian Studies (EUROSEAS) conference and the 2018 Migration, Displacement, and Belonging Research Group Seminar at the Centre for Trust, Peace, and Social Relations (CTPSR). I thank the participants at both events for their questions and comments. Thanks also to two anonymous reviewers for their very helpful suggestions. I am grateful to all the children and families in Preah Thnov, who shared their stories with me, and to those teaching at the God School, where I conducted much of this research.

1 See Heikkilä et al. 2015 for a critical examination of the term *integration*.

2 Echoing Portes and Rumbaut's (2001) reactive ethnicity theory.

3 My proposed concept of cross-border affiliations resonates with Yen Le Espiritu's (2003) concept of "symbolic transnationalism," with the caveat that in this work the idea of "home" is ambiguous. Moreover, affiliations are generated through negative encounters with the majority Khmer, hence the emphasis on dislocations.

4 "Postwar" in this instance refers to the period after the Khmer Rouge regime of 1975–1979.

5 The ruling Cambodian People's Party is the country's only political party.

6 For a detailed description of the God School, see Rumsby 2021.

7 For a discussion on how the notion of gender performativity can be applied to belonging, see Bell 1999.

8 In using the term *paper people*, children were referring to the officials who would check the paperwork related to residency and citizenship.

References

Ager, Alastair, and Alison Strang. 2008. "Understanding Integration: A Conceptual Framework." *Journal of Refugee Studies* 21, no. 2: 166–91.

Akinwumi, Akinbola E. 2006. "Review Article: A New Kind of Entanglement? Immigrants, the 'American Dream,' and the Politics of Belonging." *Geografiska Annaler, Series B: Human Geography* 88, no. 2: 249–53.

Allerton, Catherine. 2014. "Statelessness and the Lives of the Children of Migrants in Sabah, East Malaysia." *Tilburg Law Review* 19, nos. 1–2: 26–35.

Allerton, Catherine. 2017. "Impossible Children: Illegality and Excluded Belonging among Children of Migrants in Sabah, East Malaysia." *Journal of Ethnic and Migration Studies* 44, no. 7: 1081–97.

Amer, Ramses. 1994. "The Ethnic Vietnamese in Cambodia: A Minority at Risk?" *Contemporary Southeast Asia* 16, no. 2: 210–38.

Anderson, Benedict. 1991. *Imagined Communities: Reflections on the Origin and Spread of Nationalism*. London: Verso.

Ang, Chanrith, Chiara Natta, and Holm Hansen. 2014. *No School for Stateless Vietnamese Children in Cambodia: Case Study on Birth Certificates and Identification Documents Required for Exercising the Right to Education*. Phnom Penh, Cambodia: Minority Rights Organisation Penh.

Ang, Chanrith, Noémie Weill, and Jamie Chan. 2014. *Limbo on Earth: An Investigative Report on the Current Living Conditions and Legal Status of Ethnic Vietnamese in Cambodia*. Phnom Penh, Cambodia: Minority Rights Organization.

Antonsich, Marco. 2010. "Searching for Belonging: An Analytical Framework." *Geography Compass* 4, no. 6: 644–59.

Bagnoli, Anna. 2009. "Beyond the Standard Interview: The Use of Graphic Elicitation and Arts-Based Methods." *Qualitative Research* 9, no. 5: 547–70.

Beazley, Harriot. 2015. "Multiple Identities, Multiple Realities: Children Who Migrate Independently for Work in Southeast Asia." *Children's Geographies* 13, no. 3: 296–309.

Beazley, Harriot, Leslie Butt, and Jessica Ball. 2018. "'Like It, Don't Like It, You Have to Like It': Children's Emotional Responses to the Absence of Transnational Migrant Parents in Lombok, Indonesia." *Children's Geographies* 16, no. 6: 591–603.

Bell, Vikki. 1999. "Performativity and Belonging: An Introduction." *Theory, Culture, and Society* 16, no. 2: 1–10.

Berman, Jennifer S. 1996. "No Place Like Home: Anti-Vietnamese Discrimination and Nationality in Cambodia." *California Law Review* 84, no. 3: 817–74.

Bhabha, Jacqueline. 2011. "From Citizen to Migrant: The Scope of Child Statelessness in the Twenty-First Century." In *Children without a State: A Global Human Rights Challenge*, edited by Jacqueline Bhabha, 2–39. Cambridge, MA: MIT Press.

Brown, Eleanor. 2007. *The Ties That Bind: Migration and Trafficking of Women and Girls for Sexual Exploitation in Cambodia*. Phnom Penh, Cambodia: International Organisation for Migration.

Buijs, Frank J., Froukje Demant, and Atef Hamdy. 2006. *Radical and Democratic Muslims in the Netherlands*. Amsterdam: Amsterdam University Press.

Buonfino, Alessandra, and Louise Thomson. 2007. *Belonging in Contemporary Britain*. London: Commission on Integration and Cohesion.

Canzutti, Lucrezia. 2019. "Precarious (Non-)Citizens: A Historical Analysis of Ethnic Vietnamese' Access to Citizenship in Cambodia." *Journal of Ethnic and Migration Studies*, November 17. doi.org/10.1080/1369183X.2019.1690438.

Chow, Henry. 2007. "Sense of Belonging and Life Satisfaction among Hong Kong Adolescent Immigrants in Canada." *Journal of Ethnic and Migration Studies* 33, no. 3: 511–20.

de Certeau, Michel. 1984. *The Practice of Everyday Life*. Berkeley: University of California Press.

Dixon, John, and Kevin Durrheim. 2004. "Dislocating Identity: Desegregation and the Transformation of Place." *Journal of Environmental Psychology* 24, no. 4: 455–73.

Dreby, Joanna. 2015. *Everyday Illegal: When Policies Undermine Immigrant Families*. Oakland: University of California Press.

Duoos, Tori. 2012. *To Be Determined: Stories of People Facing Statelessness*. Phnom Penh, Cambodia: Jesuit Refugee Service.

Duyendak, Jan Willem, and Paul Scholten. 2010. "The Invention of the Dutch Multicultural Model and Its Effects on Integration Discourses in the Netherlands." *Perspective on Europe* 40, no. 2: 39–49.

Edwards, Penny. 1996. "Imaging the Other in Cambodian Nationalist Discourse before and during the UNTAC Period." In *Propaganda, Politics, and Violence in Cambodia: Democratic Transition under United Nations Peace-Keeping*, edited by Steve Heder and Judy Ledgerwood, 50–72. Armonk, NY: M. E. Sharpe.

Edwards, Penny. 2007. *Cambodge: The Cultivation of a Nation, 1860–1945*. Honolulu: University of Hawai'i Press.

Ehrentraut, Stefan. 2011. "Perpetually Temporary: Citizenship and Ethnic Vietnamese in Cambodia." *Ethnic and Racial Studies* 34, no. 5: 779–98.

Espiritu, Yen Le. 2003. *Home Bound: Filipino American Lives across Cultures, Communities, and Countries.* Berkeley: University of California Press.

Esser, Hartmut. 2003. "What Substance Is There to the Term 'Leitkultur'?" In *The Challenge of Diversity: European Social Democracy Facing Migration, Integration, and Multiculturalism*, edited by René Cuperus, Karl A. Duffek, and Johannes Kandel, 47–58. Innsbruck, Austria: StudienVerlag.

Frewer, Tim. 2016. "Cambodia's Anti-Vietnam Obsession: Anti-Vietnamese Sentiment Dominates Cambodia, Even among Otherwise Progressive NGOs and Political Groups." *Diplomat*, September 6. thediplomat.com/2016/09/cambodias-anti-vietnam-obsession/.

Ghorashi, Halleh. 2010. "'Dutchness' and the Migrant 'Other': From Suppressed Superiority to Explicit Exclusion?" *Focaal* 56: 106–111.

Golash-Boza, Tanya. 2019. "Punishment Beyond the Deportee: The Collatoral Consequences of Deportation." *American Behavioral Scientist* 63, no. 9: 1331–49.

Goscha, Christopher. 2012. *Going Indochinese: Contesting Concepts of Space and Place in French Indochina.* Copenhagen, Denmark: NIAS Press.

Hart, Jason, and Bex Tyrer. 2006. "Research with Children Living in Situations of Armed Conflict: Concept, Ethics, and Methods." RSC Working Paper No. 30, May. www.rsc.ox.ac.uk/files/files-1/wp30-children-living-situations-armed-conflict-2006.pdf.

Heckmann, Friedrich. 2005. "Integration and Integration Policies: IMISCOE Network Feasibility Study." www.ssoar.info/ssoar/bitstream/handle/document/19295/ssoar-2005-heckmann-integration_and_integration_policies.pdf?sequence=1&isAllowed=y&lnkname=ssoar-2005-heckmann-integration_and_integration_policies.pdf (accessed November 22, 2021).

Heikkila, Eli, Auvo Kostiainen, Johanna Leinonen, and Ismo Söderling, eds. 2015. *Participation, Integration, and Recognition: Changing Pathways to Immigrant Incorporation.* Turku, Finland: Institute of Migration.

Ho, Elaine Lynn-Ee. 2019. *Citizens in Motion: Emigration, Immigration, and Re-Migration across China's Borders.* Stanford, CA: Stanford University Press.

hooks, bell. 2009. *Belonging: A Culture of Place.* New York: Routledge.

Kleifgen, Jo Anne, and Trang Thi Huynh Le. 2007. "Vietnamese Immigrants' Shifting Patterns of Status Display at Work: Impressions from Hanoi." *Journal of Asian Pacific Communication* 17, no. 2: 259–79.

Lamont, Michèle, and Virga Molnar. 2002. "The Study of Boundaries in the Social Sciences." *Annual Review of Sociology* 28: 167–95.

Malischewski, Charlotte-Anne. 2013. "How Indian Law Produces Statelessness." McGill Human Rights Interns (blog), July 17. blogs.mcgill.ca/humanrightsinterns/2013/07/17/how -indian-law-produces-statelessness/.

Menjivar, Cecilia. 2006. "Liminal Legality: Salvadoran and Guatemalan Immigrants' Lives in the United States." *American Journal of Sociology* 111, no. 4: 999–1037.

Metzl, J. 1995. "The Vietnamese of Cambodia." *Harvard Human Rights Journal* 8: 269–75.

Nguyen, Lyma, and Christoph Sperfeldt. 2012. *Boat without Anchors: A Report on the Legal Status of Ethnic Vietnamese Minority Populations in Cambodia under Domestic and International Laws Governing Nationality and Statelessness.* Phnom Penh, Cambodia: Jesuit Refugee Service.

Nishikawa, Yukiko. 2009. "Human Security in Southeast Asia: Viable Solution or Empty Slogan?" *Security Dialogue* 40, no. 2: 213–36.

Orellana, Marjorie. 2016. *Immigrant Children in Transcultural Spaces.* London: Routledge.

Parreñas, Rhacel. 2005. "Long Distance Intimacy: Class, Gender, and Intergenerational Relations between Mothers and Children in Filipino Transnational Families." *Global Networks* 5, no. 4: 317–36.

Parsons, Laurie, and Sabina Lawreniuk. 2018. "Seeing Like the Stateless: Documentation and the Mobilities of Liminal Citizenship in Cambodia." *Political Geography* 62: 1–11.

Penninx, Rinus, and Blanca Garcés-Mascareñas. 2016. "The Concept of Integration as an Analytical Tool and as a Policy Concept." In *Integration Processes and Policies in Europe: Contexts, Levels, and Actors*, edited by Blanca Garcés-Mascareñas and Rinus Penninx, 11–29. Cham, Switzerland: Springer International.

Portes, Alejandro, and Ruben Rumbaut. 2001. *Legacies: The Story of the Immigrant Second Generation.* Berkeley: University of California Press.

Probyn, Elspeth. 1996. *Outside Belongings.* London: Routledge.

Rattansi, Ali, and Ann Phoenix. 2005. "Rethinking Youth Identities: Modernist and Postmodernist Frameworks." *Identity: An International Journal of Theory and Research* 5, no. 2: 97–123.

Rouvoet, Marjo, Melanie Eijberts, and Halleh Ghorashi. 2017. "Identification Paradoxes and Multiple Belongings: The Narratives of Italian Migrants in the Netherlands." *Social Inclusion* 5, no. 1: 105–16.

Rumbaut, Rubén G. 1994. "The Crucible Within: Ethnic Identity, Self-Esteem, and Segmented Assimilation among Children of Immigrants." *International Migration Review* 28, no. 4: 748–94.

Rumbaut, Rubén G. 2005. "Sites of Belonging: Acculturation, Discrimination, and Ethnic Identity among Children of Immigrants." *Discovering Successful Pathways in Children's*

Development: Mixed Methods in the Study of Childhood and Family Life, edited by Thomas S. Weisner, 111–64. Chicago: University of Chicago Press.

Rumsby, Charlie. 2019. "Modes of Identity and Belonging among Noncitizen Vietnamese Children Living in Cambodia." PhD diss., Coventry University.

Rumsby, Charlie. 2021. "The God School: Informal Christian Education and Emerging Aspirations among de Facto Stateless Children Living in Cambodia." *European Journal of Development Research* 33, no. 1: 89–108. doi.org/10.1057/s41287-020-00303-x.

Rydstrøm, Helle. 2001. "'Like a White Piece of Paper': Embodiment and the Moral Upbringing of Vietnamese Children." *Ethnos* 66, no. 3: 394–413.

Said, Edward. 2003. *Orientalism*. London: Penguin.

Sigona, Nando. 2016. "Everyday Statelessness in Italy: Status, Rights, and Camps." *Ethnic and Racial Studies* 39, no. 2: 263–79.

Sperfeldt, Christoph. 2017. *Report on Citizenship Law: Cambodia*. January. cadmus.eui.eu/bitstream/handle/1814/45084/GLOBALCIT_2017_02_Cambodia.pdf.

Sperfeldt, Christoph. 2020. "Minorities and Statelessness: Social Exclusion and Citizenship in Cambodia." *International Journal on Minority and Group Rights* 27, no. 1: 94–120.

Stokols, Daniel. 1990. "Instrumental and Spiritual Views of People-Environment Relations." *American Psychologist* 45, no. 5: 641–46.

United Nations Human Rights Council. 2019. "Assessing Protection of Those at Risk of Being Left Behind: Report of the Special Rapporteur on the Situation of Human Rights in Cambodia." September 2. digitallibrary.un.org/record/3863405?ln=en.

Waters, Mary C., Van C. Tran, Philip Kasinitz, and John H. Mollenkopf. 2010. "Segmented Assimilation Revisited: Types of Acculturation and Socioeconomic Mobility in Young Adulthood." *Ethnic and Racial Studies* 33, no. 7: 1168–93.

Yuval-Davis, N., and E. Kaptani. 2008. "Participatory Theatre as a Research Methodology: Identity, Performance, and Social Action Among Refugees." *Sociological Research Online*, September 30. www.socresonline.org.uk/13/5/2.html.

Children's Bodies Are Not Capital:

Arduous Cross-Border Mobilities between Shenzhen and Hong Kong

Johanna L. Waters and Maggi W. H. Leung

As we approach the Hong Kong–Shenzhen border, we are overwhelmed by the sight of dozens of school children moving towards us in crocodilian fashion, wearing matching uniforms and tags around their necks. They are moving, as they do every day, over the border from Mainland China to Hong Kong, to attend school. Twenty years ago, such mobility was rare—the few children that did this were exceptional. Today it is more like mobility on an industrial scale, involving highly choreographed movements and the necessity for docile bodies.
—Taken from field notes, June 2018

For many children, cross-border mobilities transpire not as an exception, novelty, or aberration, but as a "way of life." Mobility forms part of a young person's "habitus" (Bourdieu 1984)—a taken-for-granted form of socialization that occurs, within a household, from birth. During the past fifteen years, we have been undertaking research with young people in and from

positions 30:2   DOI 10.1215/10679847-9573383
Copyright 2022 by Duke University Press

Hong Kong, some of whom could be classified in this way, as intrinsic movers, originating from families who have, in living memory, always "moved" (see Skeldon 1994). Aihwa Ong (1999: 2) describes the Chinese in Hong Kong as

> [a] rather special kind of refugee, haunted by *memento mori* even when they seek global economic opportunities that include China. . . . Hong Kong people are driven by the memory of previous Chinese disasters and shaped by their status as colonials without the normal colonial expectation of independence. They are people always in transit, who have become "world-class practitioners of self-sufficiency." . . . For over a century, overseas Chinese have been the forerunners of today's multiply displaced subjects, who are always on the move both mentally and physically.

What does it mean to be "always on the move"? Our latest project, on cross-boundary schooling (CBS), involves a sample of children—born in Hong Kong but resident in Mainland China—who appear to embody just that. We begin with a fictionalized anecdote, taken from our recent fieldwork, to illustrate some of the key aspects of our arguments in relation to children's everyday mobilities.

> Lily is eight years old. She was born in Hong Kong but lives with her parents and sister in Shenzhen, Mainland China, a fifty-minute drive from the boundary with Hong Kong. Her sister attends school in Shenzhen, a short walk away, but Lily must engage in a daily commute of around two hours each way to Hong Kong for school. She rises every day at 5:30 a.m. to undertake this journey by bus, disembarking at the border with other children her age, crossing the boundary (passing through a checkpoint), and continuing on her journey to school. Frequently, she falls asleep on the bus and feels perpetually tired. She arrives home from school around 8:00 p.m. and must then complete any homework and go to bed. She was born in Hong Kong, her parents tell us, for two main reasons—one, to bypass the one-child policy enforced in China at that time and, two, to be able to access a "better" education system, opening up possibilities for her future (global?) mobility. Her sister, she reports, has a far easier (less tiring and strenuous) life. But Lily likes her school in Hong Kong—she has made

good friends, many of whom undertake this daily cross-border commute along with her. She has also become rather fond of the nannies employed by the bus companies to take care of the children during the daily drive.

This short story hints at the complexities of education-related mobilities, especially their quotidian, immediate, and embodied nature. Children experience these not as some seamless "flow" or abstract migration strategy, but their whole young lives are shaped by their cross-boundary schooling practices. From this point of departure, we will make three main points within the article's broader argument: (1) that mobilities exist within the habitus of many young people within East and Southeast Asia; (2) that "education" represents a primary discursive tool in the reasons given for or justifications of ongoing mobilities; and (3) that educational mobilities are often, in reality, difficult and corporeal: arduous, tiring, boring, and dispiriting (drawing on our empirical findings). This view challenges the tendency in the extant literature to depict children's bodies in the abstract as "body-capital" (discussed below). While we acknowledge that many children travel vast distances to attend school on a daily basis without crossing a border or boundary, we hope to show that the act of border crossing and the transborder habitus that exists in the region (Xu 2017a, 2017b) makes CBS a particularly compelling case.

More broadly, the article highlights the role played by children in emergent transnational topologies. Foregrounding children's movement evokes the idea of "embodied statecraft," discussed recently by Mitchell and Kallio (2017) in relation to Jennifer Hyndman's (2001) work on feminist geopolitics, where states (and borders) are made through quotidian movements. Arguably, the daily border-crossing mobilities of CBS children help make and maintain the boundary between Hong Kong and the Mainland. Furthermore, children are harbingers of *future* migration. They are migrants "in the making," and their educational mobilities have longer-term implications: for themselves, their families and the geopolitical landscape. Young people's mobilities in search of educational opportunities are increasingly prevalent, and links have been drawn between mobility for education and mobility later in life (Findlay et al. 2012). And yet their movements are, for them, immediate (about the "now" and not about the future); they are raw and felt with intensity. Over the past decade, research in social science on "educational mobilities" has tended to focus more on longer-term strategies (with the emphasis on strategizing) than on short-term experiences (cf. Forsberg, 2017a). This article attempts to focus on both—considering how cross-boundary schooling is indicative of questions around transnational migration, global householding, geopolitics, the "geo-social" and household social reproduction (Ho 2017) as well as what it signals for children's everyday, embodied experiences.

Educational Mobilities in and out of East Asia within the Habitus

According to Bourdieu (1990: 56), the habitus is "embodied history, internalized as a second nature and so forgotten as history—it is the active presence of the whole past of which it is a product." Consequently, "the most improbable practices are therefore excluded, as unthinkable, by a kind of immediate submission to order that inclines agents to make a virtue of necessity, that is, to refuse what is anyway denied and to will the inevitable" (54). Children are socialized into their particular (group) habitus. Through exposure to friends and family (occupying the same social group), they develop schema by which they learn to organize their thoughts and actions, resulting in the development of certain attitudes that appear "natural" but are, in fact, a direct consequence of their upbringing. It is another way of conceiving the process of socialization into a particular "life-world," providing individuals with a sense of their place in the world ("knowing your place") and thereby ascribing the range of necessities and possibilities that they attach to their everyday lives. For many young children in East Asia, mobility (for education) is seen as natural and necessary. And yet, while mobility (and the propensity to be mobile) *may* be part of children's habitus, how they respond to the situations they encounter through mobility is not; hence the mismatched expectations between parents and children that often occur in migrant households (particularly transnational households, where physical absence is common).

Habitus can also be used to indicate one's orientation toward a border or boundary: Xu (2017a, 2017b), for example, has considered the notion of habitus explicitly in relation to Hong Kong–Mainland China in her study of Mainland students in Hong Kong. Xu (2017b: 2) proposes the concept of "transborder habitus," where the border can indicate "spaces that belong politically to the same country, share a deep level of historic cultural and/or ethnic entanglement, but can be ideologically, linguistically and socially divergent." Many of the children undertaking CBS will have been socialized to accept such a transborder habitus.

The wider literature would suggest that many children, globally, perceive mobility or border crossing for education as unexceptional and anticipated. There has been a great deal of interest, for example, in the transnational household formations represented by so-called kirogi families, originating from South Korea. These have been defined as "families that are separated between two countries for the purpose of children's education abroad" (Lee and Koo 2006: 533; see also Kang and Abelmann 2011). Other work has considered the mobility patterns of older children—the "astronaut" families and "parachute" or "satellite kids" found in North America, New Zealand and Australia (Waters 2002, 2003; Zhou 1998). The reasons for migration, research has shown, are often multifaceted, but almost always encompass an overriding concern with children's education (Kobayashi and Preston 2007; Waters 2002). This literature often hints at the difficulties faced by these children (caused, for example, by separation from parents) but rarely explores the daily challenges and the intimate and corporeal nature of physical movement (Finn and Holton 2019). For these children, migration involves longer-term resettlement and not quotidian commuting. The physicality and materiality of travel, as well as the site of the border, have been insufficiently explained in educational mobilities (compare Xu 2017a, 2017b), and this is something we hope to redress in our research on CBS.

The Complex Meanings of "Education"

When it comes to migration, education is seldom about "knowledge," "content," or "pedagogy." The importance of education is largely symbolic (Bourdieu 1984; Goldthorpe 1996) and closely tied to capital accumulation strategies, inextricably linked to an elemental concern with social reproduction (Bourdieu 1984, 1986; Mitchell et al. 2012). In the work of sociologist Pierre Bourdieu, capital, in its various forms, is integral to societal stratification.

He writes: "The structure of the distribution of the different types and subtypes of capital at any given moment in time represents the immanent structure of the social world, i.e., the set of constraints, inscribed in the very reality of that world, which govern its functioning in a durable way, determining the chances of success for practices" (Bourdieu 1986: 242). Access to forms of capital, he suggests, determines the life chances of social groups, while the consequent distribution of life chances tends to be fixed and self-perpetuating. Capital has the propensity "to reproduce itself in identical or expanded form . . . to persist in its being . . . a force inscribed in the objectivity of things so that everything is not equally possible or impossible" (241–42).

Recent scholarship on the contemporary Chinese diaspora references the social reproduction strategies of middle-class families as they endeavor to maintain or increase their capital through migration (Leung 2013). Education is a key form of cultural capital. As Ong (1999: 18–19) has written: "Chinese entrepreneurs are not merely engaged in profit making; they are also acquiring a range of symbolic capitals [including education] that will facilitate their positioning, economic negotiation, and cultural acceptance in different geographical sites." Through CBS, households are attempting to secure the future social and economic status of their families by strategically investing in the cultural capital of their children.

Cindi Katz's (2008, 2011, 2017) project on "childhood as spectacle" articulates the ways in which children might be seen as "accumulation strategy, as commodity, as ornament and as waste" (2017: 3). She writes: "These kinds of practices smuggle with them an almost magical 'investment' in the child as oneself, one's future, and *the* future" (4). Here Katz draws on Foucault to explain the "concerted cultivation" (and its disciplining effects) that go along with the accumulation of cultural capital through the child: "The social reproductive practices associated with the concerted cultivation of children are labors of love, but they are also a means of cultivating parents in a Foucauldian sense. These cultural forms and practices of class formation make a space of conformity and competition, a realm of social life that parents often feel compelled to participate in so their children "stay in the game." All the more so when the game is unclear" (5). Education and, specifically, forms of migration tied to education are precisely about such "magical 'investment' in the child as . . . *the* future"—their future, but also their family's future.

As a form of cultural capital, education is more than just institutional-ized credentials. Cultural capital also "presupposes embodiment" (Bourdieu 1986: 244), involving a process of incorporation that, "insofar as it implies a labor of inculcation and assimilation, costs time, time which must be invested personally by the investor." Education is also, therefore, assumed to reflect embodied competences. Recent scholarship on the spatial strategies of middle- and upper-class Chinese families has made reference to the delib-erate and self-conscious fostering of cultural competences within children. Ong (1999: 91) has argued that the "would-be immigrant often acquires an intensified sense of him- or herself as body capital that can be constantly improved to meet new and shifting criteria of symbolic power." Chinese families in Hong Kong are *supposed to be* extremely knowledgeable about the types (and locations) of capital they covet. As Ong (1999: 89) has written, these families seek "the kinds of symbolic capital that have international rec-ognition and value, not only in the country of origin but also in the country of destination and especially in the transnational spaces where the itineraries of travelling businessmen and professionals intersect." However, the existing literature has tended to overlook the importance of a specific, geographically embedded market for these cultural competences and the frequent "failure" of such strategies (Waters 2015). It has also overlooked how difficult and challenging daily mobilities can be.

In sum, the literature has drawn three main points in relation to children's educational mobilities within East Asia. First, education is understood as a form of embodied cultural capital and pursued as a strategy of household social reproduction. Children are seen to embody this capital—yet the liter-ature pays scant attention to children's embodied (corporeal) experiences of educational mobility because their bodies tend to be "abstracted." We seek to avoid this failing. The second point, which is related to the first, is that the literature has stressed the future-oriented nature of educational migra-tory strategies—children's "body capital" is about *the future*. They are seen as an investment now for some future "payoff." By contrast, in this article we want to stress the immediate and present nature of children's (and parents') experiences of CBS. There is little concern with "the future"—the present is all-encompassing. And a third point emerging from the literature concerns the apparent "ease" with which Chinese families are able to engage in border crossing and live "transnational" lives. As we will explore below, however, the families that we studied stressed the difficulties they faced—how arduous CBS was and is.

Research Methods

The project on which this article primarily draws involves an in-depth qualitative examination of the daily mobility patterns of children, their families, and the infrastructure surrounding the phenomenon of cross-boundary schooling (bus companies, homestays, schools, and teachers). The field "site" is the border between Hong Kong (Special Administrative Region) and Shenzhen (Mainland China) (fig. 1) and the area of travel between home and school.

The project has involved in-depth interviews and ethnography undertaken with twelve households residing in Mainland China with at least one child commuting daily to Hong Kong for school (either now or in the recent past). These households were selected partly through personal contacts, partly by "snowballing" and by participating in a WeChat group. We have also interviewed older individuals who undertook the commute for a while and "gave up," other family members of these children, school teachers who have close contact with CBS children and border officials and have monitored public WeChat (social media) accounts and advertisements relating to CBS. Observations have been taken at different border-crossing points and different times of the day and also during travel with families moving between their homes and the border. These data are consequently a mix of detailed ethnographic fieldnotes and interview transcripts that we have analyzed thematically. We are interested in exploring the everyday realities of cross-boundary schooling—how it is experienced (by children and wider family members). And we also aim to understand the *meaning* of "education" in the context of such an ostensibly extreme daily routine and how children's and women's bodies are implicated in educational migrations.

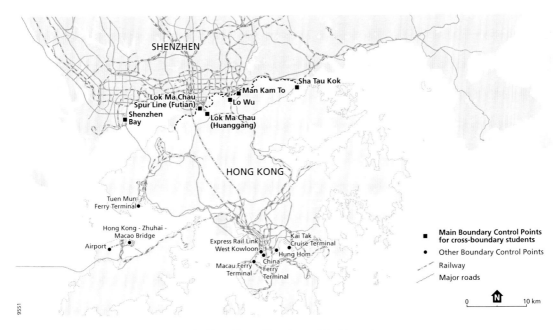

Figure 1 The Hong Kong–Shenzhen political boundary.

Daily Border Mobilities for Schooling between Hong Kong and Shenzhen

The particular case of cross-boundary schooling provides a fascinating example of the intersection of mobilities, materialities, and capital in children's education. In this project, we explore the daily "commute" undertaken by tens of thousands of children who live in Mainland China and attend school in Hong Kong. Their experience rests on the differential rights granted to citizens/residents born on one or the other side of the Hong Kong–Mainland border. As Chan and Ngan (2018: 145) note, "Even after Hong Kong became a Special Administrative Region (SAR) of China in 1997, the Hong Kong–Shenzhen border continued to operate as an international, rather than an internal, border." Cross-border schooling, therefore, involves a materially complex form of migration, enacted on a daily basis.

In the decade between 2001 and 2011, the number of babies born in Hong Kong to Mainland parents increased from 620 to 35,000 (Chee 2017). Chee notes the class background of mothers choosing to give birth over the border in Hong Kong. The early "wave" was mostly from the middle class while, more lately, mothers have been increasingly from working-class and rural backgrounds. These children, usually born to Mainland resident parents, have no right to attend school in China (they lack essential *hukou*[1]). They are Hong Kong residents (a status automatically granted to a person of Chinese descent born on Hong Kong soil since 2001), and their access to education, health care, and other social services is tied to this. Fascinatingly, in the cases we have examined, it is usual to have siblings, within the family, with different residence statuses. One child will attend school in Shenzhen and the other will commute daily over the border, creating fascinating dynamics and differential experiences of educational mobilities within the household. There are currently an estimated 30,000 so-called CBS children moving in this way, although estimates do vary.

While there has been significant media coverage of CBS in both the Chinese and English-language press, fewer academic studies have explored this phenomenon, and those that have tend to consider the psychological impacts on the children from a "social work" or "policy" perspective. Some exceptions are found in a handful of recent articles (Chan and Ngan 2018; Chee 2017; Chiu and Choi 2018). Chee (2017) considers CBS from the viewpoint of Mainland Chinese mothers, whose original decision to give birth in Hong Kong has resulted in a lifetime of being "trapped" by incessant mobilities. This standpoint—seeing educational mobilities as entrapment rather than "freedom"—is unusual yet revealing. Interestingly, the article focuses on the infrastructure of the border and border crossing, and the ways in which infrastructures "circumscribe" mothers' border-crossing experiences, yet their mobility is at the same time "compelled." In this article, mothers tended to accompany their children, who often lived in Hong Kong during the week while they attended school. However, the mothers were only in possession of a temporary (three-month) visa, which had to be renewed frequently, and this could take a few weeks to process. According to Chee (2017: 208), "these Mainland mothers see no end to their recurring border crossing ordeals." The main conclusions drawn by this article include an assertion about the enduring "power of the border" (despite this one being, in effect, an "internal" border) and the "infrastructural assemblages" (immigration, security, visas, and policing) that shape the border and border-crossing experiences (210). By contrast, Chan and Ngan (2018) focus more on the experiences of the young people involved in CBS, within the context of family strategies, resources, and constraints.

Cross-boundary schooling is experienced in various ways, not least through the physicality of transportation (by bus, on foot, by car) and the "hardness" of the border between Hong Kong and the PRC (Waters and Leung 2020). Despite the fact that Hong Kong has, for more than twenty years now, been a special administrative region of China, the border remains writ large with its imposing checkpoints, guards, customs, cameras, channels, and signage. People are very much policed over the border—it is by no means a fluid zone of travel. That said, CBS children experience a more familiar, amenable border than many other "migrants," using their electronic passes to scan themselves over in a fairly unproblematic way.

There are different ways in which young people travel to, and cross, the border. Older children travel independently, using public transportation, and often meet up with friends at the border as they proceed to cross it. We saw several smaller groups of older children during our observations at the border.

> A group of older boys sat together on the seats, apparently waiting for something or someone. Although they were "together," there was little talking amongst the group. Most of them were hunched over playing games on mobile phones. A smaller group (three) of slightly younger boys stood together away from the flows of people and talked, with their heads down. One of them kicked the wall mindlessly. They looked bored and a bit dejected. (Taken from fieldnotes, June 2018)

Younger children are nearly always accompanied in some way—either by a relative on either side of the checkpoint, by a Mainland parent on a visitor visa, or a Hong Kong resident parent. The most striking visual impression, however, is made by the children on the schoolbus—there are several licensed private bus companies offering services expressly for CBS children. These will employ a nanny ("aunty X") to accompany the children (keep them in line, keep them safe), and the children wear a name tag around their necks with the name of the nanny. The normality of CBS, however, does not mean children (or parents) find it "easy." On the contrary—our interview transcripts are full of lamentations about how "hard" the whole process is or was. In what follows, we consider the extent to which CBS is part of children's habitus, before focusing on why CBS is pursued and the physical strain it involves.

Taken for Granted: Daily Mobilities and Children's Habitus

Cross-border schooling is a "strategy" pursued by families from birth, and even prior to conception, in many cases, as the following quotations from interviews indicate:

> Even until the day I gave birth in Hong Kong, I was still hesitant and worried about the troubles and headaches later on. (YQ has two children, one born in China and one in Hong Kong.)

> She was born in Hong Kong. . . . When she was three years old, many Hong Kong–born babies went to Hong Kong for kindergarten, so we did that too. (LSC has two daughters; the younger one was born in Hong Kong.)

In 2017, the Mainland government changed the law to allow some children born in Hong Kong to attend Mainland schools. When the children in our sample were born, however, the only option for Hong Kong–resident children was to commute over the border or to pay extortionate private school fees on the Mainland. Consequently, parents had known, from the time of conception of their second child, that mobility would (out of necessity) become part of their daily lives. The families live within what Xu (2017b) has called a "transborder habitus"—where the border features in their daily lives in a way that has become almost normalized. Most of the young people we have talked to speak of the border in a matter-of-fact way. Some, however, saw their border crossing (especially those that have been doing it for more than a decade) as an "achievement" and a marker of "resilience."

Mobility is an undeniable "hallmark" of their daily lives. For many of the younger children, the school bus is a significant place (representing far more than a mere "mode of transportation") where they spend a great deal of time during the school year. The seating arrangements on the bus, the way it is decorated, the playing of nursery rhymes over the loudspeaker, the moments spent talking and more often sleeping, represent more than just "travel" (Adey 2006; Sheller and Urry 2006; Urry 2000)—they are profoundly formative experiences in children's lives (Gustafson and van der Burgt 2015; Ladru and Gustafson, 2020; Waters 2017).

Several of the families we talked to had "given up" with CBS, finding it too arduous, and instead put their child in (private) school in Shenzhen. This example from one family, in the interview transcript of a mother (YQ), makes this point very well:

> The whole process was very tiring. My husband also understood that I am tired. Because he just got up early in the morning to send us to the port [border-crossing point], he didn't send the kid to school in Hong Kong. But he realized how difficult it was for me and for the kid. . . . By the end of 2017, around November, the weather was cooler, it was harder for the child to get up, and it is more tiring for him. Once upon a time, my son said to the teacher by himself, he said, "I am too tired, I don't want to go to school, I was so tired that I want to drop out, I won't come tomorrow." Then, the teacher called me immediately. At that time, for some Fridays, he also went to interest [extracurricular] classes in Hong Kong, it was like, every Friday, he got up around 6 a.m., he finished all the classes around 4:45 p.m. in the afternoon. I picked up him at school, then sent him to the tutoring centre in Hong Kong. Sometimes he was hungry, I will allow him have dinner first then go to tutoring classes. When we were back to port, it was around 8:00 p.m. already. The child generally cannot get back home until 8:45 p.m., and he was particularly tired. A few times at the port, he lost his temper and cried.

> **Interviewer:** It is very hard.

> Indeed. He was extremely tired. Actually, it took only around 15 minutes from port to home, but you could tell, he was very tired when he cried. So that was the fourth time my husband said, let my son come back.

We will consider in more detail, below, the embodied experiences of CBS.

Here, however, we want to examine some of the reasons why parents continued to endure CBS. As noted above, in 2017 the Mainland government changed its policy, subsequently allowing children with Hong Kong residency status (born to parents with Mainland hukou and property) to apply to public schools on the PRC side of the border. Despite this shift in policy, however, many parents continued to send their children to Hong Kong for school. This reflects a general sense among families that schooling in Hong Kong is "better" and the curriculum is preferred. More specific views were given by the parents we interviewed:

> I like Hong Kong's education very much. . . . The teachers are very responsible and careful. And the class size is small. For instance, there are around twenty-five students in one class in primary school; in the Mainland there are fifty to sixty students in one class. . . . My son, although he is not an excellent student, he has more opportunities to attend activities, competitions, and international exchanges in Hong Kong schools. Besides academic work, I think, it seems that Hong Kong's schools offer more chances for the kids to develop their abilities. (ZYY, has two children. Her younger son has commuted cross-boundary for five years, since he was six years old).

> Hong Kong's education is [. . .] years ahead of the Mainland. Maybe because of the UK's influence. (LXM has two children, both born in Hong Kong. Both commute from Shenzhen for school).

Unpack this notion a little, and the usual tropes around "Westernized" schooling emerge—children are better schooled in the English language, they follow a preferred curriculum, teachers are better trained and qualified. Furthermore, children attain a less tangible form of cultural capital from spending time in Hong Kong, with other Hong Kong resident children. Despite recent massive development occurring in Shenzhen, Hong Kong retains an allure as a "cosmopolitan," Westernized city and a springboard for future mobilities. According to Xu (2017a), Hong Kong people define themselves as having an "autonomous cultural identity" involving (quoting Mathews 1997: 3) "Chineseness plus English/colonial education/colonialism" and "Chineseness plus democracy/human rights/the rule of law" (Xu 2017a:

3). When discussing Mainland Chinese (higher education) students opting to study in Hong Kong, Xu (2017a: 5) rationalizes their decision in relation to what she calls their "Hong Kong dream." This includes

> their yearning to capitalise on Hong Kong's close alignment with international practices and standards, its English-rich environment, abundant opportunities for exposure to cosmopolitan lifestyles and the chances to gain overseas experiences. The last characteristic was reflected in rich imaginations of Hong Kong as a sophisticated and inclusive society, which mirrors what Fong (2011) describes as a yearning for the "developed" world. . . . [T]his Hong Kong dream was enmeshed with these students' positioning of Hong Kong as a flexible space that would enable them to move with ease postgraduation, whether relocating abroad, remaining in Hong Kong, or returning to mainland China.

A similar dream was articulated by our research participants.

> I mean, many kids, in Mainland, they don't have the chance to see a bigger world. They don't have independent thinking. . . . I don't want my kids to become like that. . . . I hope he will become a person with independent thinking. . . . I think, now, China is developing so fast economically, but its education is quite centralized. When you implement the same education to different people, it will definitely cause problems. It is relatively easier to govern like this. And, at the same time, the system doesn't want kids to have too many their own thoughts . . . so I say, China is still a good place for money-making, but I don't want my kids to stay in this environment forever. (TY has two sons—one born in Hong Kong, the other in the United States.)

Children are assumed to acquire, by osmosis, a more global, outward-facing outlook by attending school in Hong Kong, even though a large portion of each day is actually (ironically) spent on a bus. One young man told us that by sending him to Hong Kong for schooling, his parents had assumed he would subsequently go "overseas" (to a Western institution) for university (and he did, to Canada).

Arduous Mobilities

Educational mobilities may often be future-focused strategies, but they are also, for children, very much of the present. It is therefore incumbent on us to reflect on the implications of educational strategies, described above, for children's (and parents') everyday, embodied experiences, emotional and otherwise. Very little of the literature on student mobilities has considered how difficult the experience can be (although see Abelmann and Kang 2014; Waters 2015). Rather, the focus of scholarship has tended to rest on the success of the "strategy" (to what extent capital has been accumulated and status reproduced) (Ong 1999). The privileged nature of students' backgrounds is frequently foregrounded (Findlay et al. 2012). Other mobile children, however are not privileged to the same degree and some face challenging social circumstances. In her book *Children of Global Migration,* Parreñas (2005) explores what she calls the "dismal view of transnational households." She recounts the common responses given to the question "What are the effects of overseas migration to [*sic*] the family?":

> 1. They are neglected. 2. Abandoned. 3. No one is there to watch over the children. 4. The attitudes of children change. 5. They swim in vices. 6. The values you like disappear. 7. They take on vices. 8. Men take on mistresses. 9. Like, with the children, when you leave, they are still small, and when you come back, they are much older. But they do not recognize you as their real parents. And what they want, you have to follow. They get used to having a parent abroad and they are used to always having money. 10. That's true. That's true. (43)

The children we have encountered in CBS households are undoubtedly cared for but are also, for the most part, compelled to undertake their cross-border commute against their will. One of our participants, now an adult, who undertook CBS for twelve years, lamented that he was never, ever, able to play with friends after school (having to board the bus immediately) and that his childhood was, consequently, less rich and fulfilled for that. Chee (2017) draws unambiguous conclusions about how CBS indicates a form of entrapment. However, our findings do seem to indicate that children who have undertaken CBS are relatively "successful" in their schooling and subsequent university outcomes. But more work remains to be done in understanding more precisely the function of CBS in localized class inequalities and social reproduction.

One sixteen-year-old we spoke to had been commuting for ten years. He described his commute during primary school: "From primary one to primary four I took the cross-border bus. From primary four to now I cross the border by myself. . . . [Taking the bus] it was very tiring and difficult during primary one. . . . Everyday I needed to take the bus around 6 a.m. in the morning, came back around 6 p.m. in the evening. That was the hardest time, I think." He continued later: "It was hard. Exhausting. I just wanted to have more sleep. Maybe my other classmates, they lived in Hong Kong, or nearby, they had more time to play around. I had to be in the bus." When asked how he had felt when he started to commute on his own, independently, he replied: "More freedom. Lonely." This perfectly captures the contradictions inherent in CBS—it is at once enabling and restrictive, liberating and highly exhausting. He described needing to drink coffee to stay awake in school.

Waking up early was a commonly mentioned aspect of CBS:

My son got up around 6:05. Some people asked me, why your kid gets up at 6:05 a.m. Most of the kids have to get up at 5:30 in the morning. I said because I think sleep is very important for kids. (YQ has two children. The younger one, a son, commuted for four years before returning to the Mainland to attend private school in Shenzhen a year ago.)

I never complain to my kids about it. I never tell my kids how hard it is. . . . She [daughter] is happy when she leaves home, she is happy when arriving at school; just not very happy during the trip. (LXM has two children born in Hong Kong.)

All of the families we talked to described in detail how tiring CBS was and how this impacted on all aspects of their child's life (friendships, schoolwork, leisure activities), placing huge constraints on their ability to lead what parents described as a "normal" life. A conversation with a group of younger children (ages six to eleven) also raised the issue of sleep:

Researcher: Do you think you get enough sleep every day?

A: Almost.

B: Sometimes tired. On Mondays, quite tired.

C: I am a little bit tired, every day.

Conclusions

Far from being an issue of peripheral importance, the educational mobilities of children and young people are profoundly significant for understanding the contemporary world. Education is becoming more—not less—important as a differentiator, identifier, and giver of life chances, and it is ever more closely tied to migration, globally. Crossing borders for education has geo-political and geo-social implications.

Education within the Chinese diaspora has been widely studied: the literature has tended to emphasize a number of aspects in relation to this. First, education is equated with cultural capital and social reproduction within the Chinese family or household. Second, children embody the accumulation of capital. And, third, migratory strategies related to education tend to be successful and undertaken by relatively privileged elites. Consequently, there has been a need to redress some of these misleading assumptions, as we have done in our project on CBS involving the Hong Kong–Shenzhen political border. Here, we have focused on the daily commuting of children with Hong Kong residency status living with their families in Mainland China. In this article, we have considered the extent to which daily mobilities are part of young people's habitus and why education (specifically the difference between schooling offered in Hong Kong and Mainland China) is such an important consideration in CBS. We then focused on the corporeal realities of CBS, particularly how tiring and arduous young people (and parents) find it to be. With this, we wanted to stress that for the young people themselves, the concept of "body-capital" and the importance of the future in CBS have no meaning when they are concerned with day-to-day survival. The importance of children's daily experiences needs to become more prominent, we argue, in work conceptualizing educational migration.

Notes

Johanna Waters would like to thank Sari Ishii for her kind invitation to present a version of this article in Tokyo, which was a truly memorable experience. The authors also extend their gratitude to Sari, Rhacel Parreñas, and Nicola Piper for their comments and guidance. Yunyun Qin has been a wonderful research assistant on this project, and without the support of the research participants, this project would be nothing. Thank you to all involved.

1   *Hukou* is the geographical system of household registration used in Mainland China. Possession of hukou determines access to jobs, health care, and schooling for children.

References

Abelmann, Nancy, and Jiyeon Kang. 2014. "Memoir/Manuals of South Korean Pre-College Study Abroad: Defending Mothers and Humanizing Children." *Global Networks* 14, no. 1: 1–22.

Adey, Peter. 2006. "If Mobility Is Everything Then It Is Nothing: Towards a Relational Politics of (Im)mobilities." *Mobilities* 1, no. 1: 75–94.

Bourdieu, Pierre. 1984. *Distinction: A Social Critique of the Judgement of Taste*, translated by Richard Nice. Cambridge, MA: Harvard University Press.

Bourdieu, Pierre. 1986. "The Forms of Capital." In *Handbook of Theory and Research for the Sociology of Education*, edited by John G. Richardson, 241–58. Westport, CT: Greenwood Press.

Bourdieu, Pierre. 1990. *The Logic of Practice*, translated by Richard Nice. Stanford, CA: Stanford University Press.

Chan, Anita K., and Lucille L. S. Ngan. 2018. "Investigating the Differential Mobility Experiences of Chinese Cross-Border Students." *Mobilities* 13, no. 1: 142–56.

Chee, Wai-chi 2017. "Trapped in the Current of Mobilities: China–Hong Kong Cross-Border Families." *Mobilities* 12, no. 2: 199–212.

Chew, Phyllis Ghim-Lian. 2010. "Linguistic Capital, Study Mothers, and the Transnational Family in Singapore." In *Globalization of Language and Culture in Asia: The Impact of Globalization Processes on Language*, edited by Viniti Vaish, 82–105. London: Continuum.

Chiu, Tuen Yi, and Susanne Y. P. Choi. 2018. "Frequent Border-Crossing Children and Cultural Membership." *Population, Space, and Place*, April 16. doi.org/10.1002/psp.2153.

Chua, Amy. 2011. *Battle Hymn of the Tiger Mother*. New York: Penguin.

Collins, Francis. 2008. "Of Kimchi and Coffee: Globalisation, Transnationalism, and Familiarity in Culinary Consumption." *Social and Cultural Geography* 9, no. 2: 151–69.

Cresswell, Tim. 2006. *On the Move: Mobility in the Modern Western World*. New York: Routledge.

Findlay, Allan, Russell King, Fiona M. Smith, Alistair Geddes, and Ron Skeldon. 2012. "World Class? An Investigation of Globalisation, Difference, and International Student Mobility." *Transactions of the Institute of British Geographers* 37, no. 1: 118–31.

Findlay, Allan, Laura Prazeres, David McCollum, and Helen Packwood. 2017. "'It Was Always the Plan': International Study as 'Learning to Migrate.'" *Area* 49, no. 2: 192–99.

Finn, Kirsty, and Mark Holton. 2019. *Everyday Mobile Belonging: Theorising Higher Education Student Mobilities*. London: Bloomsbury Academic.

Fong, Vanessa. 2011. *Paradise Redefined: Transnational Chinese Students and the Quest for Flexible Citizenship in the Developed World*. Stanford, CA: Stanford University Press.

Forsberg, Sara. 2017a. "Educated to Be Global: Transnational Horizons of Middle-Class Students in Kerala, India." *Environment and Planning A: Economy and Space* 49, no. 9: 2099–2115.

Forsberg, Sara. 2017b. "'The Right to Immobility' and the Uneven Distribution of Spatial Capital: Negotiating Youth Transitions in Northern Sweden." *Social and Cultural Geography* 20, no. 3: 1–21.

Goldthorpe, John H. 1996. "Class Analysis and the Reorientation of Class Theory: The Case of Persisting Differentials in Educational Attainment." *British Journal of Sociology* 47, no. 3: 481–505.

Gustafson, Katarina, and Danielle van der Burgt. 2015. "'Being on the Move': Time-Spatial Organisation and Mobility in a Mobile Preschool." *Journal of Transport Geography* 46, no. 4: 201–9.

Ho, Elaine L. E. 2017. "The Geo-Social and Global Geographies of Power: Urban Aspirations of 'Worlding' African Students in China." *Geopolitics* 22, no. 1: 15–33.

Holloway, Sarah L., Sarah L. O'Hara, and Helena Pimlott-Wilson. 2012. "Educational Mobility and the Gendered Geography of Cultural Capital: The Case of International Student Flows between Central Asia and the UK." *Environment and Planning A: Economy and Space* 44, no. 9: 2278–94.

Hyndman, Jennifer. 2001. "Towards a Feminist Geopolitics." *Canadian Geographer* 45, no. 2: 210–22.

Kang, Jiyeon, and Nancy Abelmann. 2011. "The Domestication of South Korean Pre-College Study Abroad in the First Decade of the Millennium." *Journal of Korean Studies* 16, no. 1: 89–118.

Katz, Cindi. 2008. "Cultural Geographies Lecture: Childhood as Spectacle: Relays of Anxiety and the Reconfiguration of the Child." *Cultural Geographies* 15, no. 1: 5–17.

Katz, Cindi. 2011. "Accumulation, Excess, Childhood: Toward a Countertopography of Risk and Waste." *Documents d'anàlisi geogràfica* 57, no. 1: 47–60.

Katz, Cindi. 2017. "The Angel of Geography: Superman, Tiger Mother, Aspiration Management, and the Child as Waste." *Progress in Human Geography*, May 17. doi.org/10.1177/0309132517708844.

Kenway, Jane, Johanna Fahey, Debbie Epstein, Aaron Koh, Cameron McCarthy, and Faisal Rizvi. 2017. *Class Choreographies: Elite Schools and Globalization*. New York: Springer.

Kipnis, Andrew B. 2011. *Governing Educational Desire: Culture, Politics, and Schooling in China*. Chicago: University of Chicago Press.

Kobayashi, Audrey, and Valerie Preston. 2007. "Transnationalism through the Life Course: Hong Kong Immigrants in Canada." *Asia Pacific Viewpoint* 48, no. 2: 151–67.

Ladru, Danielle Ekman, and Katarina Gustafson. 2020. "Children's Collective Embodiment—Mobility Practices and Materialities in Mobile Preschools." *Population, Space, and Place* 26, no. 3: e2322.

Lee, Sunhwa, and Mary C. Brinton. 1996. "Elite Education and Social Capital: The Case of South Korea." *Sociology of Education* 69, no. 3: 177–92.

Lee, Yean-Ju, and Hagen Koo. 2006. "'Wild Geese Fathers' and a Globalised Family Strategy for Education in Korea." *International Development Planning Review* 28, no. 4: 533–53.

Leung, Maggi W. H. 2013. "'Read Ten Thousand Books, Walk Ten Thousand Miles': Geographical Mobility and Capital Accumulation among Chinese Scholars." *Transactions of the Institute of British Geographers* 38, no. 2: 311–24.

Lo, Adrienne, Nancy Abelmann, Soo Ah Kwon, and Sumie Okazaki, eds. 2017. *South Korea's Education Exodus: The Life and Times of Early Study Abroad*. Seattle: University of Washington Press.

Marginson, Simon. 2008. "Global Field and Global Imagining: Bourdieu and Worldwide Higher Education." *British Journal of Sociology of Education* 29, no. 3: 303–15.

Mathews, Gordon. 1997. "Hèunggóngyàhn: On the Past, Present, and Future of Hong Kong Identity." *Bulletin of Concerned Asian Scholars* 29, no. 3: 3–13.

Matthews, Julie, and Ravinder Sidhu. 2005. "Desperately Seeking the Global Subject: International Education, Citizenship, and Cosmopolitanism." *Globalisation, Societies, and Education* 3, no. 1: 49–66.

Maxwell, Claire, and Peter Aggleton, eds. 2015. *Elite Education: International Perspectives*. London: Routledge.

Mitchell, Katharyne, and Kirsi Pauliina Kallio. 2017. "Spaces of the Geosocial: Exploring Transnational Topologies." *Geopolitics* 22, no. 1: 1–14.

Mitchell, Katharyne, Sallie A. Marston, and Cindi Katz, eds. 2004. *Life's Work: Geographies of Social Reproduction*. Malden, MA: Blackwell Publishing.

Ong, Aihwa. 1999. *Flexible Citizenship: The Cultural Logics of Transnationality*. Durham, NC: Duke University Press.

Park, Joseph Sung-Yui, and Sohee Bae. 2009. "Language Ideologies in Educational Migration: Korean Jogi Yuhak Families in Singapore." *Linguistics and Education* 20, no. 4: 366–77.

Parreñas, Rhacel S. 2005. *Children of Global Migration: Transnational Families and Gendered Woes*. Stanford, CA: Stanford University Press.

Robertson, Susan L. 2011. "The New Spatial Politics of (Re)Bordering and (Re)Ordering the State-Education-Citizen Relation." *International Review of Education* 57, nos. 3–4: 277–97.

Sheller, Mimi, and John Urry. 2006. "The New Mobilities Paradigm." *Environment and Planning A: Economy and Space*, February 1. doi.org/10.1068/a37268.

Skeldon, Ronald. 1994. *Reluctant Exiles? Migration from Hong Kong and the New Overseas Chinese*. Armonk, NY: M. E. Sharpe.

Urry, John. 2000. *Sociology beyond Societies: Mobilities for the Twenty-First Century*. London: Routledge.

Waters, Johanna L. 2002. "Flexible Families? 'Astronaut' Households and the Experiences of Lone Mothers in Vancouver, British Columbia." *Social and Cultural Geography* 3, no. 2: 117–34.

Waters, Johanna L. 2003. "Flexible Citizens? Transnationalism and Citizenship amongst Economic Immigrants in Vancouver." *Canadian Geographer* 47, no. 3: 219–34.

Waters, Johanna L. 2015. "Dysfunctional Mobilities: International Education and the Chaos of Movement." *Handbook of Children and Youth Studies*, edited by Johanna Wyn and Helen Cahill, 679–88. Singapore: Springer.

Waters, Johanna L. 2017. "Education Unbound? Enlivening Debates with a Mobilities Perspective on Learning." *Progress in Human Geography* 41, no. 3: 279–98.

Waters, Johanna, and Maggi W. H. Leung. 2020. "Rhythms, Flows, and Structures of Cross-Boundary Schooling: State Power and Educational Mobilities between Shenzhen and Hong Kong." *Population, Space, and Place* 26, no. 3: e2298.

Xu, Cora Lingling. 2017a. "Mainland Chinese Students at an Elite Hong Kong University: Habitus-Field Disjuncture in a Transborder Context." *British Journal of Sociology of Education* 38, no. 5: 610–24.

Xu, Cora Lingling. 2017b. "Transborder Habitus in a Within-Country Mobility Context: A Bourdieusian Analysis of Mainland Chinese Students in Hong Kong." *Sociological Review*, September 26. doi.org/10.1177/0038026117732669.

Yang, Peidong. 2018. "Compromise and Complicity in International Student Mobility: The Ethnographic Case of Indian Medical Students at a Chinese University." *Discourse: Studies in the Cultural Politics of Education*, February 7. doi.org/10.1080/01596306.2018.1435600.

Zhou, Min. 1998. "'Parachute Kids' in Southern California: The Educational Experience of Chinese Children in Transnational Families." *Educational Policy* 12, no. 6: 682–704.

Transperipheral Educational Mobility: Less Privileged South Korean Young Adults Pursuing English Language Study in a Peripheral City in the Philippines

Carolyn Areum Choi

As various observers have noted, English has become the main language of the global economy, business, technology, and politics (Pennycook 2017; Crystal 2012). Within Asia, the largest sending region of international students in the world (UNESCO 2013; Collins 2013), English as foreign language acquisition (EFL) has become a major driving force of contemporary migration and mobility flows among young people, especially in countries where English is not a native language (Nguyen 2012).[1] In a number of states including China, Japan, Vietnam, and South Korea, governments and ministries of education have implemented English language policies within formal schooling systems to usher in a new era of globalization, signaling English is the dominant language of the global economy (Nguyen 2012; Hu 2005; Park and Abelmann 2004; Kobayashi 2007). As a result, EFL is now seen as a necessity to achieve middle-class mobility in a globalizing world.

positions 30:2 DOI 10.1215/10679847-9573396
Copyright 2022 by Duke University Press

Since the turn of the twenty-first century, English language education has been integrated as part of South Korea's national strategy for building global competitiveness and collective national identity. Starting with former president Kim Young Sam's *segyehwa* campaign, which opened South Korea's doors to globalization, English was heralded as a key resource for human capital development in an increasingly precarious labor market (Park and Abelmann 2004; Schattle 2013; Sung, Park, and Choi 2013; Yoon 2015). As South Korea shifted from a developmental state to a neoliberal model of economic governance following the 1997 Asian financial crisis (Song 2009), the onus of developing English competencies was transferred from the state to individuals and their families, exacerbating inequalities for those who cannot afford to participate in private education (Abelmann, Park, and Kim 2009; Park 2011). With the highest monthly spending on private education in the world (M. Yoon 2014), South Korea among other countries in Asia has become an important social laboratory for exploring the consequences of neoliberal educational policies (Anagnost 2013; Lukacs 2015), especially its impacts among low-resourced families and students.

This article examines underexplored flows of South Korean educational mobility for English language acquisition to provincial destinations in the industrializing Asian world. Educational destinations in provincial regions of the Global South have emerged as cheaper alternatives for private educational consumption than existing options. They offer more cost-effective rates compared to those in metropolitan centers of the Global North, such as Los Angeles, Sydney, or Toronto, and also in urbanized regions of the Global South, like Manila. The commercialization of English language competencies in former colonial Anglophone countries (Ortiga 2018) or what applied linguist Braj Kachru (1992) refers to as "Outer Circle" countries, has produced low-cost options for private English language education that make private supplemental education affordable and accessible for economically constrained youth looking to participate in the global economy. Building on the growing body of literature on educational migration and international migration, my research examines the rise of peripheral cities in the Global South as emerging sites of private educational consumption for a wider swath of South Korean youth. It is also a window into understanding how students reimagine their futures more broadly and creatively in the context of emerging and expanding global markets in Asia and beyond.

Using in-depth interviews and participant-observation with South Korean educational migrants in the Philippines and South Korea, I highlight class and regional differences in a pattern of youth mobility I call "transperipheral educational mobility."[2] Transperipheral educational mobility describes a strategy pursued by less-privileged South Korean youth, largely from smaller provincial cities outside the metropolitan capital of Seoul, who opt for low-cost private English education programs in peripheral regions of the Philippines.[3] This movement is largely in response to the South Korean government's calls for global citizenship, which expects its upcoming generation of youth to bear the weight of the country's broader ambitions to become a global power. Even though the credentials that educational migrants earn in peripheral destinations can be perceived as "undervalued" in and of themselves, my research finds that these migrants' transperipheral educational mobility and their access to educational experiences in the provincial Philippines grant them the means to alternative capital building that holds value for them beyond any calculated labor market ascendance.

Educational Migrations in the Peripheries

The international migration literature has privileged the study of South to North as well as East to West flows. Informed by world-system theory (Wallerstein 2004), the literature has framed its analysis in terms of a core-periphery model, which posits an uneven distribution of global flows, goods, and materials from "peripheral" countries in the Global South to developed "core" countries in the Global North. International students have often been conflated with "skilled migrants" and subsequently incorporated into existing paradigms of core periphery. Such studies typically focus on the pattern of elite students from the Global South/East migrating to destinations in the Global North/West, where they earn educational credentials that enhance their competitiveness in professional labor markets not only back home but also abroad (Ong 1999; Brooks and Waters 2011). As such, international students are viewed as central constituents to what economists have called the "brain drain," referring to skilled professionals or international students who settle in large numbers in receiving countries of the Global North (Miyagiwa 1991). In this configuration, peripheral countries depend on core countries as centers of elite knowledge production (Altbach 1981; Quy 2010) and class reproduction. Such perspectives, however, often neglect to see the ways in which regions in the South and East can also be transformed by globalization.

With the exponential growth of international student mobilities as a major driver of international migration, the core-periphery model has become increasingly contested in the last several decades. Although countries such as the United States and the United Kingdom continue to dominate as the largest receiving regions of international students, the ever-shifting landscape of international education has increasingly moved beyond core regions, challenging existing assumptions of educational mobilities as unidirectional and elite. With Asia becoming the largest sending region of international students in the world, a growing body of work has interrogated the broader scope of the global educational landscape, documenting the rise of budget-friendly "regional educational hubs" as alternatives to the West (Collins et al. 2014; Mok 2011; Sidhu, Ho, and Yeoh 2011). Those hubs include state-supported higher educational zones in affluent Asian cities such as Singapore, Hong Kong, and Doha, while "unlikely" educational destinations in the Global South are also on the rise (Ortiga 2018). The latter includes former colonial English-speaking destinations, with places such as the Philippines and India (Ortiga 2018; Lipura, 2021) offering some of the most affordable educational opportunities in the market. By opening up analysis to a larger diversity of educational landscapes and destinations, scholars have begun to expose the inherent contradictions of the capitalist model of international education as a neutral and liberatory process (Madge, Raghuram, and Noxolo 2009) and to consider how differential pathways of migration can reflect the class and gender stratification in home societies (Xiang and Shen 2009; Park and Abelmann 2004).

Meanwhile, discussions of peripheral areas as destinations have largely focused on the movement of affluent migrants. Beginning with studies on counterurbanization, researchers have examined the relocation of people from urban to rural areas, particularly urban middle-class families who pursue more comfortable lives in the countryside (Halfacree 2008). With a focus on interregional moves within Europe, the peripheral was largely conceptualized as a romantic and idyllic countryside representing a "prominent aspiration" or an "alternative universe to that of our present postmodern capitalist world" (Halfacree 2008: 485). With the transnational turn in migration studies, recent studies on tourism and lifestyle migration have redirected their focus toward the rise of North to South relocations in designated retirement or expat hubs in peripheral regions of the Global South. Scholars exploring such flows have centered on retirees (Bozic 2006), amenity migrants (Gossnell and Abrams 2011), digital nomads (Green 2020), and residential tourists (McWatters 2008).

More contemporary work on international peripheral migrations have complicated earlier representations based on the frictionless movement of people from the Global North to the Global South (Hayes 2018; Rivers-Moore 2016). Decolonial studies researchers have situated North-South migrations within the larger context of the global division of labor between high-cost and low-cost regions, with the practices of transnational consumption and gentrification in low-cost regions reflecting a deeper history of colonial domination from northern Europe and North America (Hayes 2018; Quijano 2000). The historically higher incomes accrued to higher-cost regions reproduce the ability of people in these regions to purchase the labor power of workers from low-cost regions and lay claim to capitalistic uses of local spaces—as in the case of tourism or lifestyle migration (Hayes 2018; Ong 2006).

South Korean educational mobilities to the Philippines are another example of North to South migrations, where educational migrants maximize their relative economic power to make more consumer choices within low-cost destinations. At the same time, the shared histories of US empire and military occupation in South Korea and the Philippines add another dimension, informing contemporary social relations between South Korean migrants and Filipino locals. Following the Cold War, countries previously occupied or invaded by colonial powers were pitted against one another in the race for modernization. Upheld as the model of economic development, South Koreans came to believe that they were the only one of the few groups of people to overcome US imperialism with successful capitalistic development

(D. Kim 2016). The Philippines, on the other hand, which experienced longer periods of colonialism, were viewed by Koreans as an economically failed nation that fell outside global capitalistic society (D. Kim 2016).

Such racial histories have informed South Koreans' increasing purchasing, racial, and cultural power in the twenty-first century, producing a racial consciousness of "Koreanness" rooted in symbolic associations of geopolitical, economic, and racialized privilege and power that shape South Koreans' everyday social relations with local Filipino people.[4] In situating South Korean transperipheral mobilities within the larger context of educational mobilities and North-to-South migration, my research investigates the unexplored emergence of mobility flows to provincial cities in the Philippines as sites of educational accumulation for economically constrained educational migrants.

The Rise of Peripheral Youth on the Move to the Global South

Existing research on South Korean youth has exclusively focused on the experiences of those from metropolitan areas, largely from the global city of Seoul (Abelmann, Park, and Kim 2009; Jung 2017; Song 2007). With close to half of the country's total inhabitants, Seoul is undeniably central to any sociological study of South Korea. However, a focus on Seoul comes at the expense of the perspectives of those from peripheral cities. In advocating for perspectives of South Korean youth on the margins, I examine how their experiences of English study abroad are inflected with class, regional, educational inequalities.

During South Korea's rapid economic development and modernization phase, Seoul became the epicenter of South Korean economic and industrial life, drawing internal migrants from the countryside who left in search of education and work opportunities (Jung 2017). Rural to urban migration in South Korea set in motion regional imbalances (Jung 2017) that would later differentially impact younger populations (Jeon 2012). After decades of authoritarian control, South Korea's first civilian-elected president, Kim Young Sam, embraced globalization policies as a means to accelerate South Korea's global competition as well as distance himself from South Korea's authoritarian past (Park and Abelmann 2004). Centralizing English education was a cornerstone of his social policies for building global competitiveness and human capital development (Jeon and Lee 2006; Jung and Norton 2002; Park 2009). The state's push for English-speaking "global citizens" contributed to the rise of a multibillion-dollar private English education market in South Korea, which operates alongside formal education systems (Park and Abelmann 2004). Despite a series of moratoriums on private education, one study found that more than 70 percent of South Korean children in Seoul are enrolled in private English education (Park and Abelmann 2004).

Regional inequalities in contemporary educational migration flows are closely related to entrenched class inequalities and polarization among youth in South Korea (Kang and Abelmann 2011; Koo 2007; Yang 2018). Toward the end of the 1990s, the 1997 Asian financial crisis occurred, making way for the rise of neoliberal labor and educational structures (Song 2009). Under the guidance of the International Monetary Fund, South Korea restructured its economic systems, outsourcing factory production to the Global South and replacing lifetime employment with part-time, contractual, precarious labor (Song 2009). Youth, particularly from provincial and rural cities, bore the brunt of these changes, facing the highest rates of unemployment and irregular employment in the following decades (Cheng and Kim 2014; Chun and Han 2015; Hyundai Research Institute 2018; Song 2007; K. Yoon 2015). Youth from peripheral cities likewise faced disadvantages in terms of higher education. Despite that the majority of South Korean youth do attend college; the stratification of higher education socially and economically privileges those with degrees from colleges based in Seoul, marking them as more prestigious than those in the provinces (Abelmann, Park, and Kim 2009; Chae and Hong 2009). Youth who leave the provinces for colleges in Seoul generally tend to have better labor prospects, while those who remain behind and obtain degrees from regional, low-ranked colleges have fewer opportunities in the job market (Chae and Hong 2009).

Lee Myung Bak's presidential administration (2007–13) doubled down on existing neoliberal English educational policies, largely as a solution to youth unemployment, consequently fueling private spending on English education. Targeting populations deemed "English deficit," the state introduced a number of programs including the establishment of global English villages, the recruitment of foreign English teachers, and the introduction of youth and young adult migration programs to liberalize access to English language learning (Jeon 2012; Yoon 2015). With regard to migration, the government initiated a number of programs having to do with language exchange, internships, and labor migration (Yoon 2015). In particular, working-class youth have pursued education abroad primarily via the working holiday program, which allows young people from age eighteen to thirty to live in another country for up to two years in exchange for their low-wage labor (Chun and Han 2015).

The push for English language learning, combined with the deregulated expansion of the international educational market, produced a fertile climate for the rise of English language destinations in the "Expanding Circle" countries (Kachru 1992) of the Global South or countries where English is spoken but does not have primary-language status. Scholars studying neoliberal educational reforms in Asia have foregrounded this work, illustrating how the adoption of international education, including language education, as an economic resource has helped produce "regional educational hubs" in wealthier Asian destinations such as Singapore, Seoul, or Hong Kong that are able to retain regional higher educational student flows often bound for the West (Collins 2013; Mok 2011; Sidhu, Ho, and Yeoh 2011). In recent years, more affordable destinations such as the Philippines, India, Saipan, and even Malta have joined efforts to internationalize their education systems with international educational brokerage agencies playing an instrumental role in connecting students to these "unlikely" locations. In South Korea, for instance, educational brokers were largely successful in introducing *yonge yonsu* programs that connected the state's working holiday program with English language programs in the Philippines (Chun and Han, 2015).

Newer reports have underscored the rise of Philippines as a popular "transit destination" for foreign students to learn English or study in English language institutions at a discount (Ortiga 2018). For instance, Yasmin Ortiga (2018) illustrates how private universities in the Philippines capitalize on degree programs such as nursing and engineering that offer the best opportunities in international labor markets and are in demand among foreign students. Degree programs at private universities are not the only lure for foreign students. Capturing a larger share of the international student market are Philippine English language programs with a total of 31,000 Special Study Permits (or residency permits for short-term study) issued in 2012 (ICEF 2016). The vast majority of English language students are South Koreans and Japanese, with growing numbers from Vietnam, Taiwan, Brazil, Russia, and Libya. While most universities in the Philippines do operate auxiliary English language programs, the English language industry is likewise made up of smaller stand-alone English language schools, many of which are products of direct foreign investment and cater to a specific ethnic or national demographic of foreign students.

South Korean students make up three-fourths of the number of students who obtain special study permits in the Philippines each year (ICEF 2016). As a result, Korean-owned English language schools dominate the stand-alone English language school industry in the Philippines, the first schools having been established during the largest wave of Korean emigration to the Philippines in the 1990s. While the majority of language schools were originally based in metropolitan areas like Manila or Cebu, the surge in educational migration in the past decade has resulted in its geographical market expansion to the peripheral cities of Iloilo, Baguio, Clark, Bacolod, and Davao. EFL programs in peripheral cities boast cheaper rates, less crime, freedom from urban distractions, and adjacency to vacation destinations. Meanwhile, these locations are also in close proximity to call-center hubs, which secures a steady supply of educated, fluent English-speaking Filipino workers. Provincial educational destinations in the Global South are now productive sites of educational consumption for less-privileged South Korean educational migrants, many from provincial cities in South Korea, who desire to become global citizens but do not have the means to study in countries in the Global North.

Methods

This study's findings are based on ethnographic research conducted between 2015 to 2017 in the home country of South Korea and the host country of the Philippines. My primary fieldwork was based on participant-observation at an English language school in the Philippines. I gained access to field sites through a multistep process. First, I attended study-abroad fairs in Seoul and Busan, where I met with owners and staff of Philippine-based English language schools who later invited me to several of these institutions. I chose to undertake fieldwork at Oceanside English Language School in Bacolod in exchange for working as an unpaid volunteer tutor.[5] During my four months at Oceanside, I attended and taught classes, and lived in a student dormitory with other students.

I also carried out forty-one in-depth, semistructured interviews and demographic surveys with South Korean educational migrants studying in the Philippines. Additionally, I conducted supplemental interviews with Oceanside administrators and staff as well as Filipino tutors. The interview topics included class and family background, migration process, educational background, and past work experiences. Most of the students came from working-class or middle-class backgrounds, with a larger number of their parents involved in small business, service jobs, transportation, manufacturing, though some were in white-collar and government positions. While age varied from the twenties to the early thirties, close to half of the participants in my study were in their mid-twenties at the time of interview. While most were currently pursuing or had previously pursued a college education, almost all of them, with the exception of five individuals, were from colleges outside of Seoul. Around three-quarters of the sample of comprised migrants who were in the workforce either as part-time working students or as full-time workers, with the rest able to be nonworking, full-time college students. Most in the workforce were in the irregular, part-time, contingent labor sectors working as cashiers, servers, entry-level secretaries, and food deliverers, among other jobs, although some were white-collar workers. During 2017–18, I conducted follow-up interviews with twenty-three returnees living in their hometowns, including the South Korean cities of Busan, Iksan, Seoul, An-dong, Gumi, Pyeongtaek, and Gwangju. The interviews were conducted in Korean and audio-recorded.

English Education as a Second Shot

Every night after dinner at the cafeteria, Seungyob would rush back to his desk in the communal study room to kick-start his late-night study session, staying until midnight when the custodian would turn off the lights. In a sea of anonymous desks, Seungyob's was distinctly marked by a large stack of workbooks, a dizzy sprawl of handmade flashcards, and a giant stuffed Ryan doll—who, Seungyob jokes, is there to keep the bad spirits away.[6] Even on weekend nights when some of his friends insist that he join them for some drinks and dancing at the local karaoke bar to take the edge off the week of studying, Seungyob tends to (albeit politely) decline, putting up with the mild round of backlash from his ever-persistent friends.

But with only a couple of months left until his college entrance exam, everyone knew that nothing could break Seungyob's focus and determination. Seungyob, a high school graduate, who had in the past year completed his compulsory military service, was going to take the college entrance exam for the first time to facilitate his admission to college—as a last-ditch hope in resetting his future. Seungyob is typical of many of the South Korean youth I met in Bacolod; they are learning English language skills to better navigate their social mobility and labor prospects in South Korea. In South Korea, English language skills are part of what has been called *specsaggi* ("spec," a shortening of "specification," meaning "qualification," and "saggi" meaning "to accumulate"), which describes the varied résumé-building activities that allow pre-market job seekers to appeal to future employers (Cho 2015). Even for college seekers like Seungyob, English language skills constitute a major component of college admission exams like the College Scholastic Ability Test, the transfer student exam, and other tests. Since the dramatic shift from full-time secure employment to flexible part-time labor schemes, specsaggi has intensified, becoming a central feature of the school-to-work transitional experience for South Korean youth. It is not uncommon for many South Korean college students to delay their college graduation and set aside time to focus on collecting qualifications (Chun and Han 2015; K. Yoon 2015). English study abroad is a popular spec that young South Koreans invest in.

South Korean students I met in the Philippines profess they would have liked to have been able to study abroad for a year in the Global North—namely, in richer and more developed countries such as the United States and Australia. Pursuing English language studies in Los Angeles or Sydney would not only allow them to gain the type of spec they would need to appeal

to employers but also would fulfill their *romang* as first-time travelers—
that is, making real the fantasies of living abroad that they have seen in
Hollywood dramas. Indeed, some do plan to eventually make their way to
the Global North as labor migrants via working holiday schemes or through
coordinated study packages that allow them to study in different destinations (Choi 2021). For youth who cannot afford to study in the Global North,
English language schools in the Philippines represent a low-cost alternative
for improving English skills while fulfilling travel and cosmopolitan desires.
In contrast to Seoul-based private educational centers that cost $1,000 to
$1,500 per month for tuition alone, schools in peripheral cities in the Philip-
pines charge only $500 to $900 per month for access to a study environment
equipped with a five- to eight-hour daily class schedule, housing, home-
cooked meals three times a day, complimentary housekeeping and laundry
services, security, and three to four hours of "one-on-one" classes with Filipino English tutors (this last feature was pointed out as the biggest draw).
Tuition in the Philippines, students said, would be easily recoupable after
a few months of working part-time once they were back in South Korea.

Many schools operated "Sparta" or "Semi-Sparta" campuses, which were
meant to have a strict, disciplinary campus culture where mandatory study
hours, limited off-campus access, and "English only" zones were enforced.
Such a "no-frills" approach to study preparation has enabled students, especially low-resourced ones, to take advantage of their time in school in the
Philippines as a way to catch up on skills that they feel like they missed out
on during their previous education. While South Korean students are motivated to study English abroad because of the culture of specsaggi, they often
characterize the graduation certificates that they receive after they finish the
program in the Philippines as not counting as spec. For this reason, some
even say that they will leave it out of their résumés altogether. As Jae Yeon, a
mid-twenties college graduate from Gumi, explains, "The Philippines is not
an English speaking country. . . . A future employer might even read me as
poor because I couldn't afford to study in an English speaking country . . .
so if it's not going to count, I would rather just leave it out."

The Philippines is considered to rank lower on the English educational
destination hierarchy with speakers of English in the Philippines often perceived as not "legitimate [English] speakers" (Jang 2018). Scholars such as Il

Chull Jang (2018) and Ryuko Kubota (2009) have written about the disconnect between authenticity and legitimacy in producing English language hierarchies and how a speaker's legitimacy is often linked to nonlinguistic power relations. This was also the case for Korean American English teachers in South Korea who are often viewed as less legitimate English speakers than white English teachers (Cho 2012). The Philippine state's commercialization of English competence as an exported source of global labor—from migrant domestic workers to domestic call center workers—largely informs international perceptions about its legitimacy. The global image of Filipino English as a form of "service English" explains the deflated and resigned attitudes of South Korean students learning English in the Philippines.

Given the concern that English language study experiences in the Philippines will not be viewed as an appealing spec to prospective employers, many young people saw their experiences in the Philippines instead as a type of English language "training ground" where they could accumulate intermediate forms of educational capital. As Hobin, a mid-twenties educational migrant from Iksan, explains, "Learning English in the Philippines is not going to open the doors to a good college or a future career. It is a place where I can hole up and lock into my studies. It keeps me focused and away from all the distractions. That is what is going to get me into school, it is my scores." Aware that their overseas experiences in a peripheral city in the Philippines will not carry weight in the professional labor market back home, South Korean students still go to such a place to gain preliminary cultural capital in the form of English language skills, which they may then parlay into more "valued" credentials and qualifications (such as good English test scores or an improved English-speaking ability) once they become job seekers.

English assessment exams potentially transform the precultural capital acquired in the Philippines into valuable cultural capital. Since the introduction of English education into the South Korean primary school system in the 1990s, English has become increasingly incorporated into standardized assessment exams for high school graduation, college admission, college graduation, college transfer admissions, and the professional labor market. Regardless of whether a job requires English communication skills, major corporations such as Samsung and LG require that job applicants have good English language competency scores on tests such as the TOEIC (Test of

English for International Communication). The function of these sites as quintessential cram schools is further reinforced by the large number of college partnerships that schools have established with universities in South Korea to provide supplemental educational opportunities for students who need to meet minimum TOEIC requirements for college graduation.

A number of students at Oceanside were between one level of education and the next, taking exams with English components to get into a college or to transfer from a two-year college to a four-year college. This was the case of twenty-six-year-old Banjang from An-dong. Unlike Seungyob, Banjang dropped out of high school in his last year because of what he described as a "lack of motivation" after his father ran into financial troubles. On leaving school, Banjang began working near home as a food delivery motorist, which he did for several years, making minimum wage. He envisioned saving up enough money to start his own small pub sometime in the near future. However, the difficulty of saving money while having to support his parents put a damper on Banjang's dreams. While Banjang originally had no concrete intention of going back to school, he had a change of heart after a friend introduced him to the world of stock trading. Excited by the possibility of "big payouts" that seemed to loom ahead, he became motivated to go back to school to eventually earn a General Equivalency Diploma for high school.

However, An-dong, a smaller city in eastern South Korea, did not have a large concentration of college preparatory academies that could help him prepare for his exam. According to Banjang, most education centers were located in big cities like Seoul, and a move to Seoul for his education would cost his family thousands of dollars in housing and tuition fees each month. He also pointed out another barrier to taking up residence in a place like Seoul for college preparation: most independent housing in South Korea typically requires a large deposit of more than ten thousand dollars, an amount he and his family could not afford. Banjang settled on the Philippines as his "English and college preparation boot camp," which he could afford by using part of his savings. For Banjang, studying in the Philippines did not feel like a choice but the only way to pursue his goal of attending college.

Like Banjang, many of the students in my study represent the experiences of nonelite South Korean youth struggling to meet the increasing demands for English put on them by the South Korean state, the labor market, and society. These students are not part of the earlier the "education exodus" (Abelmann et al. 2015) undertaken by members of an earlier generation, who typically went abroad to Western countries for a second chance at success (Brooks and Waters 2009) in the South Korean labor market. Rather, the students in my study are in many ways latecomers to private education, who have been compelled to invest in English education because of changing expectations in the labor market and education system at a moment when barriers to participate in terms of travel and costs have been lowered. Many of them are from peripheral cities outside of Seoul who face more spatial, class, and education-related inequalities than metropolitan youth. Their circumstances demonstrate the ways in which class stratification becomes extended into a transnational context (Kang and Abelmann 2011) and how migrants themselves navigate the stratifying effects of educational migration hierarchies in creative ways.

Compensatory Middle-Class Consumption

"Woogahlong!" Dahae cried out in her accented Hiligaynon as she handed the passenger next to her a handful of pesos to pass down to the driver in front of the jeepney.[7] It was my first day at Oceanside, and Dahae, my roommate for the next few months, asked me to join her for dinner and drinks after classes in the center of town. While I was used to the mostly rural landscape where Oceanside was based, I was shocked to see in the center of town a spanking new, football stadium–sized mega-mall amid a flurry of street vendors, local Filipino passers-by, jeepneys, and tricycle cabs. As the bus came to a full stop, an outpouring of South Korean, Japanese, and Taiwanese students from Oceanside and other nearby English language schools gleefully stepped off the bus, some with shopping totes in hand. Filled with eager excitement, the students all began to walk through the pedestrian traffic into the entrance of the mall, marking the beginning of their weekend ritual of luxurious consumption, leisure, and middle-class living.

On the weekend, provincial educational destinations like this one in Bacolod become thriving entertainment enclaves for the residents, local tourists, and the large transient student population. In the past couple of decades, what once was a rural and unpopulated landscape of mostly sugarcane fields has dramatically transformed into a global "consumptionscape" (Ger and Belk 1996) fueled by the rise of remittance flows, call center–fueled growth, emigration, redevelopment, and tourism. Educational tourism has contributed to an accelerated expansion of consumption culture, which has become increasingly global in its provisions and spending practices. These "consumptionscapes" are anchored in local consumption practices where tourists and locals use their consumption of global goods to reposition themselves in localized gender, racial, and class hierarchies (see Ger and Belk 1996).

Consider the central square of Bacolod, which has all the features of a global consumptionscape. The mega mall is part of the largest department store chain in the Philippines that caters to international consumers, middle-class locals, and anyone else who wants to escape the heat outdoors. Inside the mega mall are several global brands and restaurants, including McDonalds, KFC, Uniqlo, Home Depot, and Roxy Surf Shop. Many of the price tags equal a fraction of the salaries of local workers. A few blocks beyond, the mega mall has spawned an entertainment district filled with pubs, karaoke bars, hostess bars, and coffee shops. The food options are international and include Korean, American, Thai, and Filipino fare. For roughly the cost of one month's worth of bus fares ($100–$200) in South Korea, South Korean youth in the low-cost corridor of Bacolod are able to participate liberally in a consumption wonderland of fine dining, self-care, and middle-class consumption that is inaccessible to them back home.

Weekend excursions were a highlight for many, including Bomi. Coming from the outskirts of Busan, this was Bomi's first time studying abroad, let alone traveling outside of South Korea. She had only been to Seoul two times in her life. Back in her hometown, Bomi told of living out a "slow death." For the past two years, she had been in and out of work, with her longest job out of college working as a personal assistant for a professor, who severely underpaid her. Bomi struggled to find a full-time job despite her degree in graphic design:

Back at home, these days, I'm probably one step above the unhoused at the subway station. I mostly eat at home and try to cut down my spending as much as I can. It's been hard for me to even meet up with my friends these days. When they go out, they eat out and get drinks. I love drinking, but I dare not go. When I get [an itch to drink], I could waste away my whole savings in one night.

Yet in the low-cost consumer market of Bacolod, Bomi can partake in a you-only-live-once lifestyle and is able to compensate for her feeling of missing out on the "ordinary" consumption practices of middle-class South Korean youth. What Bomi participates in is a transnational form of compensatory consumption, which consumer researchers have defined as a reaction to systematic lack of self-esteem or powerlessness in society (Rucker and Galinsky 2008). Frustrated by a lack of employment and an inability to spend, young people like Bomi are able to indulge in some of the middle-class leisurely pursuits and self-care practices denied to them in South Korea. For a couple of hundred dollars per month, students enjoy a wide array of consumptive activities on the weekend, including spa treatments, massages, manicures, steak dinners, desserts at upscale bakeries, and ironically, countless cups of the Korean brand Tom N Toms coffee.

Students' faux-luxurious and consumptive lifestyles lead to a form of bounded social mobility, where they experience a temporary boost in social and economic status within the context of a low-cost destination. On a typical weekend night, students will start with getting a massage at one of the massage parlors for around five dollars. After a massage, they move onto dinner at one of the nicer sit-down restaurants inside the megamall, followed by coffee at a chain coffee shop. After dinner and coffee, students will relocate to the entertainment district for a night of dancing, karaoking, and drinking. Students will also get together to do day trips at hotel resorts nearby where they can use the pool for a small fee. At least once or twice during their stay, students typically take a weekend trip to the nearby beach resorts and island destinations such as Bohol, Dumaguete, Boracay, and Cebu, trips that are often organized by the school itself. Such consumption practices are bounded within the spatial parameters of these peripheral locations of the Philippines, where South Korean youth can temporarily negotiate their lowered status within South Korea by maximizing the economic differentials between South Korea and the Philippines.

Bounded social mobility involves students' personal acts of material consumption. It also is relational and shapes the unequal social and racialized relations between South Korean students and Filipino tutors and residents. Dohye Kim's (2016) work on South Korean retiree migrants in the Philippines has elaborated on the historical dynamics of South Korean-Filipino social relations. She finds that South Koreans, who take pride in their "middle-income nation" status, often embrace a form of racial supremacy over Filipino because they believe the latter are people from a failed and economically poor nation. Furthermore, she points out that because South Koreans come into regular contact with Filipino locals in subservient positions, this intensifies their feelings of racial superiority.

While South Korean students are positioned differently from South Korean retiree migrants, economic and intra-Asian racial dynamics still inform the everyday interactions of South Korean students and Filipino tutors. Because students and tutors are similar in age, many become friendly over the course of their stay. For instance, it was not uncommon for students to lean on their Filipino tutors as sources of information or as tour guides for exploring local tourist sites and landmarks. While such forms of social interaction are not financially transactional, many South Korean students do not acknowledge the economic burden of asking their tutors to come with them on their middle-class travel excursions. Some students offered to "repay in kind" by buying cheap meals for their tutors or giving them used and new items that they brought from home, such as make-up or clothing. While students were generally well meaning and do such acts to show their appreciation, they often failed to see the unequal social relations that define relationships with locals. This was true for Sarah, a mid-twenties English tutor at Oceanside:

> I don't like to accept meals or gifts from them because over time it starts to feel awkward. They pay for me, and there's pressure. Taking them out can sometimes feel like a part-time job. . . . I just want it to be normal.

Sarah points out that tutors and students can often enter "awkward" situations of patronage. While students might feel that they are helping tutors by paying for their own outings, tutors may also feel pressured to take out their student-friends, making it feel like a "part-time job." The power dynamics and economic disparities at play underscore the larger geopolitical and racialized positionings of Filipino-South Korean social relations. In many ways, bounded social mobility highlights the contradictory ways in which working-class South Koreans empower themselves by exploiting unequal power relations with their tutors.

Such materialistic and relational consumption activities, however, are not just a hedonistic exercise. Self-care, or "healing" as the South Korean students call it, is a common consumption practice among South Korean youth in the Philippines. Such self-care for these young people is the effort to build and strengthen their own health and well-being (Fries 2013), which can include getting massages, taking vacations, and exercising regularly. The trendy catchphrase "healing" is meant to emphasize the importance of mental health, a balanced life, and healthy living in reaction to the stressful neoliberal-oriented pursuit of lucrative employment or a prestigious education. Take the example of Gee, a twenty-six-year-old social work college student from An-dong. Gee used her time in the Philippines to prioritize the physical healing activities she felt she was denied in South Korea. A nontraditional student, Gee returned to college to obtain her degree after having children. When her program offered her a scholarship to study English in the Philippines, she also saw it as an opportunity to "heal" and enrolled in a gym where she got private personal training classes—which she described as a costly activity in South Korea:

> I got a personal trainer when I joined a gym in the Philippines. PT [personal training] is expensive in South Korea. But in the Philippines, it is affordable, and the price doesn't make me feel guilty for spending money on myself. Back in South Korea, I don't put myself first, and school, work, and my kids take most of my time. I was lucky I got my parents to watch my kids while I go away for a month. I saw this as my chance to heal. I want to take advantage while I'm here.

Students complained about the emotional struggle of having to navigate the unstable job market while sometimes being responsible for others like Gee or having to endure the pressures of living at home under their parents' surveillance. Students who were burned-out from the emotional and psychological stress of their school-to-work transition were able to stop the job market clock and take stock in leisure trips or other self-preserving activities that would help them rebuild strength to continue to participate the competitive labor market of South Korea. So, even as the credentials that educational migrants earn in peripheral destinations are not considered a valuable spec, the bounded mobility students enjoy can offer a valuable experience that partly and temporarily offsets the pressures of neoliberal competition at home.

The Enterprising Self

Sometimes, compensatory consumption practices can inspire ideas for entrepreneurship or income-earning through the discovery of "business items" (Abelmann, Park, and Kim 2009) or learning skills that students can parlay into setting up a small business back home. Jesook Song's (2007) work, for example, has examined the ways in which the South Korean government promotes entrepreneurship via gig economies, venture capital companies, and creative industries among unemployed youth so they can manage the labor precarity that increased in the wake of the 1997 Asian financial crisis. However, such initiatives target youth that possess certain commodifiable educational capital such as technological skills or other forms of "creative capital." While South Korean educational migrants in the Philippines might offer another example of such ventures, the ways in which they are situated with South Korean society and the extended migration landscape offer vastly different experiences. How are such projects experienced by marginalized youth who do not have other options than to enter into self-business?

In South Korea, the connection between entrepreneurship and economic precarity is not new. Korean labor scholar Kwang-Yeong Shin (2013) explains how the self-employed in South Korea represent a large share of the precarious, insecure, and fragile class of workers, with self-employed persons having no employees of their own constituting 60 percent of the total self-employed population in 2011. Furthermore, as Myungji Yang (2018) points out, self-employment is connected to ageism in the South Korean professional labor market, small business having become the last resort for middle-class workers who were pushed into early retirement after the Asian financial crisis. Ageism in the labor market is not exclusive to older workers; younger workers in their late twenties and early thirties seeking a career change or who are coming back from living overseas also tend to turn to self-employment to make a living. In her study of Japanese women who study abroad in Western countries, Karen Kelsky (2001) describes how young women returning from advancing their studies abroad confront an experience of "aging out" in the Japanese professional labor market because they are viewed as "too old" and "overqualified" to fill the secretarial positions typically designated for women.

Many of the South Korean young people I interviewed, especially those who were in the upper-age range, discussed how being too far along in life was something they worried about when going back to South Korea. They often left their home country with hopes of acquiring global skills and credentials only to later recognize that their experience would not necessarily provide a career boost. For them, study abroad comes with the risk of exacerbating their constrained job prospects because of extended gaps in their professional work history from being overseas.

This was the case for thirty-year-old June from Goyangsi near Seoul, who was actually returning to the Philippines for a second time after undertaking a working holiday in Australia. June finished college in his late twenties because of how long it took for him to transfer from a two-year to a four-year college and complete his compulsory military service. While June had planned to transition to permanent residency, a pathway the Australian government provides for some "skilled workers" after completing a working holiday, he decided to return home after a bad breakup with his girlfriend, another South Korean on a working holiday in Australia. Before his return, June decided to do a three-month stint in the Philippines to take the time to think about what he wanted to do back home. In an interview, he was candid about the great apprehension he had about his future:

> When I go back to South Korea I will be thirty with no professional work experience. I can't use my work at the banana farm in Australia on my resume. Even if I wanted to start over from the bottom, South Korean employers don't want to hire people over thirty for entry-level

positions because it is more uncomfortable managing an older person. Your manager might be younger than you, for example, and it creates an age and positional mismatch. They prefer someone who is fresh out of college, who is more easily controlled. People over thirty are not the ideal new workers.

June's reservations about his prospects in the South Korean labor market pushed him, while he was in the Philippines, to look into small business opportunities he could pursue in South Korea. He then decided to pursue a pasta business in South Korea, pointing out that it became his favorite meal while in Australia. He planned to learn how to make pasta in South Korea from a family acquaintance who ran a small but lucrative pasta-making business, using some of the money he had saved up from his working holiday. The rest he planned to invest in the purchase of equipment that will enable him to either sell the food online or as a street vendor to reduce the cost of renting space.

Such experiences are common among South Korean youth that I interviewed in the Philippines. Some felt that they did not have the right educational credentials to obtain secure salaried jobs. Others felt that even if they had college degrees, they had missed their opportunity to apply for positions that were suitable for their age range. This was especially the case with South Koreans who were already in the workforce but had been stuck in "transitional" periods for a long time. Take, for example, Arang, a twenty-five-year-old trade school graduate from Chungju. After graduating from beauty school, Arang worked as an assistant at a hair salon while nursing dreams of starting her own salon. However, after an accident at work left her working hand injured, Arang was unemployed for several months, during which she received treatment before looking for work again. Feeling unmotivated but forced to earn an income to survive, she picked up a shift as a cashier at Dunkin' Donuts. Although she had planned to work there only temporarily, she ended up staying longer as a result of the convenience. It was only when her wealthy uncle who was concerned about Arang's future offered to send her abroad that she decided to go to the Philippines. Having never gone abroad, Arang decided to take the opportunity to figure out what she wanted to do while learning English—a "guiltless compromise" for her to stay "productive" while taking a break from the emotional stress of "figuring out a career" back home.

Having left for the Philippines close to a week and a half after her uncle offered her the opportunity, Arang remarked that she was not all that invested in learning. She consequently skipped out on classes regularly and sometimes ventured for midday trips to the mall. Arang's off-campus excursions would always involve a stop at her favorite dessert shop, where she would get a Filipino dessert called halo-halo. Calling herself a "sweets expert," Arang often talked about how it would be great to sell halo-halo in South Korea and that it was a dessert that perfectly fit the "Korean taste buds." Our frequent trips to the halo-halo shop eventually led to her becoming friendly with the owner of the shop, Hugo, a middle-aged Filipino man. During our weekly visits, Hugo would often strike up a conversation with us, and Arang would share her love for the dessert and how she wanted to sell it back in South Korea. Before Arang left, Hugo offered to give Arang a lesson in how to make halo-halo to help her introduce Filipino food to South Koreans—something, Hugo said, that would make him proud as someone who had never been to South Korea.

While Arang was not strategically looking to find a business idea, her consumption activities inspired her to think of an alternative livelihood that she could not have imagined before. Selling a single dessert, she thought, would be a lot more manageable than owning a brick-and-mortar restaurant for someone with meager resources like her, because she could save on costs by renting a kiosk or a cart or a small space inside a store or mall. Such enterprising imaginings were a common feature among South Korean youth in the older age bracket, who did not see themselves going back to school in their home country or being able to obtain a white-collar job at a large company.

Other students I met revealed more premeditated plans to maximize their time in the Philippines beyond English language learning by acquiring a new trade, skill, or craft. This was the case for thirty-one-year-old Jiman, who was working as a mid-level salesperson in South Korea before undertaking a multidestination itinerary to visit the Philippines and Australia. When his sister got married and could no longer support their parents, he decided it was the right moment to shift gears and find another job: "My parents are getting older and I need to take care of them. While I make enough for me, it's not enough to be a family man." Jiman marked his transition out of full-time employment by undertaking a multiyear, multi-destination trip, starting in the Philippines. Jiman would not only brush up on his English language skills in the Philippines but also solidify concrete career plans. In his eyes, the right move was to start his own business, which he believed was the only way a person his age could earn a higher living without going back to school. One of his ideas was to learn how to scuba dive and start a scuba-diving school back in South Korea. He planned to obtain his license in the Philippines and maximize his time scuba diving there to avoid the high fees of getting trained in Australia. Jokingly, he said that he did need to pick up an Australian English accent when he was there, so that people would find it more convincing when he called his business the "Great Barrier Reef Korea."

Because Jiman was focused on learning scuba diving, he would often miss class to take side trips to nearby beaches. Such entrepreneurial approaches demonstrate the ways in which economically constrained young people maximize their study-abroad experiences to facilitate their survival back in South Korea. Such orientations not only go against the grain of conventional adulthood norms but also challenge labor market structures that have closed off opportunities for upward mobility. Instead of passively accepting the stratifying impacts of South Korea's domestic and transnational education system, South Korean youth on the margins use educational migration to peripheral destinations to pioneer new forms of income-earning that allow them to proudly make a life for themselves in South Korea's increasingly managed neoliberal society.

Summary and Conclusion

In highlighting the experiences of transperipheral educational migrants, this study is the first of its kind to include the perspectives of provincial, working-class South Korean youth. I have demonstrated how South Korean youth with few resources who enroll in low-cost English educational programs in the Philippines challenge the stratifying effects of the segmentation encountered in transnational educational contexts; they do so by engaging in both strategic and organically experienced consumption and capital accumulation practices. In examining the transnational field of educational migration, this study has been able to expand on existing research on the transformations of the welfare state and the human implications of neoliberal policies regarding "human capital development." While a number of researchers such as Jesook Song (2007) and Nancy Abelmann and her colleagues (2009) have shed light on how recent developments in South Korean governance have proved a promising site for understanding the implementation of neoliberal policies as they affect the labor power of youth, such studies have yet to examine how such policies have not only traveled but also expanded geographically through the increasing deregulation of the international education market and the liberalization of youth travel and migration (via working holiday schemes and other state travel programs).

At first glance, transperipheral educational migrants seem caught in a catch-22. Although they are pressured by the government and prospective employers in South Korea to become fluent English-speaking "global citizens," they recognize that their "third world" English credentials obtained in the Philippines will be undervalued on their return home in a professional labor market that continues to privilege credentials from the Global North. However, I have shown that South Korean youth who take low-cost migration pathways for English education in peripheral destinations of the Global South are still able to accumulate precultural capital, engage in compensatory middle-class consumption, and gain entrepreneurial inspiration, enabling them to strategically and creatively challenge the marginal position of working-class migrants' within South Korea's highly stratified and increasingly neoliberal society.

Transperipheral educational mobility is an alternative strategy taken on by low-resourced South Korean youth, largely from outside of Seoul in smaller cities, who opt for low-cost private English education programs in peripheral locations like the Philippines in response to the demand of government and business in South Korea that they become "global citizens." I find that South Korean youth engage in low-cost migration pathways for English education with the understanding that their experiences will not be globally as legitimized as elite study abroad programs in the Global North when they return back home. Even though the credentials that educational migrants earn in peripheral locations are undervalued in and of themselves, my research reveals that transperipheral educational mobility provides forms of alternative capital-building and consumption that allows students to reimagine their futures more broadly in ways that hold value for them beyond any calculated means of labor market ascendance.

Notes

1   This is particularly true for countries in Asia with histories of US empire, colonialism, and war.

2   My use of the term *youth* refers to those aged mid-teens to mid-twenties who constitute the majority of my sample. However, as Annika Westberg (2006) states, as young people stay in education longer and postpone economic independence, age categories such as "youth" and "adulthood" become an increasingly subjective matter in which individuals older than the age of twenty-four increasingly do not see themselves as having fully transitioned into adulthood.

3   The term *peripheral* is used to refer to places beyond metropolitan areas in both South Korea and the Philippines. This includes smaller, rural, and provincial cities and locations.

4   Scholars advocate for use of the term *Filipinx* in the diaspora to challenge gendered binaries with the terms *Filipino* and *Filipina*. In this article I use the term *Filipino*, because this is how the participants referred to themselves during interviews.

5   "Oceanside" and the names of participants in my research are pseudonyms.

6   Ryan is a popular animated icon in South Korea made by the company Kakao and Friends.

7   A jeepney serves as a commuter bus in the Philippines. It is a long pick-up truck with a truck bed that can carry more than a dozen customers.

References

Abelmann, Nancy A., Soo Ah Kwon, Adrienne Lo, and Sumie Okazaki. 2015. "Introduction: South Korea's Education Exodus." In *South Korea's Education Exodus: The Life and Times of Early Study Abroad*, edited by Nancy A. Abelmann, Soo Ah Kwon, Adrienne Lo, and Sumie Okazaki, 1–21. Seattle: University of Washington Press.

Abelmann, Nancy, So Jin Park, and Hyunhee Kim. 2009. "College Rank and Neo-Liberal Subjectivity in South Korea: The Burden of Self-Development." *Inter-Asia Cultural Studies* 10, no. 2: 229–47.

Altbach, Philip G. 1981. "The University as Centre and Periphery." *Teachers College Record* 82, no. 4: 601–21.

Anagnost, Ann. 2013. "Introduction: Life-Making in Neoliberal Times." In *Global Futures in East Asia: Youth, Nation, and the New Economy in Uncertain Times,* edited by Ann Anagnost, Andrea Arai, and Hai Ren, 1–27. Stanford, CA: Stanford University Press.

Bozic, Sasa. 2006. "The Achievement and Potential of International Retirement Migration Research: The Need for Disciplinary Exchange." *Journal of Ethnic and Migration Studies* 32, no. 8: 1415–27.

Brooks, Rachel, and Johanna Waters. 2009. "A Second Chance at 'Success': UK Students and Global Circuits of Higher Education." *Sociology* 43, no. 6: 1085–1102.

Brooks, Rachel, and Johanna Waters. 2011. *Student Mobilities, Migration, and the Internationalization of Higher Education.* New York: Springer.

Chae, Jae-Eun, and Hee Kyung Hong. 2009. "The Expansion of Higher Education Led by Private Universities in Korea." *Asia Pacific Journal of Education* 29, no. 3: 341–55.

Cheng, Sealing, and Eunjung Kim. 2014. "The Paradoxes of Neoliberalism: Migrant Korean Sex Workers in the United States and 'Sex Trafficking.'" *Social Politics* 21, no. 3: 355–81.

Cho, Hae-Joang. 2015. "The Spec Generation Who Can't Say 'No': Overeducated and Underemployed Youth in Contemporary South Korea." *positions* 23, no. 3: 437–62.

Cho, John. 2012. "Global Fatigue: Transnational Markets, Linguistic Capital, and Korean-American Male English Teachers in South Korea." *Journal of Sociolinguistics* 16, no. 2: 218–37.

Chun, Jennifer Jihye, and Ju Hui Judy Han. 2015. "Language Travels and Global Aspirations of Korean Youth." *positions* 23, no. 3: 565–93.

Collins, Francis L. 2013. "Regional Pathways: Transnational Imaginaries, Infrastructures, and Implications of Student Mobility within Asia." *Asian and Pacific Migration Journal* 22, no. 4: 475–500.

Collins, Francis L., Ravinder Sidhu, Nick Lewis, and Brenda S. A. Yeoh. 2014. "Mobility and Desire: International Students and Asian Regionalism in Aspirational Singapore." *Discourse: Studies in the Cultural Politics of Education* 35, no. 5: 661–76.

Crystal, David. 2012. *English as a Global Language.* New York: Cambridge University Press.

Fries, Christopher J. 2013. "Self-Care and Complementary and Alternative Medicine as Care for the Self: An Embodied Basis for Distinction." *Health Sociology Review* 22, no. 1: 37–51.

Ger, Güliz, and Russell W. Belk. 1996. "I'd Like to Buy the World a Coke: Consumptionscapes of the 'Less Affluent World.'" *Journal of Consumer Policy* 19, no. 3: 271–304.

Gossnell, Hannah, and Jesse Abrams. 2011. "Amenity Migration: Diverse Conceptualizations of Drivers, Socioeconomic Dimensions, and Emerging Challenges." *GeoJournal* 76, no. 4: 303–22.

Green, Paul. 2020. "Thinking Within, Across, and Beyond Lifestyle Paradigms: Later-Life Mobility Histories and Practices 'in' Ubud, Bali." *Ethnography* 21, no. 2: 241–60.

Halfacree, Keith. 2008. "To Revitalise Counterurbanisation Research? Recognising an International and Fuller Picture." *Population, Space, and Place* 14, no. 6: 479–95.

Hayes, Matthew. 2018. *Gringolandia: Lifestyle Migration under Late Capitalism.* Minneapolis: University of Minnesota Press.

Hu, Guangwei. 2005. "English Language Education in China: Policies, Progress, and Problems." *Language Policy* 4, no. 1: 5–24.

Hyundai Research Institute. 2018. "Economic Week No. 18–19." www.hri.co.kr/board/report View.asp?firstDepth=1&secondDepth=1%20&numIdx=30043 (accessed November 23, 2021).

ICEF. 2016. "ELT Enrollment in the Philippines on the Rise." *ICEF Monitor.* March 14. monitor.icef.com/2016/03/elt-enrolment-in-the-philippines-on-the-rise/.

Jang, In Chull. 2018. "Legitimating the Philippines as a Language Learning Space: Transnational Korean Youth's Experiences and Evaluations." *Journal of Sociolinguistics* 22, no. 2: 216–32.

Jeon, Mihyon. 2012. "Globalization of English Teaching and Overseas Koreans as Temporary Migrant Workers in Rural Korea." *Journal of Sociolinguistics* 16, no. 2: 238–54.

Jeon, Mihyon, and Jiyoon Lee. 2006. "Hiring Native-Speaking English Teachers in East Asian Countries." *English Today* 22, no. 4: 53–58.

Jung, Minwoo. 2017. "Precarious Seoul: Urban Inequality and Belonging of Young Adults in South Korea." *positions* 25, no. 4: 745–67.

Jung, Sook Kyung, and Bonny Norton. 2002. "Language Planning in Korea: The New Elementary English Program." In *Language Policies in Education: Critical Issues*, edited by James W. Tollefson, 245–65. Mahwah, NJ: Lawrence Erlbaum.

Kachru, Braj B., ed. 1992. *The Other Tongue: English Across Cultures.* Urbana: University of Illinois Press.

Kang, Jiyeon, and Nancy Abelmann. 2011. "The Domestication of South Korean Pre-College Study Abroad in the First Decade of the Millennium." *Journal of Korean Studies* 16, no. 1: 89–118.

Kelsky, Karen. 2001. *Women on the Verge: Japanese Women, Western Dreams.* Durham, NC: Duke University Press.

Kim, Dohye. 2016. "Geographical Imagination and Intra-Asian Hierarchy between Filipinos and South Korean Retirees in the Philippines." *Philippine Studies: Historical and Ethnographic Viewpoints* 64, no. 2: 237–64.

Kobayashi, Yoko. 2007. "Japanese Working Women and English Study Abroad." *World Englishes* 26, no. 1: 62–71.

Koo, Hagen. 2007. "The Changing Faces of Inequality in South Korea in the Age of Globalization." *Korean Studies* 31, no. 1: 1–18.

Kubota, Ryuko. 2009. "Rethinking the Superiority of the Native Speaker: Toward a Relational Understanding of Power." In *The Native Speaker Concept*, edited by Neriko Musha Doerr, 233–48. Berlin: De Gruyter Mouton.

Lipura, Sarah Jane D. 2021. "Deconstructing the Periphery: Korean Degree-Seeking Students' Everyday Transformations in and through India. *Research in Comparative and International Education* 16, no. 3: 252–75. doi.org/10.1177/17454999211038769.

Lukacs, Gabriella. 2015. "Labor Games: Youth, Work, and Politics in East Asia." *positions* 23, no. 3: 381–409.

Madge, Clare, Parvati Raghuram, and Patricia Noxolo. 2009. "Engaged Pedagogy and Responsibility: A Postcolonial Analysis of International Students." *Geoforum* 40, no. 1: 34–45.

McWatters, Mason R. 2008. *Residential Tourism: (De)Constructing Paradise*. Bristol, UK: Channel View Publications.

Miyagiwa, Kaz. 1991. "Scale Economies in Education and the Brain Drain Problem." *International Economic Review* 32, no. 3: 743–59.

Mok, Ka Ho. 2011 "The Quest for Regional Hub of Education: Growing Heterarchies, Organizational Hybridization, and New Governance in Singapore and Malaysia." *Journal of Education Policy* 26, no. 1: 61–81.

Nguyen, Hoa Thi Mai. 2012. "Primary English Language Education Policy in Vietnam: Insights from Implementation." In *Language Planning in Primary Schools in Asia*, edited by Richard B. Baldauf Jr., Robert B. Kaplan, Nkonko M. Kamwangamalu, and Pauline Bryant, 131–56. London: Routledge.

Ong, Aihwa. 1999. *Flexible Citizenship: The Cultural Logics of Transnationality*. Durham, NC: Duke University Press.

Ong, Aihwa. 2006. *Neoliberalism as Exception: Mutations in Citizenship and Sovereignty*. Durham, NC: Duke University Press.

Ortiga, Yasmin. 2018. "Constructing a Global Education Hub: The Unlikely Case of Manila." *Discourse: Studies in the Cultural Politics of Education* 39, no. 5: 767–81.

Park, Joseph Sung-Yul. 2009. *The Local Construction of a Global Language: Ideologies of English in South Korea*. Berlin: De Gruyter Mouton.

Park, Joseph Sung-Yul. 2011. "The Promise of English: Linguistic Capital and the Neoliberal Worker in the South Korean Job Market." *International Journal of Bilingual Education and Bilingualism* 14, no. 4: 443–55.

Park, So Jin, and Nancy Abelmann. 2004. "Class and Cosmopolitan Striving: Mothers' Management of English Education in South Korea." *Anthropological Quarterly* 77, no. 4: 645–72.

Pennycook, Alastair. 2017. *The Cultural Politics of English as an International Language.* London: Routledge.

Quijano, Anibal. 2000. "Coloniality of Power and Eurocentrism in Latin America." *International Sociology* 15, no. 2: 215–32.

Quy, N. T. K. 2010. "Beyond Center Periphery Higher Education Development in South East Asia." *Journal of the Pacific Circle Consortium for Education* 22, no. 2: 21–36.

Rivers-Moore, Megan. 2016. *Gringo Gulch: Sex, Tourism, and Social Mobility in Costa Rica.* Chicago: University of Chicago Press.

Rucker, Derek D., and Adam D. Galinsky. 2008. "Desire to Acquire: Powerlessness and Compensatory Consumption." *Journal of Consumer Research* 35, no. 2: 257–67.

Schattle, Hans. 2015. "Global Citizenship as a National Project: The Evolution of *Segye Shimin* in South Korean Public Discourse." *Citizenship Studies* 19, no: 1: 53–68.

Shin, Kwang-Yeong. 2013. "Economic Crisis, Neoliberal Reforms, and the Rise of Precarious Work in South Korea." *American Behavioral Scientist* 57, no. 3: 335–53.

Sidhu, Ravinder, K. C. Ho, and Brenda Yeoh. 2011. "Emerging Education Hubs: The Case of Singapore." *Higher Education* 61, no. 1: 23–40.

Song, Jesook. 2007. "'Venture Companies,' 'Flexible Labor,' and the 'New Intellectual': The Neoliberal Construction of Underemployed Youth in South Korea." *Journal of Youth Studies* 10, no. 3: 331–51.

Song, Jesook. 2009. *South Koreans in the Debt Crisis: The Creation of a Neoliberal Welfare Society.* Durham, NC: Duke University Press.

Sung, Youl-Kwan, Minjeong Park, and Il-Seon Choi. 2013. "National Construction of Global Education: A Critical Review of the National Curriculum Standards for South Korean Global High Schools." *Asia Pacific Education Review* 14, no. 3: 285–94.

UNESCO. 2013. "The International Mobility of Students in Asia and the Pacific." unesdoc.unesco.org/images/0022/002262/226219e.pdf (accessed November 23, 2021).

Wallerstein, Immanuel Maurice. 2004. *World-Systems Analysis: An Introduction.* Durham, NC: Duke University Press.

Westberg, Annika. 2004. "Forever Young? Young People's Conception of Adulthood: The Swedish Case." *Journal of Youth Studies* 7, no. 1: 35–53.

Xiang, Biao, and Wei Shen. 2009. "International Student Migration and Social Stratification in China." *International Journal of Educational Development* 29, no. 5: 513–22.

Yang, Myungji. 2018. *From Miracle to Mirage: The Making and Unmaking of the Korean Middle Class, 1960–2015*. Ithaca, NY: Cornell University Press.

Yoon, Kyong. 2015. "A National Construction of Transnational Mobility in the 'Overseas Working Holiday Phenomenon' in Korea." *Journal of Intercultural Studies* 36, no. 1: 71–87.

Yoon, Min-sik. 2014. "Korea Has Highest Reliance on Private Education Market in OECD: Report." *Korean Herald*, September 10.

Contributors

Jessica Ball, MPH, PhD, is a professor with the School of Child and Youth Care at the University of Victoria, Canada. She has taught, consulted, and completed research on the determinants of marginalization of children and youth on three continents, focusing primarily on Southeast Asia. Her recent studies have addressed outcomes of transnational labor migration for children and families in Indonesia as well as the experiences of forced migration among young people from Myanmar and the Middle East who are living in Thailand and Malaysia (www.youthmigrationproject.com).

Harriot Beazley is an associate professor of human geography at the University of the Sunshine Coast Maroochydore. Her research interests are located within social and development geography and children's geographies in Southeast Asia and the Pacific.

Amanda R. Cheong is an assistant professor of sociology at the University of British Columbia. Her research examines the relationships between legal status and inequality, with a focus on undocumented, stateless, and refugee populations. She is currently working on a

positions 30:2 DOI 10.1215/10679847-9573410
Copyright 2022 by Duke University Press

book project, tentatively titled *Omitted Lives*, that explores the causes and consequences of exclusion from civil registration systems.

Carolyn Areum Choi is a Guarini Dean's postdoctoral fellow in Asian and Asian American studies at Dartmouth College. Her research examines how race, class, education, and migration intersect across the Asian diaspora, and her current book project looks at the rise of South Korean labor and educational mobilities in intra-Asian and different Anglo-American settler contexts.

Sari K. Ishii is a professor at the College of Sociology, Rikkyo University, Tokyo. Her research interests include minorities, transnationalism, citizenship, and statelessness. Her work has focused on migration and tourism in East and Southeast Asia, especially Thailand and Japan.

Misaki Iwai is a professor with the Department of Asian Languages, Kanda University of International Studies, Chiba, Japan. Her research interests are in the fields of family relations, care, and transnational marriage migration, with a special focus on Vietnam.

Maggi W. H. Leung is a professor of international development studies with the Department of Geography, Spatial Planning, and International Development at the University of Amsterdam. Her research focuses on the uneven geographies of migration and development, Chinese diaspora, and the internationalization of education.

Rhacel Salazar Parreñas is a professor of sociology and gender and sexuality studies at the University of Southern California. Her areas of interest include gender, labor, migration, family, and economic sociology.

Nicola Piper, formerly a professor of international migration and founding director of the Sydney Asia Pacific Migration Centre at the University of Sydney, Australia, is a Global Professorial Research Fellowship awardee, funded by the British Academy, at the Queen Mary University of London. Her key research interests are global and regional governance of labor migration, advocacy politics, and gendered migration.

Charlie Rumsby is a fellow at the *Sociological Review Journal*, based at Keele University, and has a visiting research fellowship with the Anthropology Department at the London School of Economics and Political Science. Her recent work explores identity and belonging among Vietnamese children living as de facto stateless in Cambodia, and it covers themes such as citizenship, human rights, morality, religious conversion, ethnicity, and intergenerational mobilities.

Johanna L. Waters is a professor of human geography at University College London, where she is the codirector of the Migration Research Unit. She specializes in migration, transnationalism, and (international) education. Her work has largely focused on East Asia and trans-Pacific educational mobilities.